Investment Statistics Locator

by Karen J. Chapman

Phoenix ● New York

ORYX PRESS

1988

The rare Arabian Oryx is believed to have inspired the myth of the unicorn. This desert antelope became virtually extinct in the early 1960s. At that time several groups of international conservationists arranged to have 9 animals sent to the Phoenix Zoo to be the nucleus of a captive breeding herd. Today the Oryx population is over 500, and herds have been returned to reserves in Israel, Jordan, and Oman.

Library of Congress Cataloging-in-Publication Data

Chapman, Karen J.
    Investment statistics locator.

    Includes index.
    1. Investments—United States—Statistics—Periodicals—Indexes.   I. Title.
Z7164.C18C47   1988   [HG4910]   332.6'0973   87-24746
ISBN 0-89774-367-9

Contents

Introduction

A large number of the reference questions being asked in today's libraries are requests for business information, and a large number of these are for investment statistics: stock prices, price-earnings ratios, dividend information, and so on. There are a number of standard reference sources available to answer these questions, but each provides a unique collection of data presented at varying frequencies. Reference librarians and library users may find themselves looking in two or three sources before finding one that presents exactly the data required. The purpose of *Investment Statistics Locator* is to eliminate that searching. Twenty-two standard sources of investment statistics are indexed, and the frequency of the data is given in each entry. After checking a heading in this book, the librarian or researcher will be able to go straight to the source where the information is given. This should be an especially useful tool for beginning reference or business librarians or for general reference librarians who are not business specialists, as well as for library users who need investment information but don't know where to start.

Headings are arranged in alphabetical order, with entries under individual headings arranged in order of decreasing frequency. Where the same information is found in multiple sources, the sources are listed in alphabetical order. The titles of the sources are abbreviated, and a key can be found on page 9. Within the entries, abbreviations are usually avoided; where they appear, they are alphabetized as written. Numerals are alphabetized as if spelled out. Cross-references are provided for increased access. Little attempt has been made to standardize the vocabulary used across sources, so most entries appear with the same wording as is used in the source from which they were taken.

Sources Guide

For those not already familiar with all the sources indexed in the *Investment Statistics Locator*, a brief guide to each source follows, including basic descriptive information, as well as notes related to the effective use of each source.

To use *Investment Statistics Locator*, first look up the general category needed—e.g., Dow Jones Industrial Average—then find the entry that corresponds to the exact information required—e.g., payout ratio. The entry presents the frequency of the data, along with the source where they can be found. The example entry appears as shown:

> ### Dow Jones Industrial Average
>
> **Payout ratio**
> quarterly - *Barron's*

Thus, quarterly payout ratios for the Dow Jones Industrial Average are reported in *Barron's*. Below is information on the 22 sources covered in this book.

Amex Fact Book. New York: American Stock Exchange. Annual.
   Description: Gives statistical information on the activity of the American Stock Exchange. This volume also gives a year-end list of stocks registered on the exchange, with price and volume information for each stock.
   Use Notes: This source has both a Table of Contents and an Index, which together provide access to the statistics.

Analyst's Handbook. New York: Standard & Poor's. Annual with monthly supplements.
   Description: Provides about 20 financial statistics on a per share basis for the various industry categories contained in the Standard & Poor's 500. Information is given on an annual basis for 30 years or as long as the category has been used. Income statements, balance sheets, and financial ratios for the past six years are also presented for each category on a per share basis.

Use Notes: The Table of Contents provides access to the industry information given in this source. Additional income statement and balance sheet information for industrial groups is given at the end.

Bank and Quotation Record. Arlington, MA: National News Services. Monthly.

Description: Gives stock market quotations from a number of exchanges, including New York, American, Boston, Midwest, Pacific, Toronto, and Philadelphia. Quotations for OTC securities in various categories and other pertinent statistics, such as the New York Stock Exchange Common Stock Index, are also given.

Use Notes: The Table of Contents on the first page guides the user in locating the various exchange listings in the body of the source as well as the market statistics printed on the inside covers.

Barron's National Business and Financial Weekly. Chicopee Falls, MA: Barron's Publishing Company. Weekly.

Description: Contains an enormous number of investment statistics, along with articles of interest to investors. The newspaper carries quotations from each of the major exchanges and selected listings from regional and foreign exchanges. Listings for bonds, mutual funds, and government securities are also given. Barron's Market Laboratory, a special section at the end of the newspaper, provides detailed statistics on the various Dow Jones averages and exchange activity as well as numerous other statistical indicators.

Use Notes: Most of the statistics given in this source are in the latter part of the issue in the Market Week section. An index precedes the section, which includes the various exchange listings and Barron's Market Laboratory, on the the last few pages. The Market Laboratory contains a huge number of market indicators generally grouped by stocks, bonds, and economic indicators.

Bond Guide. New York: Standard & Poor's. Monthly.

Description: Gives information on individual bond issues, such as price range, interest dates, and Standard & Poor's rating. Foreign bonds, municipal bonds, and other securities are also included.

Use Notes: Listings for securities are arranged in this source by type of security—e.g., foreign securities, corporate bonds, etc.—which are shown in the Table of Contents. Securities are listed in each section in alphabetical order by issuing body. Useful tables explaining the entries are shown on the inside covers.

Commercial and Financial Chronicle. Arlington, MA: National News Service. Weekly.

Description: Gives daily stock and bond prices for issues traded on the major exchanges and a few regional exchanges. The newspaper also shows the price-earnings ratio and indicated annual dividend for each stock.

Use Notes: There is no Table of Contents for this source, but the order in which the exchange listings are printed seems fairly consistent from issue to issue. New York Stock Exchange stock listings are shown first.

Daily Stock Price Record. New York: Standard & Poor's. Quarterly.

Description: Gives daily information on major financial indicators, such as the Standard & Poor's 500 and its components, and individual stock prices and volume. For each stock, earnings and dividends for that quarter are reported.

Use Notes: This source is issued in three parts: New York Stock Exchange, American Stock Exchange, and Over-the-Counter. An explanatory sample page introduces the volume, and tables of stock market indicators follow. The main part of the volume is composed of entries for stocks in alphabetical order by company name.

Financial Dynamics. Denver, CO: Standard & Poor's Compustat Services. Loose-leaf.

Description: Provides a large amount of quantitative information on individual companies and industries on a yearly and quarterly basis. Balance sheet and income statement information is presented in some detail for the last 10 years.

Use Notes: This source is also issued in several volumes. The *Industry Composite* gives aggregate financial information for individual industries, arranged in alphabetical order by industry. The other volumes contain company information, with the companies grouped by industry. An index appears at the beginning of Volume 1. For each industry, there are three sections of financial information: quarterly financial analyses, annual financial analyses, and industry comparisons. In the first two sections, each company appears on a separate sheet. In the third, all companies are grouped into a single table for ease of comparison. Each volume of *Financial Dynamics* has an extensive glossary in the front which explains virtually every line of information given.

Moody's Bond Record. New York: Moody's Investors Service. Monthly.

Description: Provides Moody's ratings and other important financial statistics for a large number of securities, including corporate bonds, convertible bonds, commercial paper, preferred stock, and municipal and other government bonds.

Use Notes: Securities are listed in this source by category—e.g., municipal bonds, industrial development revenue bonds, etc. Categories are listed in the Table of Contents inside the front cover. By far the largest section is that containing corporate bonds, in which the bonds are listed alphabetically by company and within company by type of bond and date of maturity.

Moody's Bond Survey. New York: Moody's Investors Service. Weekly.

Description: Gives changes in Moody's ratings of bonds and preferred stocks. Recent and prospective offerings are described. Several Moody's averages are also shown.

Use Notes: Ratings information, announcements of prospective and recent corporate bond offerings, and other useful tables appear at the beginning of each issue. The Table of Contents covers only issues for which more extensive write-ups are given. Moody's Yield Averages are shown on the last page.

Moody's Dividend Record. New York: Moody's Investors Service. Semiweekly plus supplements, cumulative, and annual.

Description: Lists dividends announced on common and preferred stocks and bond funds. Other information, such as tax status of dividends and dividend changes, is also presented.

Use Notes: A brief Table of Contents is shown at the beginning of the Cumulative Issue. In each issue, new dividends are listed first. The largest section is "Dividends Declared," in which stocks are listed with their dividend payments in alphabetical order by company name.

Moody's Handbook of Common Stocks. New York: Moody's Investors Service. Quarterly.
Description: Gives an overview of a company's current financial condition, including a description of its business, quarterly information on earnings and dividends, and 10 years of selected financial statistics.
Use Notes: The introductory material in this source, which includes tables of stock indexes and a fairly extensive guide to using the book, can be accessed quickly by using the Table of Contents. The main body of the source, one-page reports on over 900 companies, is arranged in alphabetical order by company name.

Moody's Industrial Manual. New York: Moody's Investors Service. Annual.
Description: Covers industrial companies on the New York and American Stock Exchanges. An overview of the company, its history and line of business, financial information, and a description of its long-term debt are given for most companies, although the length of the entries varies.
Use Notes: The statistics from this source that are covered in *Investment Statistics Locator* are taken from the blue pages bound in the center of the first volume. Information in the central blue pages can be found by using the Table of Contents which appears on the first page of that section.

NASDAQ Fact Book. Washington, DC: National Association of Securities Dealers. Annual.
Description: Provides statistical information on NASDAQ activity. It includes a list of NASDAQ securities, with yearly volume and price information for each.
Use Notes: The Table of Contents at the beginning of this source provides adequate access to the statistics shown.

New York Stock Exchange Fact Book. New York: New York Stock Exchange. Annual.
Description: Contains a huge number of statistics on New York Stock Exchange activity. Detailed information is given for the most recent year, often on a monthly basis, and a more general historical section provides information as far back as 1900. Information on other exchanges is sometimes provided for comparison.
Use Notes: The Table of Contents and the Index provide access for this source. A special historical section of more important statistics appears at the end.

New York Times. New York: New York Times. Daily.
Description: Gives stock and bond quotations from all major and selected regional and foreign exchanges in the business section of the daily edition. Numerous other statistics, such as the Dow Jones averages and measures of trading activity on the major exchanges, are also given.
Use Notes: Investment statistics are presented in the Business section of this newspaper.

NYSE Fact Book—see *New York Stock Exchange Fact Book*

Quarterly Dividend Record—see *Standard & Poor's Quarterly Dividend Record*

Security Owner's Stock Guide. New York: Standard & Poor's. Monthly.

Description: Provides a great deal of investment information in a compact format. This publication covers more than 5,300 common and preferred stocks and more than 425 mutual fund issues. Information on price range, dividends, earnings, etc., is reported for each stock, and similar useful information is provided for each mutual fund.

Use Notes: The bulk of this source is the Common and Preferred Stock section, in which stocks are arranged alphabetically by company name. A short mutual fund section follows. A convenient guide to using the Stock Guide appears inside the back cover.

Security Price Index Record. New York: Standard & Poor's. Annual.

Description: Gives detailed tables of all Standard & Poor's Indexes. Part of *Standard & Poor's Statistical Service,* the volume also shows price-earnings ratios and yields of major indexes. Other statistics presented include the Dow Jones averages and stock and bond sales on the New York Stock Exchange.

Use Notes: A fairly detailed index found at the beginning of the volume provides excellent access to the tables of indexes, yields, prices, etc., which appear in the source.

S & P Bond Guide—see *Bond Guide*

S & P Stock Guide—see *Security Owner's Stock Guide*

S & P Stock Reports—see *Standard & Poor's Stock Reports*

Standard & Poor's Quarterly Dividend Record. New York: Standard & Poor's. Quarterly and annual cumulation.

Description: Shows dividend payments on publicly owned American and Canadian stocks. Other information related to dividend payments, such as tax status of dividends, stock dividends offered, and dividends per share of Standard & Poor's indexes, is also presented.

Use Notes: Dividend payments are shown in alphabetical order by company name. Other tables and lists can be found by using the Table of Contents.

Standard & Poor's Stock Reports. New York: Standard & Poor's. Quarterly.

Description: Provides a concise but thorough overview of stock traded on the New York and American Stock Exchanges and over-the-counter. For each stock, such basic information as address, officers, recent price, ticker symbol, and a description of the company and its current condition is given, as well as 10 years of per share, income, and balance sheet data. Quarterly information on sales, earnings, and dividends is also provided.

Use Notes: The *Stock Reports* are issued in three parts: New York Stock Exchange, American Stock Exchange, and Over-the-Counter. Each volume presents two-page descriptions of companies traded on that exchange, in alphabetical order by company name. A glossary explaining the terms used appears at the beginning of each volume.

Value Line. New York: Arnold Bernhard & Company. Weekly.

Description: Presents a great deal of financial information on individual companies and a lesser amount for individual industries. Part 1, Summary & Index, has lists of stocks covered and some current information on each, as well as lists of stocks in various categories, such as highest price-earnings ratios, widest discounts from book value, etc. Part 2, Selection & Opinion, highlights particular stocks or economic indicators and gives tables of market statistics. Part 3, Ratings & Reports, gives a limited number of statistics on individual industries and a great deal of information on individual companies.

Use Notes: *Value Line* is published in three parts. Part 1, Summary & Index, lists the companies and industries covered and gives page numbers where they can be found in the other two parts. Brief information about each company is also given. Part 1 contains several tables grouping stocks into categories like "Highest P/Es," "Untimely Stocks," etc. The last three or four pages of Part 2, Selection & Opinion, contain statistics on stock market activity. Part 3, Ratings & Reports, gives detailed information on industries and individual companies within the industries. Because it is issued in 13 "editions," each covering different industries and companies, the user is recommended always to start with Part 1, Summary & Index.

Wall Street Journal. Chicopee Falls, MA: Wall Street Journal. Daily.

Description: Provides quotations for stocks and bonds on all major and selected regional exchanges. This newspaper gives measures of trading activity on major exchanges, foreign exchange rates, stock indexes, and many more useful investment statistics.

Use Notes: The statistics in the *Journal* are in the second section. Many market indicators are given on the next-to-last page, and others are scattered throughout the exchange listings pages. The section is most easily read back-to-front.

List of Periodical Title Abbreviations

AH	Analyst's Handbook
AmexFB	American Stock Exchange Fact Book
Barron's	Barron's National Business and Financial Weekly
BG	Bond Guide
BQR	Bank and Quotation Record
CFC	Commercial and Financial Chronicle
DSPR	Daily Stock Price Record
FD	Financial Dynamics
MBR	Moody's Bond Record
MBS	Moody's Bond Survey
MDR	Moody's Dividend Record
MHCS	Moody's Handbook of Common Stock
MIM	Moody's Industrial Manual
NASDAQFB	NASDAQ Fact Book
NYSEFB	New York Stock Exchange Fact Book
NYT	New York Times
SOSG	Security Owner's Stock Guide
SPIR	Security Price Index Record
SPQDR	Standard & Poor's Quarterly Dividend Record
SPSR	Standard & Poor's Stock Reports
VL	Value Line Investment Survey
WSJ	Wall Street Journal

Index

A

Accounts payable

Individual companies
quarterly and yearly - *VL*

Individual industries
per share, yearly - *AH*

Accrued expenses

Individual industries
per share, yearly - *AH*

Active stocks—*see* Most active stocks

Additions to stock

Individual companies and industries
yearly - *FD*

Adjustable rate mortgage

Base rates
weekly - *Barron's*

Adjusted available for common dividends

Individual companies and industries
moving 12 months, quarterly, and
yearly - *FD*

Percentage of sales
individual companies and industries,
moving 12 months, quarterly, and
yearly - *FD*

Adjusted rate revenue bonds

Ratings, Moody's
monthly - *MBR*
new, weekly - *MBS*
reviewed and confirmed, weekly -
MBS
reviewed and revised, weekly - *MBS*
withdrawn, weekly - *MBS*

Administrative expenses—*see*
Selling, general and administrative
expenses

ADRs—*see* American Depository
Receipts

Advance-decline line

American Stock Exchange
daily and 10-day total, daily - *DSPR*

New York Stock Exchange
daily and 10-day total, daily - *DSPR*

Value Line stocks
cumulative, weekly, graph - *VL*

Advance planning (ENR)

Construction
weekly - *Barron's*

Advance volume

American Stock Exchange
daily - *NYT, WSJ*

NASDAQ
daily - *WSJ*

New York Stock Exchange
daily - *NYT, WSJ*

Advances

American Stock Exchange
leaders, stocks listed, daily - *NYT,
WSJ*
number, daily - *Barron's, DSPR, NYT,
WSJ*
number, weekly - *Barron's*

Bonds
Amex, number, daily - *Barron's, WSJ*
NYSE, number, daily - *Barron's, NYT,
WSJ*

Common stocks
NYSE, number, daily - *Barron's*

Domestic bonds
NYSE, number, daily - *WSJ*

Dow Jones companies
number, weekly - *Barron's*

**Dow Jones Industrial Average
companies**
number, weekly - *Barron's*

**Dow Jones Transportation Average
companies**
number, weekly - *Barron's*

Dow Jones Utilities Average companies
number, weekly - *Barron's*

NASDAQ
leaders, stocks listed, daily - *NYT,
WSJ*
number, daily - *Barron's, DSPR, NYT,
WSJ*
number, weekly - *Barron's*

New York Stock Exchange
leaders, stocks listed, daily - *NYT,
WSJ*
number, daily - *Barron's, DSPR, NYT,
WSJ*
number, weekly - *Barron's*

Value Line stocks
number, weekly - *VL*

Advances and investments

Individual companies and industries
yearly - *FD*

Percentage of assets
individual companies and industries,
yearly - *FD*

To unconsolidated subsidiaries
individual industries, per share, yearly
- *AH*

Advertising expense

Individual companies and industries
yearly - *FD*

Advertising industry

Financial statistics
yearly - *VL*

Aerospace Companies Index

Standard & Poor's
weekly, monthly, and yearly - *SPIR*
component companies, yearly - *SPIR*
range, yearly - *SPIR*

Aerospace/defense industry

Financial statistics
yearly - *AH, VL*

Aerospace industry

Financial statistics
yearly - *FD*

After-tax cash flow

Per dollar average gross plant
individual companies and industries,
yearly - *FD*

Per dollar average invested capital
individual companies and industries,
yearly - *FD*

After-tax margin

Change, effect on earnings per share
individual companies and industries,
yearly - *FD*

After-tax return on average
invested capital

Individual companies and industries
yearly - *FD*

After-tax return on average total assets

Individual companies and industries
yearly - *FD*

After-tax return on common equity

Change, effect on earnings per share
individual companies and industries,
   yearly - *FD*

After-tax return on equity

Individual companies and industries
yearly - *FD*

After-tax return on invested capital

Change, effect on earnings per share
individual companies and industries,
   yearly - *FD*

Individual companies and industries
yearly - *FD*

Agefi Stock Index—*see* France, Agefi Stock Index

Aggressive growth mutual funds

Sales
monthly - *Barron's*

Air freight industry

Financial statistics
yearly - *AH*

Air transport

Barron's Group Stock Averages
weekly - *Barron's*
component companies and weights,
   irregularly - *Barron's*
range, yearly - *Barron's*

Air transport industry

Financial statistics
yearly - *VL*

Aircraft manufacturing

Barron's Group Stock Averages
weekly - *Barron's*
companies and weights, irregularly -
   Barron's
range, yearly - *Barron's*

Airline Index

daily - *WSJ*

Stock index options, Amex
calls, number, yearly - *AmexFB*
close, monthly and yearly - *AmexFB*
contracts, number and daily average,
   yearly - *AmexFB*
puts, number, yearly - *AmexFB*

Airline industry

Financial statistics
yearly - *AH*

All-Ordinary Stock Index—*see* Australia, All-Ordinary Stock Index

Alternate energy/coal industry

Financial statistics
yearly - *VL*

Aluminum Index

Standard & Poor's
weekly, monthly, and yearly - *SPIR*
component companies, yearly - *SPIR*
range, yearly - *SPIR*

Aluminum industry

Financial statistics
yearly - *AH, VL*

American Depository Receipts

Listings
by originating country, daily - *WSJ*

NASDAQ
number, by originating country, yearly
   - *NASDAQFB*
volume leaders, yearly - *NASDAQFB*
volume leaders, dollar volume and
   closing price, yearly - *NASDAQFB*
volume leaders, share volume and
   closing price, yearly - *NASDAQFB*

South African
listings, weekly - *Barron's*

American furniture—*see* Furniture

American paintings (1800 - pre-World War II)—*see* Paintings

American Stock Exchange

Advance-decline line
daily and 10-day total, daily - *DSPR*

Advance volume
daily - *NYT, WSJ*

Advances
leaders, stocks listed, daily - *NYT, WSJ*
number, daily - *Barron's, DSPR, NYT, WSJ*
number, weekly - *Barron's*

Bonds
advances, number, daily - *Barron's, WSJ*
declines, number, daily - *Barron's, WSJ*
highs, new, number, daily - *Barron's, WSJ*
interest periods, individual bonds, weekly - *CFC*
interest periods, individual bonds, monthly - *BQR*
issues traded, number, daily - *WSJ*
listings, daily - *NYT, WSJ*
listings, weekly - *Barron's, CFC*
listings, monthly - *BQR*
lows, new, number, daily - *Barron's, WSJ*
number listed, daily - *Barron's*
price range, individual bonds, weekly and year to date - *CFC*
price range, individual bonds, 52 weeks - *Barron's*
ratings, individual bonds, weekly - *CFC*
ratings, individual bonds, monthly - *BQR*
sale price range, individual bonds, monthly and year to date - *BQR*
sales, daily and weekly - *Barron's*
sales, individual bonds, daily - *NYT*
sales, individual bonds, weekly - *Barron's*
sales, individual bonds, monthly and year to date - *BQR*

unchanged bond prices, number, daily - *Barron's, WSJ*
volume, dollars, daily - *WSJ*
volume, dollars, monthly - *BQR*
volume, dollars, year to date - *BQR, WSJ*
volume, individual bonds, daily - *WSJ*
yield, individual bonds, daily - *NYT, WSJ*
yield, individual bonds, weekly - *Barron's, CFC*
yield, individual bonds, monthly - *BQR*

Calls
contracts exercised, number, monthly and yearly - *AmexFB*
number and daily average, monthly and yearly - *AmexFB*
number, by type of option, monthly and yearly - *AmexFB*
open interest, daily - *NYT, WSJ*
open interest, weekly - *Barron's*
open interest, monthly and yearly - *AmexFB*
volume, daily - *NYT, WSJ*
volume, weekly - *Barron's*

Canadian issues
number, yearly - *AmexFB*
volume, yearly - *AmexFB*
volume, percentage of total volume, yearly - *AmexFB*

Common stock and warrant issues
market value, aggregate, yearly - *AmexFB*
number, yearly - *AmexFB*
prices, average, yearly - *AmexFB*
shares outstanding, number, yearly - *AmexFB*

Companies
number, yearly - *NASDAQFB*

Corporate bonds
bonds outstanding, principal amount, yearly - *AmexFB*
market value, yearly - *AmexFB*
number of issues, yearly - *AmexFB*
price, average, yearly - *AmexFB*
volume, principal amount, yearly - *AmexFB*

Customers
odd lots, purchases, weekly - *Barron's*
odd lots, sales, weekly - *Barron's*
odd lots, short sales, weekly - *Barron's*

Decline volume
daily - *NYT, WSJ*

Declines
leaders, stocks listed, daily - *NYT, WSJ*
number, daily - *Barron's, DSPR, NYT, WSJ*
number, weekly - *Barron's*

Dividends
indicated annual, individual stocks, weekly - *CFC*
indicated annual, individual stocks, monthly - *BQR*
individual stocks, weekly - *Barron's*

Earnings
individual stocks, yearly - *Barron's*

Floor traders
purchases, weekly - *Barron's*
sales, weekly - *Barron's*
short sales, weekly - *Barron's*

Foreign issues
number, yearly - *AmexFB*
volume, yearly - *AmexFB*
volume, percentage of total volume, yearly - *AmexFB*

Government bonds
volume, principal amount, yearly - *AmexFB*

High
individual companies, yearly - *AmexFB*

Highs, new
number, daily - *Barron's, DSPR, NYT, WSJ*
number, weekly - *Barron's*
stocks listed, weekly - *Barron's*

Issues traded
number, daily - *NYT, WSJ*

Large block transactions
number, daily - *Barron's, WSJ*
number, yearly - *AmexFB*
volume, yearly - *AmexFB*
volume, dollars, yearly - *AmexFB*
volume, dollars, percentage of total dollar volume, yearly - *AmexFB*
volume, percentage of total volume, yearly - *AmexFB*

Listing requirements
yearly - *AmexFB*

Listings
daily - *CFC, NYT, WSJ*
weekly - *Barron's*
monthly - *BQR*

Low
individual companies, yearly - *AmexFB*

Lows, new
number, daily - *Barron's, DSPR, NYT, WSJ*
number, weekly - *Barron's*
stocks listed, weekly - *Barron's*

Market value
aggregate and individual companies, yearly - *AmexFB*

Market Value Index
daily - *NYT*
monthly - *AmexFB*
geographic subindices, close and composition, yearly - *AmexFB*
industrial subindices, close and composition, yearly - *AmexFB*
range, monthly, chart and graph - *MHCS*

Members
buy/sell, net, weekly - *Barron's*
purchases, weekly - *Barron's*
purchases and sales, yearly - *AmexFB*
purchases and sales, percentage of total trading, yearly - *AmexFB*
sales, weekly - *Barron's*
sales, range and last, yearly - *AmexFB*
short sales, weekly - *Barron's*
volume, percentage of total volume, weekly - *Barron's*

Most active equity options
calls, listed, weekly - *Barron's*
puts, listed, weekly - *Barron's*

Most active options
yearly - *AmexFB*
contracts traded, number, yearly - *AmexFB*
listed, daily - *NYT, WSJ*
sales, individual options, daily - *NYT, WSJ*

Most active stocks
daily - *NYT, WSJ*
weekly - *Barron's*
price, daily and 10-day average, daily - *DSPR*

New common stock listings
weekly - *Barron's*
yearly - *AmexFB*

Number of stocks listed
daily and weekly - *Barron's*
yearly - *AmexFB, NASDAQFB*

Odd lots
purchases and sales, yearly - *AmexFB*
purchases and sales, percentage of total
   trading, yearly - *AmexFB*

Options
contracts, volume, monthly and yearly
   - *AmexFB*
contracts traded, number and daily
   average, by type of option, monthly
   and yearly - *AmexFB*
customer participation, monthly and
   yearly - *AmexFB*
customer participation, percentage of
   total options trading, monthly and
   yearly - *AmexFB*
expiration cycle, individual companies
   - *AmexFB*
firm participation, monthly and yearly
   - *AmexFB*
firm participation, percentage of total
   options trading, monthly and yearly
   - *AmexFB*
listing date, individual companies,
   yearly - *AmexFB*
listings, daily - *NYT, WSJ*
listings, weekly - *Barron's*
listings, monthly - *BQR*
market maker participation, monthly
   and yearly - *AmexFB*
market maker participation, percentage
   of total options trading, monthly
   and yearly - *AmexFB*
new listings, yearly - *AmexFB*
open interest, monthly - *AmexFB,
   BQR*
premium per contract, average, yearly -
   AmexFB
sales, monthly - *BQR*
settlement value, yearly - *AmexFB*
underlying companies, number, yearly
   - *AmexFB*
underlying stock, volume, monthly and
   yearly - *AmexFB*
volume, total and daily average,
   monthly and yearly - *AmexFB*
volume, percentage of underlying
   stock, monthly and yearly - *AmexFB*

Options principal membership sales
range and last, yearly - *AmexFB*

Percentage leaders, winners and losers
daily - *WSJ*
weekly - *Barron's*

Price-earnings ratio, individual stocks
daily - *NYT, WSJ*
weekly - *Barron's, CFC*
monthly - *BQR*

Price range, individual stocks
daily - *NYT, WSJ*
weekly - *Barron's, CFC*
year to date - *CFC*
latest 52 weeks - *Barron's, NYT, WSJ*
yearly - *AmexFB*

Public
short sales, weekly - *Barron's*

Puts
contracts exercised, monthly and yearly
   - *AmexFB*
number, by type of option, monthly
   and yearly - *AmexFB*
open interest, daily - *NYT, WSJ*
open interest, weekly - *Barron's*
open interest, monthly - *AmexFB*
open interest, yearly - *AmexFB*
volume, daily - *NYT, WSJ*
volume, weekly - *Barron's*
volume, total and daily average,
   monthly and yearly - *AmexFB*

Sale price range, individual stocks
monthly and year to date - *BQR*

Sales
daily - *Barron's*
yearly - *NYSEFB*
individual stocks, daily - *NYT, WSJ*
individual stocks, weekly - *Barron's,
   CFC*
individual stocks, monthly and year to
   date - *BQR*
market value of shares, yearly -
   NYSEFB
market value of shares, percentage of
   all exchanges' sales, yearly -
   NYSEFB
percentage of all exchanges' sales,
   yearly - *NYSEFB*
volume, monthly - *BQR*

Seat prices
monthly - *BQR*

Seats outstanding
number, monthly - *BQR*

Shares outstanding
number, aggregate and individual
   companies, yearly - *AmexFB*

Short interest
monthly - *DSPR*

Short interest ratio
weekly - *Barron's*
monthly - *DSPR*

Short ratio
members/public, weekly - *Barron's*
specialists/public, weekly - *Barron's*

Short sales
weekly - *Barron's*

Short-term trading index
daily - *Barron's*

Size distribution of transactions
yearly - *AmexFB*

Specialists
number, yearly - *AmexFB*
number per unit, average, yearly -
   AmexFB
number stocks per unit, average, yearly
   - *AmexFB*
options, contracts per transaction,
   average number, by type of option,
   yearly - *AmexFB*
options, number per unit, average,
   yearly - *AmexFB*
options, trade-to-trade price variations,
   by type of option, yearly - *AmexFB*
participation rate, yearly - *AmexFB*
participation rate, options, by type of
   option, yearly - *AmexFB*
purchases, weekly - *Barron's*
sales, weekly - *Barron's*
sales and purchases, yearly - *AmexFB*
shares per transaction, average, yearly -
   AmexFB
short sales, weekly - *Barron's*
stabilization rate, yearly - *AmexFB*
trade-to-trade price variations, yearly -
   AmexFB
units, yearly - *AmexFB*

Stock dividends
year to date - *BQR*

Stock index options
calls, open interest, individual indexes,
   daily - *NYT, WSJ*
calls, volume, individual indexes, daily
   - *NYT, WSJ*
listings, daily - *NYT, WSJ*
puts, open interest, individual indexes,
   daily - *NYT, WSJ*
puts, volume, individual indexes, daily
   - *NYT, WSJ*

Stock price
average, yearly - *AmexFB*
individual stocks, daily - *DSPR*

Stock splits
year to date - *BQR*
yearly - *AmexFB*

Ticks, closing
daily - *Barron's*

Turnover ratio
yearly - *AmexFB*

Unchanged stock prices
number, daily - *Barron's, DSPR, NYT,*
   WSJ
weekly - *Barron's*

Volume
daily - *Barron's, DSPR, NYT, WSJ*
10-day average, daily - *DSPR*
weekly - *Barron's, VL*
daily average, weekly - *Barron's*
10-week average - *VL*
monthly - *BQR*
monthly, chart - *MHCS, MIM*
year to date - *BQR, NYT*
yearly - *AmexFB, NASDAQFB*
daily average, yearly - *AmexFB*
composite, daily - *WSJ*
dollars, yearly - *AmexFB, NASDAQFB*
dollars, percentage of all exchanges'
   volume, yearly - *NASDAQFB*
individual companies, yearly -
   AmexFB
NYSE-listed stock, monthly and yearly
   - *NYSEFB*
NYSE-listed stock, percentage of all
   exchanges' volume, yearly -
   NYSEFB
percentage of all exchanges' trading,
   yearly - *NASDAQFB*
percentage of NYSE volume, weekly
   and 10-week average - *VL*

Volume leaders
volume and price, average, yearly -
   NASDAQFB
volume and price, individual
   companies, yearly - *NASDAQFB*

Warrant and common stock issues
market value, aggregate, yearly -
   AmexFB
number, yearly - *AmexFB*
price, average, yearly - *AmexFB*
shares outstanding, number, yearly -
   AmexFB

Yield, individual stocks
daily - *NYT, WSJ*
weekly - *Barron's, CFC*
monthly - *BQR*

American Stock Exchange Clubs

Schedule of companies to be discussed
date and place, weekly - *Barron's*

American Stock Exchange companies

Assets
average and median, yearly - *AmexFB*
10 leading companies, yearly -
   AmexFB

Dividend reinvestment plans
listed, yearly - *SPQDR*

Employees
number, average and median, yearly -
   AmexFB

Headquarters states
yearly - *AmexFB*

Market value
average and median, yearly - *AmexFB*
10 leading companies, yearly -
   AmexFB

Net income
average and median, yearly - *AmexFB*
10 leading companies, yearly -
   AmexFB

Price gain
10 leading companies, yearly -
   AmexFB

Sales
average and median, yearly - *AmexFB*
10 leading companies, yearly -
   AmexFB

Share volume
10 leading companies, yearly -
   AmexFB

Shareholders' equity
average and median, yearly - *AmexFB*
10 leading companies, yearly -
   AmexFB

Shares outstanding
10 leading companies, yearly -
   AmexFB

Ticker symbols
quarterly - *MHCS, SPSR, VL*
yearly - *AmexFB*

American Stock Exchange Index

daily - *Barron's, DSPR, WSJ*
weekly - *Barron's*

Range
weekly - *Barron's*

American Stock Exchange Index System

Price Level Index
daily - *BQR*

Volume of trading
daily - *BQR*

Amortization and depreciation

Change, year to year
individual companies and industries,
   moving 12 months, quarterly, and
   yearly - *FD*

Individual companies and industries
moving 12 months, quarterly, and
   yearly - *FD*

Per dollar average gross plant
individual companies and industries,
   yearly - *FD*

Per dollar average invested capital
individual companies and industries,
   yearly - *FD*

Per share, annual growth rate
individual companies and industries,
   latest year, 3 years, 5 years, and 10
   years - *FD*

Percentage of sales
individual companies and industries,
   moving 12 months, quarterly, and
   yearly - *FD*

Percentage of value added
individual companies and industries,
   yearly - *FD*

Amortization, depreciation, and depletion

Change, effect on earnings per share
individual companies and industries,
   yearly - *FD*

Individual companies and industries
yearly - *FD*

Per share
change, individual companies and
  industries, yearly - *FD*
individual companies and industries,
  yearly - *FD*
least squares growth rate and
  coefficient of determination,
  individual companies and
  industries, 5-year and 10-year - *FD*

Percentage of average gross plant
individual companies and industries,
  yearly - *FD*

Percentage of sales
individual companies and industries,
  yearly - *FD*

Amount outstanding

Bonds
individual bonds, monthly - *MBR*

Corporate bonds
individual bonds, monthly - *BG*

Foreign bonds
individual bonds, monthly - *BG*

Amsterdam, ANP-CBS General Index

daily - *NYT*
weekly - *Barron's*
yearly - *NYSEFB*

Amsterdam Stock Exchange

Listings, selected stocks
daily - *NYT, WSJ*
weekly - *Barron's*

Statistics
yearly - *NYSEFB*

Amusement companies stock price index

quarterly, graph - *MHCS*

Annuities

Variable
listings, weekly - *Barron's*

ANP-CBS General Index—*see*
  Amsterdam, ANP-CBS General
  Index

Apparel companies stock price index

quarterly, graph - *MHCS*

Apparel industry

Financial statistics
yearly - *VL*

Applications—*see* Listing
  applications

Appreciation potential

All stocks, estimated
last market high and last market low -
  VL
median, weekly and 26 weeks - *VL*

High
stocks listed, weekly - *VL*

Argentine austral

Exchange rate
daily - *NYT, WSJ*
weekly - *Barron's*

Argentine peso

Exchange rate
daily - *BQR*

Art Index, Sotheby's—*see* Sotheby's
  Art Index

Asian Development Bank securities

Listings
daily - *NYT, WSJ*
weekly - *Barron's, CFC*

Ratings
Standard & Poor's, monthly - *BG*

Yield, individual issues
daily - *NYT, WSJ*
weekly - *Barron's, CFC*

Asked price

Individual stocks
when not traded, daily - *DSPR*

Asset ratio

Liquid, mutual funds
monthly - *Barron's*

Asset value—*see* Net asset value

Assets

After-tax return
individual companies and industries,
  yearly - *FD*

Amex companies
average and median, yearly - *AmexFB*
10 leading companies, yearly -
  AmexFB

Banks
10 leading, New York City, weekly -
  WSJ

Current
individual companies, monthly - *BG*
individual companies, quarterly - *FD,
  VL*
individual companies, yearly - *FD,
  SPSR, VL*
individual industries, yearly - *FD*
individual industries, per share, yearly
  - *AH*

Gross
individual companies and industries,
  yearly - *FD*
per employee, average, individual
  companies and industries, yearly -
  FD
percentage of invested capital,
  individual companies and
  industries, yearly - *FD*

Individual companies
quarterly - *FD*
yearly - *FD, SPSR*

Individual industries
yearly - *FD*
per share, yearly - *AH*

Money market mutual funds
weekly and monthly - *Barron's*

Mutual funds
monthly - *Barron's*

**Mutual funds (excluding money market
  and limited maturity municipal bond
  funds)**
monthly - *Barron's*

Net, mutual funds
individual funds, yearly - *SOSG*
per share, percentage change, yearly -
  SOSG

NYSE companies, aggregate
yearly - *NYSEFB*
percentage of all US companies' assets,
  yearly - *NYSEFB*

NYSE member organizations
yearly - *NYSEFB*

Operating
net, per employee, average, individual
  companies and industries, yearly -
  FD
net, per share, annual growth rate,
  individual companies and
  industries, latest year, 3 years, 5
  years, and 10 years - *FD*
pretax return, individual companies
  and industries, yearly - *FD*

Per share, annual growth rate
individual companies and industries,
  latest year, 3 years, 5 years, and 10
  years - *FD*

Percentage equivalent to common equity
individual companies, quarterly - *FD*

Percentage equivalent to debt
individual companies, quarterly - *FD*

Percentage of industry assets
individual companies, yearly - *FD*

Pretax return
individual companies and industries,
  yearly - *FD*

Return on
individual bank corporations, average,
  yearly - *MHCS*
individual companies, yearly - *SPSR*
individual industries, yearly - *AH*

Sales per dollar average
individual companies and industries,
  yearly - *FD*

Turnover
individual industries, yearly - *AH*

US companies, aggregate
yearly - *NYSEFB*

Austral, Argentine—*see* Argentine
  austral

Australia, All-Ordinary Stock Index

weekly - *Barron's*

Australia, Share Price Index

daily - *NYT*
yearly - *NYSEFB*

Australia, Sydney Stock Exchange

Listings, selected stocks
selected stocks, weekly - *Barron's*

Australian dollar

Exchange rate
daily - *BQR, NYT, WSJ*
weekly - *Barron's*

Australian/Japanese diversified industry

Financial statistics
yearly - *VL*

Australian Stock Exchange Association

Statistics
yearly - *NYSEFB*

Austrian schilling

Exchange rate
daily - *BQR, NYT, WSJ*
weekly - *Barron's*

Auto and truck industry

Financial statistics
yearly - *VL*

Auto industry (original equipment manufacturing)

Financial statistics
yearly - *FD*

Auto Parts Index (after market)

Standard & Poor's
weekly, monthly, and yearly - *SPIR*
component companies, yearly - *SPIR*
range, yearly - *SPIR*

Auto Parts Index (original equipment manufacturing)

Standard & Poor's
weekly, monthly, and yearly - *SPIR*
component companies, yearly - *SPIR*
range, yearly - *SPIR*

Auto parts industry (after market)

Financial statistics
yearly - *AH*

Auto parts industry (original equipment manufacturing)

Financial statistics
yearly - *AH, FD, VL*

Auto parts industry (replacement)

Financial statistics
yearly - *FD, VL*

Auto Trucks & Parts Index

Standard & Poor's
weekly, monthly, and yearly - *SPIR*
component companies, yearly - *SPIR*
range, yearly - *SPIR*

Automobile industry

Financial statistics
yearly - *AH, FD*

Production
US domestic units, weekly - *Barron's*

Automobile industry (excluding General Motors)

Financial statistics
yearly - *AH*

Automobile industry (truck)

Financial statistics
yearly - *FD*

Automobile industry (trucks and parts)

Financial statistics
yearly - *AH*

Automobiles Index

Standard & Poor's
weekly, monthly, and yearly - *SPIR*
component companies, yearly - *SPIR*
range, yearly - *SPIR*

Automobiles Index (excluding General Motors)

Standard & Poor's
weekly, monthly, and yearly - SPIR
component companies, yearly - *SPIR*
range, yearly - *SPIR*

B

Backlog

Factory orders
monthly - *Barron's*

Orders, individual companies and industries
yearly - *FD*

Baht, Thai

Exchange rate
daily - *WSJ*
weekly - *Barron's*

Balance sheet

Individual companies
quarterly - *FD*
yearly - *FD, SPSR*

Individual industries
yearly - *FD*
per share, yearly - *AH*

NYSE member organizations
yearly - *NYSEFB*

Balance sheet debt

Individual companies and industries
yearly - *FD*

Balance sheet leverage

Individual companies and industries
yearly - *FD*

Change, effect on earnings per share
individual companies and industries, yearly - *FD*

Balanced mutual funds

Sales
monthly - *Barron's*

Bank credit cards

Interest rates
individual banks, weekly - *Barron's*

Bank deposit ratings

Moody's
changes, individual banks, monthly - *MBR*
new, weekly - *MBS*
reviewed and confirmed, weekly - *MBS*
reviewed and revised, weekly - *MBS*
withdrawn, weekly - *MBS*

Bank-finance-insurance bonds

Number of issues
weekly, six weeks, and projection - *MBS*

Volume
dollars, weekly, six weeks, and projection - *MBS*

Bank for Cooperatives securities

Listings
monthly - *BQR*

Yield
monthly - *BQR*

Bankers acceptances

Bought outright
dollars, weekly - *WSJ*

Held under repurchase plan
dollars, weekly - *WSJ*

Rates
daily - *NYT, WSJ*
weekly - *Barron's*
prime, daily - *BQR*

Banking industry

Financial statistics
composite, yearly - *VL*
Midwest, yearly - *VL*
Texas, yearly - *VL*

Banks

Assets
10 leading New York City banks,
  weekly - *WSJ*

Barron's Group Stock Averages
weekly - *Barron's*
companies and weights, irregularly -
  Barron's
range, yearly - *Barron's*

Bonds
NASDAQ, monthly - *BQR*
yield, individual bonds, monthly -
  BQR

Book value per share
individual bank corporations, yearly -
  MHCS

Deposits
individual bank corporations, yearly -
  MHCS

International, bonds, NYSE
issuers, number, yearly - *NYSEFB*
issues, number, yearly - *NYSEFB*
market value, yearly - *NYSEFB*
par value, yearly - *NYSEFB*

Large commercial
statistics, weekly - *Barron's*

Liabilities
10 leading New York City banks,
  weekly - *WSJ*

Loans
individual bank corporations, yearly -
  MHCS

NASDAQ
price-earnings ratios, individual stocks,
  monthly - *BQR*

New York City
financial statistics, yearly - *AH*

Outside New York City
financial statistics, yearly - *AH*

Return on average assets
individual bank corporations, yearly -
  MHCS

Banks and trust companies

Securities, listings
NASDAQ, monthly - *BQR*

Barron's Best Grade Bonds Index

weekly, graph - *Barron's*

Barron's Confidence Index

daily - *Barron's*
weekly - *DSPR*

**Yield gap, vs. Dow Jones Industrial
  Average**
weekly - *Barron's*

Barron's 50-Stock Average

weekly - *Barron's*

Best grade bond yields
weekly - *Barron's*

Dividend yield
year end, weekly - *Barron's*

Earnings
year end, weekly - *Barron's*
five-year average, weekly - *Barron's*
quarterly projected, weekly - *Barron's*
annualized projected, weekly - *Barron's*

Earnings yield
year end, weekly - *Barron's*

Price-earnings ratio
year end actual, weekly - *Barron's*
five-year average, weekly - *Barron's*
annualized projected, weekly - *Barron's*

Ratio, bond/stock yields
weekly - *Barron's*

Barron's Group Stock Averages—*see also* specific industries
weekly - *Barron's*

Companies and weights
irregularly - *Barron's*

Range
yearly - *Barron's*

Barron's Intermediate Grade Bonds Index

weekly, graph - *Barron's*

Barron's Low-Priced Index

weekly - *Barron's, DSPR*

Component companies
irregularly - *Barron's*

Volume
weekly - *Barron's, DSPR*
percentage of Dow Jones Industrials volume, weekly - *Barron's, DSPR*

Basel Stock Exchange—*see* Switzerland, Basel Stock Exchange

Belgian franc

Exchange rate
daily - *BQR, NYT, WSJ*
weekly - *Barron's*

Belgium, Brussels Stock Exchange

Listings, selected stocks
daily - *NYT, WSJ*
weekly - *Barron's*

Belgium, Brussels Stock Index

daily - *NYT*
weekly - *Barron's*

Best grade bonds

Volume
percentage of NYSE volume, weekly - *Barron's*

Best Grade Bonds Index, Barron's—*see* Barron's

Best-performing stocks

Last 13 weeks
listed, weekly - *VL*

Beta

Individual companies
quarterly - *SPSR, VL*
yearly - *FD*

Beverage industry

Financial statistics
yearly - *VL*

Beverages Index (brewers)

Standard & Poor's
weekly, monthly, and yearly - *SPIR*
component companies, yearly - *SPIR*
range, yearly - *SPIR*

Beverages Index (distillers)

Standard & Poor's
weekly, monthly, and yearly - *SPIR*
component companies, yearly - *SPIR*
range, yearly - *SPIR*

Beverages Index (soft drinks)

Standard & Poor's
weekly, monthly, and yearly - *SPIR*
component companies, yearly - *SPIR*
range, yearly - *SPIR*

Beverages industry (brewers)

Financial statistics
yearly - *AH, FD*

Beverages industry (distillers)

Financial statistics
yearly - *AH, FD*

Beverages industry (soft drinks)

Financial statistics
yearly - *AH, FD*

Bid/ask services

New York Stock Exchange
number, yearly - *NYSEFB*

Bid price

Individual stocks
when not traded, daily - *DSPR*

Biggest free-flow cash generators

Stocks listed
weekly - *VL*

Bills, Treasury—*see* Treasury bills

Bolivar, Venezuelan—*see*
Venezuelan bolivar

Bond Average, Dow Jones—*see*
Dow Jones Bond Average

Bond Average, Dow Jones Industrial—*see* Dow Jones
Industrial Bond Average

Bond Average, Dow Jones Utilities—*see* Dow Jones Utilities
Bond Average

Bond Buyer Municipal Bond Index

weekly - *Barron's*

Bond Buyer 20-Bond Index

weekly - *Barron's*

Bond form

Corporate bonds
monthly - *BG*

Bond funds

Dividends
amount paid, individual funds,
    monthly - *MDR*
payment dates, individual funds,
    monthly - *MDR*
record dates, individual funds,
    monthly - *MDR*

Bond offerings

weekly - *Barron's*

Bond prices

Standard & Poor's High Grade Composite Index
weekly, monthly, and yearly - *SPIR*
range, yearly - *SPIR*

Bond yield

Minus average earnings yield
weekly, last market bottom, and last
    market top - *VL*
range, 13-week and 50-week - *VL*

Moody's
by rating groups, monthly and yearly -
    MIM

Standard & Poor's Index
by rating groups, weekly, monthly, and
    yearly - *SPIR*
range, by rating groups, yearly - *SPIR*

Bonds—*see also* types of bonds, (e.g.,
    Corporate bonds, Industrial bonds,
    etc.)

American Stock Exchange
advances, number, daily - *Barron's,
    WSJ*
declines, number, daily - *Barron's,
    WSJ*
highs, new, number, daily - *Barron's,
    WSJ*
interest periods, individual bonds,
    weekly - *CFC*
interest periods, individual bonds,
    monthly - *BQR*
issues traded, number, daily - *WSJ*
listings, daily - *NYT, WSJ*
listings, weekly - *Barron's, CFC*
listings, monthly - *BQR*
lows, new, number, daily - *Barron's,
    WSJ*
number listed, daily - *Barron's*
price range, individual bonds, weekly
    and year to date - *CFC*
price range, individual bonds, 52
    weeks - *Barron's*
ratings, weekly - *CFC*
ratings, monthly - *BQR*
sale price range, individual bonds,
    monthly and year to date - *BQR*
sales, daily and weekly - *Barron's*
sales, monthly - *BQR*
sales, individual bonds, weekly -
    Barron's
sales, individual bonds, monthly and
    year to date - *BQR*

unchanged bond prices, number, daily
- *Barron's, WSJ*
volume, dollars, daily - *WSJ*
volume, dollars, monthly - *BQR*
volume, dollars, year to date - *BQR,
WSJ*
volume, individual bonds, daily - *WSJ*
yield, individual bonds, daily - *NYT,
WSJ*
yield, individual bonds, weekly -
Barron's, CFC
yield, individual bonds, monthly -
BQR

Amount outstanding
individual bonds, monthly - *MBR*

Banks
yield, individual bonds, monthly -
BQR

Best grade
volume, percentage of NYSE volume,
weekly - *Barron's*
yield, Barron's 50-Stock Average,
weekly and monthly - *Barron's*

Call prices
monthly - *MBR*

Chronological list
classified according to Moody's ratings,
yearly - *MIM*

Convertible, industrial
yearly - *MIM*

Federal tax status
individual bonds, monthly - *MBR*

Finance companies
yield, individual bonds, monthly -
BQR

Foreign stock exchanges
domestic, par value, for selected
exchanges, yearly - *NYSEFB*

Insurance companies
yield, individual bonds, monthly -
BQR

Interest dates
individual bonds, monthly - *MBR*

Intermediate grade
volume, percentage of NYSE volume,
weekly - *Barron's*
yield, weekly - *Barron's*

Issue dates
individual bonds, monthly - *MBR*

Legal status
individual bonds, monthly - *MBR*

NASDAQ
listings, monthly - *BQR*

New issues
daily - *NYT*

New York Stock Exchange
advances, number, daily - *Barron's,
NYT, WSJ*
declines, number, daily - *Barron's,
NYT, WSJ*
highs, new, daily - *Barron's, NYT, WSJ*
interest period, individual bonds,
weekly - *CFC*
interest period, individual bonds,
monthly - *BQR*
issuers, number, yearly - *NYSEFB*
issues traded, daily - *NYT, WSJ*
listings, daily - *NYT, WSJ*
listings, weekly - *Barron's, CFC*
listings, monthly - *BQR*
lows, new, daily - *Barron's, NYT, WSJ*
market value, all listed bonds, yearly -
NYSEFB
number listed, daily - *Barron's*
par value, all listed bonds, total and
daily average, monthly - *NYSEFB*
par value, all listed bonds, yearly -
NYSEFB
price, average, yearly - *NYSEFB*
price range, individual bonds, weekly
and year to date - *CFC*
price range, individual bonds, 52
weeks - *Barron's*
private placements, yearly - *NYSEFB*
ratings, weekly - *CFC*
ratings, monthly - *BQR*
sale price range, individual bonds,
monthly and year to date - *BQR*
sales, daily and weekly - *Barron's*
sales, monthly - *BQR*
sales, year to date - *WSJ*
sales, individual bonds, daily - *NYT*
sales, individual bonds, weekly -
Barron's
sales, individual bonds, monthly and
year to date - *BQR*
transactions, par value, monthly and
yearly - *SPIR*
unchanged bond prices, number, daily
- *Barron's, NYT, WSJ*
volume, weekly and monthly - *Barron's*
volume, dollars, daily - *NYT, WSJ*
volume, dollars, monthly - *BQR*
volume, dollars, year to date - *BQR,
NYT, WSJ*

volume, dollars, yearly - *NYT*
volume, individual bonds, daily - *WSJ*
volume, par value, total and daily
    average, yearly - *NYSEFB*
volume, par value and date, records,
    yearly - *NYSEFB*
yield, individual bonds, daily - *NYT,
    WSJ*
yield, individual bonds, weekly -
    Barron's, CFC
yield, individual bonds, monthly -
    BQR

Number of issues
weekly, six weeks, and projection -
    MBS

Pacific Stock Exchange
listings, selected bonds, daily - *NYT,
    WSJ*
sales, selected individual bonds, daily -
    NYT, WSJ

Price range
individual bonds, since issue and year
    to date - *MBR*

Price when issued
individual bonds - *MBR*

**Railroad companies, domestic, newly
issued**
Moody's Weighted Averages of Yields,
    yearly - *MIM*

Ratings
changes, weekly - *Barron's*
Moody's, explanation and key,
    monthly - *MBR*
Moody's, individual bonds, monthly -
    MBR
Standard & Poor's, changes, monthly -
    BG
Standard & Poor's, changes, potential,
    monthly - *BG*
Standard & Poor's, definitions,
    monthly - *BG*

Sinking fund provision
individual bonds, monthly - *MBR*

Tax-free
listings, daily - *WSJ*
listings, weekly - *Barron's*
yield, individual bonds, daily - *WSJ*
yield, individual bonds, weekly -
    Barron's

Transportation
yield, individual bonds, monthly -
    BQR

Treasury—*see* Treasury bonds

US savings
semiannual yield, weekly - *Barron's*

Volume
dollars, weekly, six weeks, and
    projection - *MBS*

Yield, individual bonds
when issued - *MBR*
monthly - *MBR*

Bonds and preferred stock

Number of issues
weekly, six weeks, and projection -
    MBS

Volume
dollars, weekly, six weeks, and
    projection - *MBS*

Book value

Banks
individual corporations, per share,
    quarterly - *MHCS*

Change, annual rate
individual companies, past 5 years,
    past 10 years, and projection - *VL*

Common equity
individual companies and industries,
    yearly - *FD*
per share, annual growth rate,
    individual companies and
    industries, latest year, 3 years, 5
    years, and 10 years - *FD*
percentage of invested capital,
    individual companies and
    industries, yearly - *FD*

Common stock
individual industries, per share, yearly
    - *AH*

Individual companies
per share, yearly - *SOSG, VL*
per share, projections - *VL*

Individual industries
per share, yearly - *AH*

Preferred stock
individual industries, per share, yearly
    - *AH*

Return
individual industries, percentage,
   yearly - *AH*

Utilities
individual companies, yearly - *MHCS*

Widest discounts from
stocks listed, weekly - *VL*

Boosts

Dividend payment
weekly - *Barron's*

Borrowings from Federal Reserve

daily average of two-week period -
   Barron's, WSJ

Seasonal
weekly - *Barron's, WSJ*

Boston Stock Exchange

Listings
daily - *NYT, WSJ*
weekly - *Barron's*
monthly - *BQR*

Price range
individual stocks, year to date -
   Barron's

Sale price range
individual stocks, monthly and year to
   date - *BQR*

Sales
daily - *NYT, WSJ*
individual stocks, daily - *NYT, WSJ*
individual stocks, monthly and year to
   date - *BQR*

Seat prices
monthly - *BQR*

Seats outstanding
monthly - *BQR*

Volume
monthly and year to date - *BQR*
NYSE-listed stock, daily - *NYT, WSJ*
NYSE-listed stock, weekly - *Barron's*
NYSE-listed stock, monthly and yearly
   - *NYSEFB*
NYSE-listed stock, percentage of all
   exchanges' volume, yearly -
   NYSEFB

Brazilian cruzado

Exchange rate
daily - *NYT, WSJ*

Brazilian cruzeiro

Exchange rate
weekly - *Barron's*

Brazilian novo cruzeiro

Exchange rate
daily - *BQR*

Brewing companies stock price index

quarterly, graph - *MHCS*

British American Depository Receipts

Listings
daily - *WSJ*

British pound

Exchange rate
daily - *BQR, NYT, WSJ*
weekly - *Barron's*

Forward exchange rates
daily - *NYT, WSJ*
weekly - *Barron's*

British prime rate

daily - *WSJ*
weekly - *Barron's*

British Stock Index—*see* headings
   beginning United Kingdom,
   Financial Times

Broadcast media industry

Financial statistics
yearly - *AH*

Broadcasting/cable TV industry

Financial statistics
yearly - *VL*

Broker call loans

Rates
daily - *NYT*

Brokerage companies

Securities
net capital ratio, individual companies,
  yearly - *MHCS*
percentage earned on net worth,
  individual companies, yearly -
  MHCS

Brokerage Firms Index

Standard & Poor's
weekly, monthly, and yearly - *SPIR*
component companies, yearly - *SPIR*
range, yearly - *SPIR*

Brussels Stock Exchange—*see*
  Belgium, Brussels Stock Exchange

Brussels Stock Index—*see*
  Belgium, Brussels Stock Index

Buenos Aires Stock Exchange

Listings, selected stocks
daily - *NYT*

Building construction

monthly and yearly - *SOSG*

Building contracts (Dodge)

monthly - *Barron's*

Building industry

Financial statistics
yearly - *VL*

Building material and equipment

Barron's Group Stock Averages
weekly - *Barron's*
companies and weights, irregularly -
  Barron's
range, yearly - *Barron's*

Building Materials Index

Standard & Poor's
weekly, monthly, and yearly - *SPIR*
component companies, yearly - *SPIR*
range, yearly - *SPIR*

Building Materials Index (air conditioning)

Standard & Poor's
weekly, monthly, and yearly - *SPIR*
component companies, yearly - *SPIR*
range, yearly - *SPIR*

Building Materials Index (cement)

Standard & Poor's
weekly, monthly, and yearly - *SPIR*
component companies, yearly - *SPIR*
range, yearly - *SPIR*

Building Materials Index (diversified)

Standard & Poor's
weekly, monthly, and yearly - *SPIR*
component companies, yearly - *SPIR*
range, yearly - *SPIR*

Building Materials Index (roofing and wallboard)

Standard & Poor's
weekly, monthly, and yearly - *SPIR*
component companies, yearly - *SPIR*
range, yearly - *SPIR*

Building materials industry

Financial statistics
yearly - *AH*

Building materials industry (cement)

Financial statistics
yearly - *FD*

Building materials industry (heat, air conditioning and plumbing)

Financial statistics
yearly - *FD*

Building supplies industry

Financial statistics
yearly - *VL*

Business failures

Number
5-week moving average, weekly -
   Barron's

Business incorporations

Dun & Bradstreet, new incorporations
monthly - *Barron's*

Business inventories—*see*
   Inventories

Business sales—*see* Sales

Buy/sell

American Stock Exchange
members, net, weekly - *Barron's*

New York Stock Exchange
members, net, weekly - *Barron's*

C

Cable TV/broadcasting
   industry—*see* Broadcasting/cable
   TV industry

CAC General Index—*see* France,
   CAC General Index

Calendar

Ex-dividend dates
yearly - *SPQDR*
5-day settlement plan, yearly - *MDR*

Call loans

Broker
rates, daily - *NYT*

NYSE collateral
rates, range, daily - *BQR*

Call money

Rates
daily - *WSJ*

Call price

Bonds
individual bonds, monthly - *MBR*

Corporate bonds
individual bonds, monthly - *BG*

Foreign bonds
individual bonds, monthly - *BG*

Preferred stock
individual stocks, monthly - *MBR*

Sinking fund
corporate bonds, individual bonds,
   monthly - *BG*
foreign bonds, individual bonds,
   monthly - *BG*

Calls—*see also* Options

American Stock Exchange
contracts exercised, number, monthly
   and yearly - *AmexFB*
number and daily average, monthly
   and yearly - *AmexFB*
number, by type of option, monthly
   and yearly - *AmexFB*
number traded, total and daily average,
   yearly - *AmexFB*
open interest, monthly and yearly -
   AmexFB

Most active equity options
listed, by exchange, weekly - *Barron's*

Open interest
by exchange and type of option, daily -
   NYT, WSJ
by exchange and type of option,
   weekly - *Barron's*

Stock index options
open interest, by exchange, individual
   indexes, daily - *NYT, WSJ*

volume, by exchange, individual
    indexes, daily - *NYT, WSJ*

Volume
by exchange and type of option, daily -
    NYT, WSJ
by exchange and type of option,
    weekly - *Barron's*
compared to put volume, Chicago
    Board Options Exchange, weekly,
    last market bottom, and last market
    top - *VL*
compared to put volume, Chicago
    Board Options Exchange, range,
    13-week and 50-week - *VL*

Canada, Montreal Stock Exchange

Listings
weekly - *Barron's*
selected stocks, daily - *NYT, WSJ*

Sales
daily - *NYT, WSJ*
selected individual stocks, daily - *NYT,
    WSJ*

Canada, Toronto Stock Exchange

Dividend, indicated annual
individual stocks, monthly - *BQR*

Listings
daily - *CFC, NYT, WSJ*
weekly - *Barron's*
monthly - *BQR*

Price-earnings ratio
individual stocks, weekly - *CFC*
individual stocks, monthly - *BQR*

Sale price range
individual stocks, monthly and year to
    date - *BQR*

Sales
individual stocks, daily - *NYT, WSJ*
individual stocks, weekly - *CFC*
individual stocks, monthly and year to
    date - *BQR*

Seat prices
monthly - *BQR*

Seats outstanding
number, monthly - *BQR*

Yield
individual stocks, weekly - *CFC*
individual stocks, monthly - *BQR*

Canada, Toronto Stock Index

daily - *NYT*
weekly - *Barron's*

Canada, Winnipeg Commodity Exchange

Seat prices
monthly - *BQR*

Canadian dollar

Exchange rate
daily - *BQR, NYT, WSJ*
weekly - *Barron's*

Forward exchange rates
daily - *NYT, WSJ*
weekly - *Barron's*

Canadian energy industry

Financial statistics
yearly - *VL*

Canadian issues—*see* Issues

Canadian municipal bonds—*see* Municipal bonds

Canadian Oil and Gas Exploration Index

Standard & Poor's
weekly, monthly, and yearly - *SPIR*
component companies, yearly - *SPIR*
range, yearly - *SPIR*

Canadian prime rate

daily - *WSJ*
weekly - *Barron's*

Canadian Stock Index

daily - *NYT*
weekly - *Barron's*

Capacity

Petroleum production
one day each week - *Barron's*

Steel production
one day each week - *Barron's*

Capital

Invested
after-tax return, change, effect on
earnings per share, individual
companies and industries, yearly -
FD
after-tax return, individual companies
and industries, yearly - *FD*
individual companies and industries,
yearly - *FD*
per employee, average, individual
companies and industries, yearly -
FD
per share, annual growth rate,
individual companies and
industries, latest year, 3 years, 5
years, and 10 years - *FD*
percentage of common equity (book
value), individual companies and
industries, yearly - *FD*
percentage of long-term debt,
individual companies and
industries, yearly - *FD*
percentage of minority interest,
deferred taxes, and investment tax
credit, individual companies and
industries, yearly - *FD*
percentage of nonredeemable preferred
stock, individual companies and
industries, yearly - *FD*
percentage of redeemable preferred
stock, individual companies and
industries, yearly - *FD*
pretax return, change, effect on
earnings per share, individual
companies and industries, yearly -
FD
pretax return, individual companies
and industries, yearly - *FD*

New
price, average, yearly - *MIM*

New York Stock Exchange
member organizations, yearly -
NYSEFB

Percentage earned on
highest, stocks listed, weekly - *VL*

Senior
individual companies, yearly - *MHCS*

Working
change, individual companies and
industries, yearly - *FD*
incremental dollars of sales per
incremental dollar of working

capital, individual companies and
industries, yearly - *FD*
individual companies, yearly - *FD,
MHCS, VL*
individual companies, projections - *VL*
individual companies, per share, yearly
- *AH*
individual industries, yearly - *FD, VL*
individual industries, projections - *VL*
percentage of sales, individual
companies and industries, yearly -
FD
sales per dollar average, individual
companies and industries, yearly -
FD

Capital expenditures

Individual companies
yearly - *FD, SPSR*

Individual industries
yearly - *FD*
per share, yearly - *AH*

Percentage of average gross plant
individual companies and industries,
yearly - *FD*

Capital flow, net

International transactions
foreign stocks, NYSE, quarterly and
yearly - *NYSEFB*
US stocks, NYSE, quarterly and yearly
- *NYSEFB*

Capital Goods Index

Standard & Poor's
weekly, monthly, and yearly - *SPIR*
component groups, yearly - *SPIR*
range, yearly - *SPIR*

Capital ratio, net

**Individual securities brokerage
companies**
yearly - *MHCS, SPSR*

Capital spending

Per share
individual companies, yearly and
projection - *VL*

Capital structure

Individual companies
quarterly - *VL*

Capital surplus

Individual industries
per share, yearly - *AH*

Capitalization

Individual companies
yearly - *MHCS, SPSR*

Capitalized leases—*see* Leases

Cash

Individual companies
yearly - *SPSR*

Treasury holdings
Federal Reserve banks, daily - *WSJ*

Cash accounts

Credit balance
NYSE, quarterly - *NYSEFB*

Free credit balance
NYSE, monthly - *Barron's*

Cash and equivalent

Individual companies
monthly - *BG*
quarterly - *FD*

Individual industries
per share, yearly - *AH*

Mutual funds
yearly - *SOSG*

Percentage of assets
individual companies and industries,
    yearly - *FD*

Percentage of sales
individual companies and industries,
    yearly - *FD*

Ratio to current liabilities
individual companies, quarterly and
    5-year average - *VL*

Cash and short-term investments

Individual companies and industries
yearly - *FD*

Cash and short-term securities

Mutual funds
monthly - *Barron's*

Cash assets

Individual companies
quarterly - *VL*
yearly - *VL*

Cash dividends

Individual companies and industries
yearly - *FD*

Cash flow

After-tax
per dollar average gross plant,
    individual companies and
    industries, yearly - *FD*
per dollar average invested capital,
    individual companies and
    industries, yearly - *FD*

Change, annual rate
individual companies, past 5 years,
    past 10 years, and projections - *VL*

Individual companies and industries
quarterly, moving 12 months, and
    yearly - *FD*

Per employee
individual companies and industries,
    yearly - *FD*

Per share
annual growth rate, individual
    companies and industries, latest
    year, 3 years, 5 years, and 10 years -
    FD
change, year to year, individual
    companies and industries, quarterly,
    moving 12 months, and yearly - *FD*
individual companies, quarterly,
    moving 12 months, and yearly - *FD,
    VL*
individual companies, projections - *VL*
individual industries, quarterly,
    moving 12 months, and yearly - *FD*
least squares growth rate and
    coefficient of determination,

individual companies and
industries, 5-year and 10-year - *FD*

Percentage equivalent to dividends
per share, individual companies and
industries, yearly - *FD*

Percentage of industry cash flow
individual companies, yearly - *FD*

Percentage of sales
individual companies and industries,
quarterly, moving 12 months, and
yearly - *FD*

Pretax
per dollar average gross plant,
individual companies and
industries, yearly - *FD*
per dollar average invested capital,
individual companies and
industries, yearly - *FD*

Ratio of price to
range, individual companies and
industries, yearly - *FD*

Cash generators

Free flow, biggest
stocks listed, weekly - *VL*

Cash holdings

Treasury
Federal Reserve banks, weekly - *WSJ*

Cash position

Individual companies
quarterly and 5-year average - *VL*

Cash prices

Commodities
daily - *NYT, WSJ*

Cement industry

Financial statistics
yearly - *VL*

Ceramics—*see* Continental ceramics

Certificates of deposit

Rates
daily - *BQR, WSJ*
average, weekly - *Barron's*

Resale
90 days, rates, weekly - *Barron's*

Secondary market offerings
rates, daily - *NYT*

Top savings deposit yields
weekly - *Barron's*

Changes

Bond ratings
weekly - *Barron's, MBS*
monthly - *MBR, BG*

Book value, annual rate
individual companies, past 5 years,
past 10 years, and projections - *VL*

Cash flow, annual rate
individual companies, past 5 years,
past 10 years, and projections - *VL*

Commercial paper ratings
Moody's, weekly - *MBS*
Moody's, monthly - *MBR*

Common stock ratings
Standard & Poor's, monthly - *SOSG*

Company names
weekly - *Barron's*
monthly - *SOSG*
quarterly - *MHCS*
year to date - *BQR*
NYSE, yearly - *NYSEFB*

Dividends, annual rate
individual companies, past 5 years,
past 10 years, and projections - *VL*

Dividends, comparative
monthly, quarterly, semiannually, 9
months, and yearly - *MDR*

Earnings, annual rate
individual companies, past 5 years,
past 10 years, and projections - *VL*

Mutual fund names
weekly - *Barron's*

Preferred stock ratings
Moody's, weekly - *MBS*
Standard & Poor's, monthly - *SOSG*

Sales, annual rate
individual companies, past 5 years,
    past 10 years, and projections - *VL*

Charge

Mutual funds
sales, maximum, percentage, yearly -
    SOSG

Charges, fixed

Times earnings
individual companies, yearly - *BG*
interim, individual companies, yearly -
    BG

Chemicals

Barron's Group Stock Averages
weekly - *Barron's*
companies and weights, irregularly -
    Barron's
range, yearly - *Barron's*

Chemicals Index

Standard & Poor's
weekly, monthly, and yearly - *SPIR*
component companies, yearly - *SPIR*
range, yearly - *SPIR*

Chemicals Index (miscellaneous)

Standard & Poor's
weekly, monthly, and yearly - *SPIR*
component companies, yearly - *SPIR*
range, yearly - *SPIR*

Chemicals industry

Financial statistics
yearly - *AH, FD*

Chemicals industry (basic)

Financial statistics
yearly - *VL*

Chemicals industry (diversified)

Financial statistics
yearly - *AH, VL*

Chemicals industry (miscellaneous)

Financial statistics
yearly - *FD*

Chemicals industry (specialty)

Financial statistics
yearly - *VL*

Chicago Board of Trade

Listings
weekly - *Barron's*

Seat prices
monthly - *BQR*

Seats outstanding
number, monthly - *BQR*

Chicago Board Options Exchange

Calls
open interest, by type of option, daily -
    NYT, WSJ
open interest, by type of option,
    weekly - *Barron's*
volume, by type of option, daily -
    NYT, WSJ
volume, by type of option, weekly -
    Barron's

Listings
daily - *NYT, WSJ*
weekly - *Barron's*
monthly - *BQR*

Most active equity options
calls, listed, weekly - *Barron's*
puts, listed, weekly - *Barron's*

Most active options
listed, daily - *NYT, WSJ*
sales, individual options, daily - *NYT,
    WSJ*

Open interest
monthly - *BQR*

Options
price ranges, monthly and since issue -
    BQR

Puts
open interest, by type of option, daily -
    NYT, WSJ
open interest, by type of option,
    weekly - *Barron's*

volume, by type of option, daily -
NYT, WSJ
volume, by type of option, weekly -
Barron's
volume, compared to call volume,
weekly, last market bottom, and last
market top - *VL*
volume, compared to call volume,
range, 13-week and 50-week - *VL*

Sales
monthly - *BQR*

Seat prices
monthly - *BQR*

Seats outstanding
number, monthly - *BQR*

Stock index options
calls, open interest, individual indexes,
daily - *NYT, WSJ*
calls, volume, individual indexes, daily
- *NYT, WSJ*
puts, open interest, individual indexes,
daily - *NYT, WSJ*
puts, volume, individual indexes, daily
- *NYT, WSJ*

Chicago Board Options Exchange Equity Index

Put-call ratio
weekly - *Barron's*

Chicago Mercantile Exchange

Listings
weekly - *Barron's*

Seat prices
monthly - *BQR*

Seats outstanding
number, monthly - *BQR*

Chilean escudo

Exchange rate
daily - *BQR*

Chilean official exchange rate

daily - *WSJ*
weekly - *Barron's*

Chilean peso

Exchange rate
daily - *NYT*

Chinese yuan

Exchange rate
daily - *WSJ*
weekly - *Barron's*

Cincinnati Stock Exchange

Seat prices
monthly - *BQR*

Seats outstanding
number, monthly - *BQR*

Volume, NYSE-listed stock
daily - *NYT, WSJ*
weekly - *Barron's*
monthly and yearly - *NYSEFB*
percentage of all exchanges' trading in
NYSE-listed stock, yearly - *NYSEFB*

Civil labor force

monthly - *Barron's*

Civilian employment

monthly and annual average - *SOSG*

Closed-end bond funds

Listings
weekly - *Barron's*

Closed-end investment companies

Barron's Group Stock Averages
weekly - *Barron's*
companies and weights, irregularly -
Barron's
range, yearly - *Barron's*

Closed-end stock funds

Listings
weekly - *Barron's*

Coal/alternate energy industry

Financial statistics
yearly - *VL*

Coal Index (bituminous)

Standard & Poor's
weekly, monthly, and yearly - *SPIR*
component companies, yearly - *SPIR*
range, yearly - *SPIR*

Coal industry

Financial statistics
yearly - *AH*

Coal industry (bituminous)

Financial statistics
yearly - *FD*

Coffee-Sugar-Cocoa Exchange

Listings
weekly - *Barron's*

Seat prices
monthly - *BQR*

Seats outstanding
number, monthly - *BQR*

Collateral securing debt—*see* Debt

Colombian peso

Exchange rate
daily - *NYT, WSJ*
weekly - *Barron's*

Free exchange rate
daily - *BQR*

Combined ratio

Insurance companies
individual companies, yearly - *MHCS*

Comex—*see* New York Commodity Exchange

Commercial and miscellaneous companies

Security issues
dollars, yearly - *MIM*

Commercial paper

Amount outstanding
weekly - *MBS, WSJ*

Dealer placed
rates, daily - *BQR, NYT*
rates, weekly - *Barron's, MBS*
rates, weekly, graph - *MBR, MBS*

Directly placed
rates, daily - *BQR*
rates, weekly - *MBS*

Financial companies
amount outstanding, weekly - *WSJ*
rates, daily - *NYT*

General Motors Acceptance Corporation
rates, daily - *WSJ*
rates, weekly - *Barron's*

High-grade
rates, weekly - *Barron's*

Issuer agreements terminated
listed, weekly - *MBS*

New issues
listed, weekly - *MBS*

Nonfinancial companies
amount outstanding, weekly - *WSJ*

Rate spread
vs. prime rate, weekly - *MBS*

Rates
daily - *WSJ*

Ratings
Moody's, changes, individual issues,
    weekly - *MBS*
Moody's, changes, individual issues,
    monthly - *MBR*
Moody's, explanation and key,
    monthly - *MBR*
Moody's, individual issues, monthly -
    MBR
Standard & Poor's, definitions,
    monthly - *BG*
Standard & Poor's, individual
    companies, yearly - *FD*

Commerzbank Index—*see* West Germany, Commerzbank Index

Commodities

Cash prices
daily - *NYT, WSJ*

Scrap, Prices, Moody's Index
monthly - *MIM*
monthly, graph - *MIM*
yearly - *MIM*

Commodity futures

Listings
by exchange, daily - *NYT, WSJ*
by exchange, weekly - *Barron's*

Open interest
individual commodities, daily - *WSJ*

Volume
individual commodities, daily - *WSJ*

Commodity Price Index

Moody's Daily
average, monthly and yearly - *MIM*
range, monthly - *MIM*
range, monthly, graph - *MIM*
range, yearly - *MIM*

Commodity Research Bureau Futures Index

daily - *NYT, WSJ*

Common dividends

Individual industries
per share, yearly - *AH*

Common earnings—*see* Earnings

Common equity

And surplus
individual companies, yearly - *MHCS*
percentage of capitalization, individual
    companies, yearly - *MHCS*

Book value
individual companies and industries,
    yearly - *FD*
per share, annual growth rate,
    individual companies and
    industries, latest year, 3 years, 5
    years, and 10 years - *FD*

percentage of invested capital,
    individual companies and
    industries, yearly - *FD*

Individual companies
quarterly - *FD*
yearly - *FD, SPSR*

Individual industries
yearly - *FD*

Internal growth
individual companies and industries,
    yearly - *FD*

Per share
individual companies and industries,
    yearly - *FD*
individual companies and industries,
    average, yearly - *FD*
ratio of price to, range, individual
    companies and industries, yearly -
    FD

Percentage of assets
individual companies, quarterly and
    yearly - *FD*
individual industries, yearly - *FD*

Percentage of current liabilities
individual companies and industries,
    yearly - *FD*

Percentage of invested capital
individual companies and industries,
    yearly - *FD*

Pretax return
individual companies and industries,
    yearly - *FD*

Return
percentage of S&P 400 return,
    individual companies and
    industries, yearly - *FD*
percentage of S&P industry relatives,
    individual companies, yearly - *FD*

Common stock

American Stock Exchange
new listings, yearly - *AmexFB*

Book value
individual industries, per share, yearly
    - *AH*

Corporate
issues, dollars, yearly - *MIM*

New York Stock Exchange
cash dividends, number paying, yearly
- *NYSEFB*
dividends, estimated aggregate cash
payments, yearly - *NYSEFB*
dividends, longevity of record, by
number of consecutive years, yearly
- *NYSEFB*
market value, by industry, yearly -
NYSEFB
market value, domestic companies,
yearly - *NYSEFB*
new listings, companies and dates,
yearly - *NYSEFB*
new listings, number, yearly - *NYSEFB*
number of issues listed, yearly -
NYSEFB
number of issues listed, by industry,
yearly - *NYSEFB*
number of shares listed, by industry,
yearly - *NYSEFB*
removals, number, yearly - *NYSEFB*
yield, median, yearly - *NYSEFB*
yield, median, records, yearly -
NYSEFB
yields, number of issues, by
percentages, yearly - *NYSEFB*

Public Utilities
Yield, Moody's Averages, weekly -
MBS
Yield, Moody's Averages, range, yearly
- *MBS*

Ratings
Standard & Poor's, monthly - *SOSG*
Standard & Poor's, changes, monthly -
SOSG
Standard & Poor's, definitions,
monthly - *SOSG*

Shares outstanding
individual companies, quarterly and
yearly - *VL*

Common stock and warrant issues

American Stock Exchange
market value, aggregate, yearly -
AmexFB
number of issues, yearly - *AmexFB*
price, average, yearly - *AmexFB*
shares outstanding, number, yearly -
AmexFB

Common stock equivalents

Per share
individual companies and industries,
yearly - *FD*

Savings due to
individual companies and industries,
yearly - *FD*

Common Stock Index

High Grade, Standard & Poor's
weekly, monthly, and yearly - *SPIR*
component companies, yearly - *SPIR*
range, yearly - *SPIR*

New York Stock Exchange—*see* New
York Stock Exchange Common
Stock Index

Common stock splits

New York Stock Exchange
yearly - *NYSEFB*

Communications companies

Security issues
dollars, yearly - *MIM*

Communications Equipment/ Manufacturers Index

Standard & Poor's
weekly, monthly, and yearly - *SPIR*
component companies, yearly - *SPIR*
range, yearly - *SPIR*

Communications equipment/ manufacturers industry

Financial statistics
yearly - *AH*

Companies

American Stock Exchange
number, yearly - *NASDAQFB*

Barron's 50-Stocks Average
irregularly - *Barron's*

Barron's Group Stock Averages
irregularly - *Barron's*

Barron's Low-Priced Stock Index
irregularly - *Barron's*

Dealings suspended
listed, weekly - *Barron's*

Domestic
number with shares listed on selected
foreign stock exchanges, yearly -
NYSEFB

Dow Jones averages
irregularly - *Barron's*
quarterly - *DSPR*

Dow Jones bond averages
irregularly - *Barron's*

NASDAQ
headquarters states, yearly -
NASDAQFB
number, yearly - *NASDAQFB*
number, percentage increase, latest 10
years - *NASDAQFB*

NASDAQ National List
typical company profile, yearly -
NASDAQFB

NASDAQ NMS
typical company profile, yearly -
NASDAQFB

New York Stock Exchange
assets, aggregate, yearly - *NYSEFB*
assets, aggregate, percentage of all US
companies' assets, yearly - *NYSEFB*
net income, aggregate, yearly -
NYSEFB
net income, aggregate, percentage of all
US companies' net income, yearly -
NYSEFB
number, yearly - *NASDAQFB,*
NYSEFB
number, by industry, yearly - *NYSEFB*
percentage of all US companies, yearly
- *NYSEFB*
revenues, aggregate, yearly - *NYSEFB*
revenues, aggregate, percentage of all
US companies' revenues, yearly -
NYSEFB
sales, aggregate, yearly - *NYSEFB*
sales, aggregate, percentage of all US
companies' sales, yearly - *NYSEFB*

Ratings
Standard & Poor's, individual
companies, quarterly - *SPSR*

United States
assets, aggregate, yearly - *NYSEFB*
net income, aggregate, yearly -
NYSEFB
number, yearly - *NYSEFB*

revenues, aggregate, yearly - *NYSEFB*
sales, aggregate, yearly - *NYSEFB*

Company name changes—*see*
Changes

Compensating balances

Individual companies and industries
yearly - *FD*

Competitive municipal bonds

Number of issues
weekly, six weeks, and projection -
MBS

Volume
dollars, weekly, six weeks, and
projection - *MBS*

Composite Average, Dow
Jones—*see* Dow Jones Composite
Average

Composite Indicator,
NASDAQ—*see* NASDAQ
Composite Index

Composite Indicator, New York
Stock Exchange—*see* New York
Stock Exchange Common Stock
Index

Composite Index, New York
Stock Exchange—*see* New York
Stock Exchange Common Stock
Index

Composite volume

American Stock Exchange
daily - *WSJ*

Compound yield

Money market funds
weekly - *Barron's*

Compounded growth rates

New York Stock Exchange
volume, yearly - *NYSEFB*

Computer and Business Equipment Index

Standard & Poor's
weekly, monthly, and yearly - *SPIR*
component companies, yearly - *SPIR*
range, yearly - *SPIR*

Computer and Business Equipment Index (excluding IBM)

Standard & Poor's
weekly, monthly, and yearly - *SPIR*
component companies, yearly - *SPIR*
range, yearly - *SPIR*

Computer and business equipment industry

Financial statistics
yearly - *AH*

Computer and business equipment industry (excluding IBM)

Financial statistics
yearly - *AH*

Computer and peripherals industry

Financial statistics
yearly - *VL*

Computer Services Index

Standard & Poor's
weekly, monthly, and yearly - *SPIR*
component companies, yearly - *SPIR*
range, yearly - *SPIR*

Computer services industry

Financial statistics
yearly - *AH*

Computer software and services industry

Financial statistics
yearly - *VL*

Computer Technology Index

daily - *WSJ*

Amex, stock index options
calls, number, yearly - *AmexFB*
close, monthly and yearly - *AmexFB*
contracts, number and daily average,
   yearly - *AmexFB*
puts, number, yearly - *AmexFB*

Confidence Index—*see* Barron's Confidence Index

Conglomerates

Financial statistics
yearly - *AH, FD*

Conglomerates Index

Standard & Poor's
weekly, monthly, and yearly - *SPIR*
component companies, yearly - *SPIR*
range, yearly - *SPIR*

Conservative stocks

Grouped by relative safety ratings
weekly - *VL*

Consolidated tape volume

NYSE-listed stock
monthly and yearly - *NYSEFB*
distribution, by exchange, yearly -
   NYSEFB

Consolidations and mergers

New York Stock Exchange
companies and dates, yearly - *NYSEFB*

Construction

Building
monthly and yearly - *SOSG*

Spending
monthly - *Barron's*

Statistics
monthly - *Barron's*

Consumer Price Index

monthly - *Barron's*

Consumers' Goods Index

Standard & Poor's
weekly, monthly, and yearly - *SPIR*
component groups, yearly - *SPIR*
range, yearly - *SPIR*

Container and packaging industry

Financial statistics
yearly - *VL*

Containers Index (metal and glass)

Standard & Poor's
weekly, monthly, and yearly - *SPIR*
component companies, yearly - *SPIR*
range, yearly - *SPIR*

Containers Index (paper)

Standard & Poor's
weekly, monthly, and yearly - *SPIR*
component companies, yearly - *SPIR*
range, yearly - *SPIR*

Containers industry (metal and glass)

Financial statistics
yearly - *AH*

Containers industry (paper)

Financial statistics
yearly - *AH*

Continental and French furniture—*see* Furniture

Continental ceramics

Sotheby's Art Index
weekly - *Barron's*

Continental silver—*see* Silver

Contract specifications

New York Futures Exchange
for NYSE stock index futures, yearly - *NYSEFB*
for NYSE stock index options on futures, yearly - *NYSEFB*

New York Stock Exchange
for NYSE Composite Index and NYSE Double Index options, yearly - *NYSEFB*

Contracts

American Stock Exchange
calls, volume, yearly - *AmexFB*
options, volume, monthly and yearly - *AmexFB*
puts, volume, yearly - *AmexFB*
stock index options, number and daily average, by index, yearly - *AmexFB*

Contracts exercised

American Stock Exchange
calls, yearly - *AmexFB*
puts, yearly - *AmexFB*

Contracts per transaction

Specialists, Amex
options, number, by type of option, average, yearly - *AmexFB*

Contracts traded

American Stock Exchange
gold options, number and daily average, monthly - *AmexFB*
options, number and daily average, by type of option, yearly - *AmexFB*

Contribution

International
individual companies, yearly - *FD*

Convertible bonds

Amount outstanding
individual bonds, monthly - *BG*

Conversion information
individual bonds, monthly - *BG*

Form of bonds
individual bonds, monthly - *BG*

Industrial issues
yearly - *MIM*

Interest dates
individual bonds, monthly - *BG*

New issues registered
monthly - *BG*
amount, individual bonds, monthly -
   BG
ratings, Standard & Poor's,
   preliminary, monthly - *BG*

Price
individual bonds, monthly - *BG*

Price range
individual bonds, year to date - *BG*

Privileges changing and/or expiring
monthly - *BG*

Rate
individual bonds, monthly - *BG*
Standard & Poor's, monthly - *BG*

Yield
individual bonds, monthly - *BG*

Convertible offerings

New
weekly - *Barron's*

Convertible stock

Industrial issues
yearly - *MIM*

Copper Index

Standard & Poor's
weekly, monthly, and yearly - *SPIR*
component companies, yearly - *SPIR*
range, yearly - *SPIR*

Copper industry

Financial statistics
yearly - *AH, VL*

Corporate bond mutual funds

Sales
monthly - *Barron's*

Corporate bonds

American Stock Exchange
amount outstanding, yearly - *AmexFB*
market value, aggregate, yearly -
   AmexFB
number of issues, yearly - *AmexFB*
price, average, yearly - *AmexFB*

volume, principal amount, yearly -
   AmexFB

Amount outstanding
individual bonds, monthly - *BG*

Bond form
monthly - *BG*

Call price
individual bonds, monthly - *BG*
sinking fund, individual bonds,
   monthly - *BG*

Distributed, yield
by rating groups, monthly, graph -
   MBR
composite and by rating groups,
   monthly - *MBS*

Eligibility
monthly - *BG*

Exchange where traded
individual bonds, monthly - *BG*

Foreign, NYSE
market value, yearly - *NYSEFB*
market value, by geographic region,
   yearly - *NYSEFB*
number of issuers, yearly - *NYSEFB*
number of issues, yearly - *NYSEFB*
par value, yearly - *NYSEFB*

Interest dates
individual bonds, monthly - *BG*

Issues
dollars, yearly - *MIM*

New York Stock Exchange
volume, dollars, daily - *WSJ*
volume, individual bonds, daily - *WSJ*
yield, individual bonds, daily - *WSJ*

Newly issued
amount, by rating groups, monthly,
   chart - *MBR*
amount, composite and by rating
   groups, monthly - *MBS*
Yield, Moody's Average, by rating
   groups, monthly, graph - *MBR*
Yield, Moody's Average, composite
   and by rating groups, monthly -
   MBS, MIM

Offerings
weekly - *Barron's*

Price
individual bonds, monthly - *BG*

Price range
individual bonds, yearly - *BG*

Privately placed
issues, dollars, yearly - *MIM*

Prospective offerings
ratings, Moody's, weekly - *MBS*
statistics, individual bonds, weekly -
    MBS

Publicly offered
issues, dollars, yearly - *MBR, MIM*

Ratings
Moody's, explanation and key,
    monthly - *MBR*
Standard & Poor's, monthly - *BG*
Standard & Poor's, by class of debt,
    individual companies, yearly - *FD*
Standard & Poor's, definitions,
    monthly - *BG*

Recent offerings
ratings, Moody's, weekly - *MBS*
statistics, individual bonds, weekly -
    MBS

Redemption provisions
individual bonds, monthly - *BG*

Statistics
individual bonds, monthly - *MBR*

Underwriter
individual bonds, monthly - *BG*

United States, NYSE
market value, yearly - *NYSEFB*
number of issuers, yearly - *NYSEFB*
number of issues, yearly - *NYSEFB*
par value, yearly - *NYSEFB*

Year of original offering
individual bonds, monthly - *BG*

Yield
by rating groups, monthly, graph -
    MBR
individual bonds, monthly - *BG*
Moody's Average, Aaa, weekly, last
    market bottom, and last market top
    - *VL*
Moody's Average, Aaa, range, 13-week
    and 50-week - *VL*
Moody's Average, by rating groups,
    weekly, graph - *MBR, MBS*
Moody's Average, by rating groups,
    monthly, graph - *MBR*
Moody's Average, composite and by
    rating groups, daily - *MBS*

Moody's Average, composite and by
    rating groups, monthly and yearly -
    MIM
Moody's Average, range, composite
    and by rating groups, yearly - *MBS*
Standard & Poor's Index, by rating
    groups, weekly and monthly - *BG*
Standard & Poor's Index, by rating
    groups, range, weekly - *BG*

Yield spread
Aaa vs. Treasury bonds, weekly, graph
    - *MBS*
among rating groups, weekly, graph -
    MBS
Salomon government/corporate yield
    spread, weekly - *Barron's*

Corporate bonds and foreign bonds

Number of issues
weekly, six months, and projection -
    MBS

Volume
dollars, weekly, six weeks, and
    projection - *MBS*

Corporate common stock issues

dollars, yearly - *MIM*

Corporate offerings

Week's probable
weekly - *Barron's*

Corporate preferred stock issues

dollars, yearly - *MIM*

Corporate securities

Amount issued
dollars, yearly - *MIM*

Ratings
Moody's, changes, monthly - *MBR*
Moody's, new, weekly - *MBS*
Moody's, reviewed and confirmed,
    weekly - *MBS*
Moody's, reviewed and revised, weekly
    - *MBS*
Moody's, withdrawn, weekly - *MBS*

Corporations—*see also* Companies

New York Stock Exchange
member organizations, number, yearly
- *NYSEFB*

Cosmetics Index

Standard & Poor's
weekly, monthly, and yearly - *SPIR*
component companies, yearly - *SPIR*
range, yearly - *SPIR*

Cosmetics industry

Financial statistics
yearly - *AH*

Cosmetics/toiletries industry

Financial statistics
yearly - *VL*

Cost of goods sold

Individual companies
quarterly and yearly - *FD*

Individual industries
yearly - *FD*

Percentage of sales
individual companies and industries,
quarterly, moving 12 months, and
yearly - *FD*

Cost of goods sold expense margin

Change
effect of earnings per share, individual
companies and industries, yearly -
FD

Cost of Living Index

monthly and annual average - *SOSG*

Costs and expenses

Individual industries
per share, yearly - *AH*

Cotton consumption

monthly and annual average - *SOSG*

Coverage

Fixed charge
Individual companies and industries,
yearly - *FD*

Pretax interest
individual companies and industries,
yearly - *FD*

Credit

Extended
Federal Reserve banks, weekly -
Barron's, WSJ

Federal
adjusted, weekly - *Barron's*

Federal Reserve banks
weekly - *WSJ*

Security
quality, NYSE, monthly, graph -
NYSEFB

Credit balance

Cash accounts
free, NYSE, monthly - *Barron's*
NYSE, quarterly - *NYSEFB*

Margin accounts
NYSE, monthly and quarterly -
NYSEFB

New York Stock Exchange
customers, monthly - *Barron's*
customers, records, yearly - *NYSEFB*

Credit cards

Bank
interest rates, individual banks, weekly
- *Barron's*

Credit Suisse Stock Index—*see*
Switzerland, Credit Suisse Stock
Index

Creditwatch

monthly - *BG*

Crude oil

Domestic
inventories, weekly - *Barron's*

Cruzado, Brazilian—*see* Brazilian cruzado

Cruzeiro, Brazilian—*see* Brazilian cruzeiro

Cruzeiro, novo, Brazilian—*see* Brazilian novo cruzeiro

Currencies, foreign—*see* individual headings for specific currencies (e.g., Argentine austral; Belgian franc; Mexican peso; etc.)

Currency gains

Individual companies
quarterly and yearly - *FD*

Individual industries
yearly - *FD*

Currency in circulation

weekly - *Barron's, WSJ*

Currency losses

Individual companies
quarterly and yearly - *FD*

Individual industries
yearly - *FD*

Current assets

Individual companies
monthly - *BG*
quarterly - *FD, VL*
yearly - *FD, SPSR, VL*

Individual industries
yearly - *FD*
per share, yearly - *AH*

Ratio to current liabilities
individual companies, quarterly and five-year average - *VL*

Current liabilities

Individual companies
monthly - *BG*
quarterly - *VL*
yearly - *FD, SPSR, VL*

Individual industries
yearly - *FD*
per share, yearly - *AH*

Current portion of long-term debt

Individual companies and industries
yearly - *FD*

Individual industries
per share, yearly - *AH*

Current position

Individual companies
quarterly - *VL*
yearly - *FD, SPSR, VL*

Current ratio

Individual companies
quarterly and yearly - *FD*

Individual industries
yearly - *AH, FD*

Customer assistance

Disbursements, NYSE
yearly - *NYSEFB*

Customer participation

American Stock Exchange
options, monthly and yearly - *AmexFB*
options, percentage of total options trading, monthly and yearly - *AmexFB*

Customers

New York Stock Exchange
credit balance, monthly - *Barron's*
credit balance, records, yearly - *NYSEFB*
margin debt, monthly - *Barron's*
margin debt, records, yearly - *NYSEFB*
odd lots, purchases, daily - *WSJ*
odd lots, purchases, number of shares and value, monthly - *NYSEFB*
odd lots, sales, number of shares and value, monthly - *NYSEFB*
odd lots, short sales, monthly and yearly - *NYSEFB*

Czechoslovakian koruna

Exchange rate
daily - *BQR*

D

Danish krone

Exchange rate
daily - *BQR, NYT, WSJ*
weekly - *Barron's*

Declared
dividends, individual companies,
    quarterly - *MHCS, QDR, SPSR*

Ex-dividend
calendar, yearly - *SPQDR*
individual companies, twice weekly -
    MDR
individual companies, quarterly -
    MHCS, SPQDR, SPSR

Payable
dividends, individual companies,
    weekly - *Barron's*
dividends, individual companies,
    quarterly - *MHCS, QDR, SPSR*

Record
dividends, individual companies, twice
    weekly - *MDR*
dividends, individual companies,
    weekly - *Barron's*
dividends, individual companies,
    quarterly - *MHCS*

Dates

Significant historical
NYSE - *NYSEFB*

Days receivables outstanding

Individual companies and industries
yearly - *FD*

Dealer-placed commercial paper

Rates
daily - *BQR, NYT*
weekly - *Barron's, MBS*

weekly, graph - *MBR, MBS*

Dealings suspended

Companies
listed, weekly - *Barron's*

Debit status

Margin accounts
NYSE, number, quarterly - *NYSEFB*

Debt

Analysis
individual companies and industries,
    yearly - *FD*

Balance sheet
individual companies and industries,
    yearly - *FD*

Collateral securing
NYSE, monthly and quarterly -
    NYSEFB
records, yearly - *NYSEFB*

Due
individual companies, quarterly and
    yearly - *VL*

Due in five years
individual companies, most recent
    quarter - *VL*

Funded
ratio to net property, individual
    companies, monthly - *BG*

Individual companies
quarterly - *VL*

Long-term
current portion, individual companies
    and industries, yearly - *FD*
current portion, individual industries,
    per share, yearly - *AH*
individual companies, monthly - *BG*
individual companies, quarterly - *FD,
    VL*
individual companies, yearly - *FD,
    MHCS, SPSR, VL*
individual companies, projections - *VL*
individual industries, yearly - *AH, FD,
    VL*
individual industries, projections - *VL*
individual industries, per share, yearly
    - *AH*
issuance, individual companies and
    industries, yearly - *FD*

maturing in five years, individual
companies and industries, yearly -
FD
percentage of capitalization, individual
companies, yearly - *MHCS, SPSR*
percentage of invested capital,
individual companies and
industries, yearly - *FD*
reduction, individual companies and
industries, yearly - *FD*
tied to prime, percentage, individual
companies and industries, yearly -
FD

Margin
NYSE, monthly - *DSPR, NYSEFB*
NYSE, quarterly - *NYSEFB*
NYSE, customers, monthly - *Barron's*
NYSE, customers, records, yearly -
NYSEFB

Outstanding
public, weekly - *Barron's*

Percentage of assets
individual companies, quarterly - *FD*

Percentage of capital
individual companies, quarterly - *VL*

Ratio of collateral to
NYSE, monthly - *Barron's*

Ratio to total assets
individual industries, yearly - *AH*

Short-term
individual companies, quarterly - *FD*
individual companies and industries,
average, yearly - *FD*
individual utilities, yearly - *MHCS*
interest, individual companies and
industries, average, yearly - *FD*
percentage of total debt, individual
companies and industries, yearly -
FD

Subject to limit
Public, weekly - *Barron's*

Declared date, dividends

Individual stocks
quarterly - *MHCS, QDR, SPSR*

Decline volume

American Stock Exchange
daily - *NYT, WSJ*

NASDAQ
daily - *WSJ*

New York Stock Exchange
daily - *NYT, WSJ*

Declines

American Stock Exchange
leaders, stocks listed, daily - *NYT,
WSJ*
number, daily - *Barron's, DSPR, NYT,
WSJ*
number, weekly - *Barron's*

Bonds
Amex, number, daily - *Barron's, WSJ*
NYSE, number, daily - *Barron's, NYT,
WSJ*

Common stocks
NYSE, number, daily - *Barron's*

Domestic bonds
NYSE, daily - *WSJ*

Dow Jones companies
number, weekly - *Barron's*

Dow Jones Industrial companies
number, weekly - *Barron's*

Dow Jones Transportation companies
number, weekly - *Barron's*

Dow Jones Utilities companies
number, weekly - *Barron's*

NASDAQ
leaders, stocks listed, daily - *NYT,
WSJ*
number, daily - *Barron's, DSPR, NYT,
WSJ*

New York Stock Exchange
leaders, stocks listed, daily - *NYT,
WSJ*
number, daily - *Barron's, DSPR, NYT,
WSJ*
number, weekly - *Barron's*

Value Line stocks
number, weekly - *VL*

Defense/aerospace industry—*see*
Aerospace/Defense industry

Deferred income tax

Individual companies
yearly - *MHCS*

Individual industries
per share, yearly - *AH*

Percentage of capitalization
individual companies, yearly - *MHCS*

Deferred taxes

Individual companies and industries
yearly - *FD*

Percentage of invested capital
individual companies and industries,
  yearly - *FD*

Deferred taxes and investment tax credit

Individual companies and industries
yearly - *FD*

Deferred taxes, minority interest and investment tax credit

Percentage of invested capital
individual companies and industries,
  yearly - *FD*

Deflator

Gross National Product
quarterly - *Barron's*

Department stores

Retail companies stock price index
quarterly, graph - *MHCS*

Sales
monthly and yearly - *SOSG*

Depletion, depreciation and amortization—*see* Depreciation, depletion and amortization

Deposits

Banks
individual corporations, yearly -
  MHCS

Foreign
with Federal Reserve banks, weekly -
  WSJ

Treasury
with Federal Reserve banks, weekly -
  Barron's, WSJ

Depreciation

Change
effect on earnings per share, individual
  companies and industries, yearly -
  FD

Individual companies
quarterly - *FD*
yearly - *VL, SPSR*
projections - *VL*

Individual industries
yearly - *VL*
projections - *VL*
per share, yearly - *AH*

Percentage of average gross plant
individual companies and industries,
  yearly - *FD*

Percentage of average net plant
individual companies and industries,
  yearly - *FD*

Percentage of gross assets
individual companies and industries,
  yearly - *FD*

Depreciation and amortization

Change
year to year, individual companies and
  industries, quarterly, moving 12
  months, and yearly - *FD*

Individual companies and industries
quarterly, moving 12 months, and
  yearly - *FD*

Per dollar average gross plant
individual companies and industries,
  yearly - *FD*

Per share
annual growth rate, individual
  companies and industries, latest
  year, 3 years, 5 years, and 10 years -
  FD

Percentage of sales
individual companies and industries, quarterly, moving 12 months, and yearly - *FD*

Percentage of value added
individual companies and industries, yearly - *FD*

Depreciation, depletion and amortization

Change
effect on earnings per share, individual companies and industries, yearly - *FD*

Individual companies and industries
yearly - *FD*

Per share
change, individual companies and industries, yearly - *FD*
individual companies and industries, yearly - *FD*
least squares growth rate and coefficient of determination, individual companies and industries, 5 year and 10 year - *FD*

Percentage of average gross plant
individual companies and industries, yearly - *FD*

Percentage of sales
individual companies and industries, yearly - *FD*

Depth, market—*see* Market depth

Deutsche mark—*see* West German mark

Diamond/gold industry (South African)—*see* Gold/diamond industry (South African)

Differential, return—*see* Return differential

Dinar, Jordanian—*see* Jordanian dinar

Dinar, Kuwaiti—*see* Kuwaiti dinar

Dinar, Yugoslav—*see* Yugoslav dinar

Directly placed commercial paper—*see* Commercial paper

Dirham, United Arab Emirates—*see* United Arab Emirates dirham

Disbursements

Customer assistance
NYSE, yearly - *NYSEFB*

Discontinued operations

Individual companies and industries
yearly - *FD*

Discontinued operations and extraordinary items—*see* Extraordinary items and discontinued operations

Discount and variety stores

Retail companies stock price index
quarterly, graph - *MHCS*

Discount bills

Listings
monthly - *MBR*

Discount from book value

Widest
stocks listed, weekly - *VL*

Discount from liquidating value

Stocks listed
weekly - *VL*

Discount rate

daily - *NYT, WSJ*
weekly - *Barron's*
weekly, graph - *MBR, MBS*

Distributed corporate bonds—*see* Corporate bonds

Distributed industrial bonds—*see* Industrial bonds

Distributed public utility bonds—*see* Public utility bonds

Distributed railroad bonds—*see* Railroad bonds

Distribution

American Stock Exchange
by size, yearly - *AmexFB*

Auto
imports, monthly - *Barron's*
US, domestic units, monthly - *Barron's*

Consolidated tape trades
participating markets, yearly - *NYSEFB*

Consolidated tape volume
yearly - *NYSEFB*

Durable goods
monthly - *Barron's*

Institutional/intermediary share volume
NYSE, yearly - *NYSEFB*
other exchanges (excluding NYSE), yearly - *NYSEFB*

Machine tool
monthly - *Barron's*

New York Stock Exchange
volume, by days, yearly - *NYSEFB*
volume, most active stocks, yearly - *NYSEFB*

Statistics
monthly - *Barron's*

Distributions

Exchange
NYSE, number and total shares, yearly - *NYSEFB*

Mutual funds
from investment income, per share, yearly - *SOSG*
from security profits, per share, yearly - *SOSG*

New York Stock Exchange
special methods, number and total shares, yearly - *NYSEFB*
stock, yearly - *NYSEFB*

Secondary
NYSE, number and total shares, yearly - *NYSEFB*

Dividend factor

Preferred
individual companies and industries, yearly - *FD*

Dividend information

Mutual funds
weekly - *Barron's*

Dividend payment boosts

weekly - *Barron's*

Dividend payout

Individual companies
yearly - *MHCS*

Dividend rate

Annual
individual companies and industries, moving 12 months and yearly - *FD*

Individual stocks
quarterly - *QDR*

NASDAQ
individual stocks, indicated 12-month, quarterly - *DSPR*

Dividend records

Longevity
NYSE, common stocks, yearly - *NYSEFB*

Dividend reinvestment plans

Amex and NYSE companies
listed, yearly - *MDR, QDR*

Dividend yield

Barron's 50-Stock Average
year end, weekly - *Barron's*

Dow Jones Industrial Average
weekly - *VL*
quarterly and yearly - *Barron's*
last market bottom and last market top - *VL*
range, 13-week and 50-week - *VL*

Dow Jones Transportation Average
quarterly - *Barron's*

Dow Jones Utilities Average
quarterly - *Barron's*

Individual companies
quarterly - *VL*
moving 12 months and yearly - *FD*
average annual, yearly and projections
  - *VL*
range, yearly - *FD*

Individual industries
moving 12 months and yearly - *FD*
average annual, yearly and projections
  - *VL*
range, yearly - *AH, FD*

NASDAQ National List
individual companies, weekly -
  Barron's

Value Line stocks
median, weekly, last market bottom,
  and last market top - *VL*
median, range, 13-week and 50-week -
  VL

Dividends

American Stock Exchange
individual stocks, daily - *NYT, WSJ*
individual stocks, weekly - *Barron's*
individual stocks, year to date - *BQR*
individual stocks, indicated annual,
  monthly - *BQR*

Barron's 50-Stock Average
year end, weekly - *Barron's*

Cash
individual companies and industries,
  yearly - *FD*

Change, annual rate
individual companies, past 5 years -
  VL

Changes
individual stocks, twice weekly - *MDR*

Dates
individual stocks, weekly - *Barron's*
individual stocks, quarterly - *MHCS,
  QDR, SPSR*
preferred stock, individual stocks,
  monthly - *MBR*

Declared date
individual stocks, twice weekly - *MDR*
individual stocks, quarterly - *MHCS,
  QDR, SPSR*

Decreased
number of companies, monthly - *QDR*

Dow Jones Industrial Average
quarterly and 12 months - *Barron's*

Dow Jones Transportation Average
quarterly and 12 months - *Barron's*

Dow Jones Utilities Average
quarterly and 12 months - *Barron's*

Ex-dividend date
individual stocks, twice weekly - *MDR*
individual stocks, quarterly - *MHCS,
  QDR, SPSR*

Extra
number of companies, monthly - *QDR*

Highest estimated
relative to current price, stocks listed,
  weekly - *VL*

Increased
number of companies, monthly - *QDR*

Individual stocks
latest and year ago, weekly - *VL*
daily - *NYT, WSJ*
weekly - *Barron's*
quarterly - *QDR, SPSR*
indicated annual, weekly - *CFC*
indicated annual, monthly - *MHCS*
interim, quarterly - *MHCS*

Midwest Stock Exchange
individual stocks, weekly - *Barron's*
individual stocks, indicated annual,
  weekly - *CFC*
individual stocks, indicated annual,
  monthly - *BQR*

Mutual funds
indicated annual, individual funds,
  weekly - *CFC*
indicated annual, individual funds,
  monthly - *BQR*

NASDAQ NMS
individual stocks, daily - *NYT, WSJ*
individual stocks, weekly - *Barron's*

New York Stock Exchange
common stock, estimated aggregate
  cash payments, yearly - *NYSEFB*
common stock, number paying cash
  dividends during year, yearly -
  NYSEFB
individual stocks, daily - *NYT, WSJ*
individual stocks, weekly - *Barron's*

individual stocks, year to date,
   monthly - *BQR*
individual stocks, indicated annual,
   weekly - *CFC*
individual stocks, indicated annual,
   monthly - *BQR*
preferred stock, estimated aggregate
   cash payments, yearly - *NYSEFB*
preferred stock, number paying cash
   dividends during year, yearly -
   NYSEFB

Omitted
number of companies, monthly - *QDR*

Pacific Stock Exchange
individual stocks, weekly - *Barron's*
individual stocks, indicated annual,
   weekly - *CFC*
individual stocks, indicated annual,
   monthly - *BQR*

Payable date
current week listed - *Barron's*
individual stocks, twice weekly - *MDR*
individual stocks, weekly - *Barron's*
individual stocks, quarterly - *MHCS,
   QDR, SPSR*

Percentage of earnings
individual industries, yearly - *AH*

Preferred
individual industries, per share, yearly
   - *AH*

Record date
individual stocks, twice weekly - *MDR*
individual stocks, weekly - *Barron's*
quarterly - *MHCS*

Reported
daily - *WSJ*

Resumed
number of companies, monthly - *QDR*

Standard & Poor's 500
quarterly - *SPIR*

Standard & Poor's 400
quarterly - *SPIR*

Standard & Poor's Railroads Index
quarterly - *SPIR*

Standard & Poor's Utilities Index
quarterly - *SPIR*

Stock
NYSE companies, number, by
   percentages, yearly - *NYSEFB*

NYSE companies, resulting in increase
   in stock list, number, yearly -
   NYSEFB

Stock of record date
individual stocks, quarterly - *QDR,
   SPSR*

Tax status
individual stocks, yearly - *QDR*

Toronto Stock Exchange
individual stocks, weekly - *Barron's*
individual stocks, indicated annual,
   weekly - *CFC*
individual stocks, indicated annual,
   monthly - *BQR*

Yield—*see* Dividend yield

Dividends declared

Individual stocks
twice weekly - *MDR*

Dividends declared or pending

Companies listed
year to date - *MDR*

Dividends per share

Individual industries
yearly - *AH*

Individual stocks
quarterly - *DSPR*
yearly - *MHCS, SPSR*
indicated annual rate, quarterly -
   DSPR

**Percentage of available for common
   stock dividends**
individual companies and industries,
   quarterly, moving 12 months, and
   yearly - *FD*

Percentage of cash flow
individual companies and industries,
   quarterly, moving 12 months, and
   yearly - *FD*

Standard & Poor's Financial Index
monthly - *QDR*

Standard & Poor's 500
quarterly - *QDR*

Standard & Poor's 400
monthly - *QDR*

Standard & Poor's Transportation Index
monthly - *QDR*

Standard & Poor's Utilities Index
monthly - *QDR*

Utilities
monthly, graph - *MHCS*

Dollar, Australian—*see* Australian dollar

Dollar, Canadian—*see* Canadian dollar

Dollar, Hong Kong—*see* Hong Kong dollar

Dollar, Malaysian—*see* Malaysian dollar

Dollar, New Zealand—*see* New Zealand dollar

Dollar, Singaporean—*see* Singaporean dollar

Dollar, Taiwanese—*see* Taiwanese dollar

Domestic auto distribution

monthly - *Barron's*

Domestic auto production

one day each week - *Barron's*

Domestic bonds

New York Stock Exchange
advances, number, daily - *WSJ*
declines, number, daily - *WSJ*
highs, new, number, daily - *WSJ*
issues traded, number, daily - *WSJ*
lows, new, number, daily - *WSJ*
unchanged bond prices, number, daily - *WSJ*
volume, dollars, daily and year to date - *NYT*

Domestic companies

Listed on selected foreign stock exchanges
number, yearly - *NYSEFB*

Domestic crude oil inventories—*see* Inventories

Domestic industrial bonds

Newly Issued
yield, Moody's Weighted Averages, yearly - *MIM*

Domestic railroad bonds

Newly Issued
yield, Moody's Weighted Averages, yearly - *MIM*

Domestic utility bonds

Newly Issued
yield, Moody's Weighted Averages, yearly - *MIM*

Dow Jones Bond Average

daily - *Barron's, WSJ*

Component companies
irregularly - *Barron's*

Range
monthly - *Barron's*
yearly - *WSJ*

Yield
weekly - *Barron's, DSPR*

Dow Jones Composite Average

half-hourly - *Barron's*
hourly - *WSJ*
daily - *Barron's, BQR, DSPR, NYT, WSJ*
weekly - *Barron's*
yearly - *Barron's*

Change
daily - *BQR, WSJ*
percentage, daily - *WSJ*

Close (composite) of 10 most active stocks
average, daily - *Barron's*

Companies listed
quarterly - *DSPR*
irregularly - *Barron's*

Range
daily - *Barron's, DSPR*
weekly - *Barron's*
monthly - *SPIR*
yearly - *Barron's*

**Ratio of 10 most active stocks
(composite) to total trading**
daily - *Barron's*

Stocks
advances, number, weekly - *Barron's*
declines, number, weekly - *Barron's*
sales, weekly - *Barron's*
unchanged stock prices, number,
    weekly - *Barron's*

Volume
daily - *DSPR, WSJ*

Dow Jones Futures Index

daily - *Barron's, WSJ*

Dow Jones Industrial Average

half-hourly - *Barron's*
hourly - *WSJ*
daily - *Barron's, BQR, DSPR, NYT,
    WSJ*
daily, graph - *WSJ*
weekly - *Barron's*
weekly, graph - *WSJ*
monthly - *Barron's*
monthly, graph - *MIM*
quarterly and yearly - *Barron's*

Change
daily - *BQR, WSJ*
actual, quarterly - *Barron's*
percentage, daily - *WSJ*
percentage, quarterly - *Barron's*

Companies listed
daily - *WSJ*
quarterly - *DSPR*
irregularly - *Barron's*

Dividend yield
quarterly - *Barron's*

Dividends
quarterly and 12 months - *Barron's*

Earnings
quarterly and 12 months - *Barron's*

Financial statistics
yearly - *FD*

Payout ratio
quarterly - *Barron's*

Price-earnings ratio
weekly, monthly, and quarterly -
    Barron's

Range
daily - *Barron's, DSPR*
weekly - *Barron's*
monthly, chart - *MHCS, SPSR*

Range and dates
yearly - *Barron's*

Sales
weekly - *Barron's*

Stocks
advances, number, weekly - *Barron's*
declines, number, weekly - *Barron's*
earnings per share, net, individual
    stocks, quarterly and latest four
    quarters - *Barron's*
unchanged stock prices, number,
    weekly - *Barron's*

Ticks
closing, daily - *Barron's*

Volume
daily - *DSPR, WSJ*

Yield
weekly - *Barron's, DSPR*
average, monthly - *Barron's*

Yield gap
vs. Barron's Confidence Index, weekly
    - *Barron's*

Dow Jones Industrial Bond Average

daily and weekly - *Barron's*

Companies listed
irregularly - *Barron's*

Yield
weekly - *Barron's*

Dow Jones Spot Commodities Index

daily - *WSJ*

Dow Jones Transportation Average

half-hourly - *Barron's*
hourly - *WSJ*
daily - *Barron's, BQR, DSPR, NYT, WSJ*
daily, chart - *WSJ*
weekly - *Barron's*
weekly, chart - *WSJ*
quarterly and yearly - *Barron's*

Change
daily - *BQR, WSJ*
percentage, daily - *WSJ*

Companies listed
daily - *WSJ*
quarterly - *DSPR*
irregularly - *Barron's*

Dividend yield
quarterly - *Barron's*

Dividends
quarterly and 12 months - *Barron's*

Earnings
quarterly and 12 months - *Barron's*

Payout ratio
quarterly - *Barron's*

Price-earnings ratio
weekly, monthly, and quarterly - *Barron's*

Range
daily - *Barron's, DSPR*
weekly - *Barron's*
monthly - *SPIR*

Range and dates
yearly - *Barron's*

Sales
weekly - *Barron's*

Stocks
advances, number, weekly - *Barron's*
declines, number, weekly - *Barron's*
earnings per share, net, individual stocks, quarterly and latest four quarters - *Barron's*
unchanged stock prices, number, weekly - *Barron's*

Volume
daily - *DSPR, WSJ*

Yield
weekly - *Barron's*

Dow Jones Utilities Average

hourly - *Barron's, WSJ*
daily - *Barron's, BQR, DSPR, NYT, WSJ*
daily, chart - *WSJ*
weekly - *Barron's*
weekly, chart - *WSJ*
quarterly and yearly - *Barron's*

Change
daily - *BQR, WSJ*
percentage, daily - *WSJ*

Companies listed
daily - *WSJ*
quarterly - *DSPR*
irregularly - *Barron's*

Dividend yield
quarterly - *Barron's*

Dividends
quarterly and 12 months - *Barron's*

Earnings
quarterly and 12 months - *Barron's*

Payout ratio
quarterly - *Barron's*

Price-earnings ratio
weekly, monthly, and quarterly - *Barron's*

Range
daily - *DSPR*
weekly - *Barron's*
monthly - *SPIR*

Sales
yearly - *Barron's*

Stocks
advances, number, weekly - *Barron's*
declines, number, weekly - *Barron's*
unchanged stock prices, number, weekly - *Barron's*

Volume
daily - *DSPR, WSJ*

Yield
weekly - *Barron's*

Dow Jones Utilities Bond Average

daily and weekly - *Barron's*

Companies listed
irregularly - *Barron's*

Yield
weekly - *Barron's*

Drachma, Greek—*see* Greek
drachma

Drugs

Barron's Group Stock Averages
weekly - *Barron's*
companies and weights, irregularly -
Barron's
range, yearly - *Barron's*

Drugs Index

Standard & Poor's
weekly, monthly, and yearly - *SPIR*
component companies, yearly - *SPIR*
range, yearly - *SPIR*

Drugs industry

Financial statistics
yearly - *AH, VL*

Drugs industry (medical and hospital supply)

Financial statistics
yearly - *FD*

Drugs industry (proprietary)

Financial statistics
yearly - *FD*

Drugstore industry

Financial statistics
yearly - *VL*

Durable goods

Distribution
monthly - *Barron's*

New orders received
monthly - *Barron's*

Durable manufacturing production

monthly - *Barron's*

Dutch guilder

Exchange rate
daily - *BQR, NYT, WSJ*
weekly - *Barron's*

Dutch Stock Index—*see*
Amsterdam, ANP-CBS General
Index

E

Earnings

American Stock Exchange
individual companies, yearly - *Barron's*

Barron's 50-Stock Average
yearly and five-year average, weekly -
Barron's
quarterly projected, weekly - *Barron's*
annualized projected, weekly - *Barron's*

Common
individual companies, quarterly -
SPSR
individual industries, per share,
yearly - *AH*

Dow Jones Industrial Average
quarterly and 12 months - *Barron's*

Dow Jones Transportation Average
quarterly and 12 months - *Barron's*

Dow Jones Utilities Average
quarterly and 12 months - *Barron's*

Fixed charges times
individual companies, yearly - *BG*
individual companies, interim,
monthly - *BG*

Individual companies
change, annual rate, past 5 years, past
10 years, and projections - *VL*
estimated, 12 months - *VL*
interim, quarterly - *MHCS*
selected companies, daily - *NYT, WSJ*

NASDAQ NMS
individual stocks, yearly - *Barron's*

New York Stock Exchange
individual stocks, yearly - *Barron's*

Percentage of net worth
individual companies and industries,
   yearly and projections - *VL*
individual securities brokerage
   companies, yearly - *MHCS*

Percentage of operating revenues
utilities, yearly - *AH*

Percentage of sales
individual industries, yearly - *AH*

Percentage of total capital
individual companies and industries,
   yearly and projections - *VL*

Predictability
individual companies, current - *VL*

Retained
individual companies and industries,
   yearly - *FD*
individual industries, per share, yearly
   - *AH*

S&P 500 companies
quarterly - *SPIR*

S&P 400 companies
quarterly - *SPIR*

Standard & Poor's Railroads Index companies
quarterly - *SPIR*

Standard & Poor's Utilities Index companies
quarterly - *SPIR*

Unconsolidated subsidiaries
equity in, individual companies and
   industries, yearly - *FD*

Yield
Barron's 50-Stock Average, year end,
   weekly and monthly - *Barron's*

Earnings per share

Dow Jones Industrial Average
individual companies, net, quarterly
   and latest four quarters - *Barron's*

Dow Jones Transportation Average
individual companies, net, quarterly
   and latest four quarters - *Barron's*

Dow Jones Utilities Average
individual companies, net, quarterly
   and latest four quarters - *Barron's*

Fully diluted, excluding extraordinary items and discontinued operations
change, individual companies and
   industries, yearly - *FD*
change, year to year, individual
   companies and industries, quarterly,
   moving 12 months, and yearly - *FD*
individual companies and industries,
   quarterly, moving 12 months, and
   yearly - *FD*
least squares growth rate and
   coefficient of determination,
   individual companies and
   industries, 5-year and 10-year - *FD*

Fully diluted, individual companies
quarterly - *FD*

Individual companies
most recently reported four quarters -
   DSPR
quarterly and projections - *VL*
yearly - *FD, MHCS, SPSR, VL*
yearly, projections - *VL*
change, yearly - *FD*

Individual companies and industries
residual change, yearly - *FD*
sources of change, yearly - *FD*

Individual industries
yearly - *AH, FD*
change, yearly - *AH*

Utilities
monthly, graph - *MHCS*

Earnings per share primary

Excluding extraordinary items and discontinued operations
change, effect on earnings per share,
   individual companies and
   industries, yearly - *FD*
change, year to year, individual
   companies and industries, quarterly,
   moving 12 months, and yearly - *FD*
individual companies and industries,
   quarterly, moving 12 months, and
   yearly - *FD*
least squares growth rate and
   coefficient of determination,
   individual companies and
   industries, 5-year and 10-year - *FD*
per share, annual growth rate,
   individual companies and
   industries, latest year, 3 years, 5
   years, and 10 years - *FD*

percentage of S&P 400 earnings per share primary, individual companies and industries, yearly - *FD*
percentage of S&P industrial earnings per share primary, individual companies, yearly - *FD*

Including extraordinary items and discontinued operations
change, individual companies and industries, yearly - *FD*
individual companies and industries, yearly - *FD*
least squares growth rate and coefficient of determination, individual companies and industries, 5-year and 10-year - *FD*
per share, annual growth rate, individual companies and industries, latest year, 3 years, 5 years, and 10 years - *FD*

Sources of change
individual companies, quarterly - *FD*

Eating places industry

Financial statistics
yearly - *FD*

Ecuadorian sucre

Exchange rate
daily - *NYT, WSJ*
weekly - *Barron's*

Effective tax rate

Individual companies
yearly - *SPSR*

Egyptian pound

Exchange rate
daily - *BQR, NYT*

Electric power industry

Financial statistics
yearly - *AH*

Electric power production

one day each week - *Barron's*
quarterly and yearly - *SOSG*

Electric utility industry

Financial statistics
Central, yearly - *VL*
East, yearly - *VL*
West, yearly - *VL*

Electrical and Electronic Index (major companies)

Standard & Poor's
weekly, monthly, and yearly - *SPIR*
component companies, yearly - *SPIR*
range, yearly - *SPIR*

Electrical and electronic industry (major companies)

Financial statistics
yearly - *AH*

Electrical equipment

Barron's Group Stock Averages
weekly - *Barron's*
companies and weights, irregularly - *Barron's*
range, yearly - *Barron's*

Electrical Equipment Index

Standard & Poor's
weekly, monthly, and yearly - *SPIR*
component companies, yearly - *SPIR*
range, yearly - *SPIR*

Electrical equipment industry

Financial statistics
yearly - *AH, VL*

Electronics Index (instrumentation)

Standard & Poor's
weekly, monthly, and yearly - *SPIR*
component companies, yearly - *SPIR*
range, yearly - *SPIR*

Electronics Index (semiconductors/components)

Standard & Poor's
weekly, monthly, and yearly - *SPIR*
component companies, yearly - *SPIR*
range, yearly - *SPIR*

Electronics industry

Financial statistics
yearly - *VL*

Electronics industry (defense)

Financial statistics
yearly - *AH*

Electronics industry (diversified)

Financial statistics
yearly - *FD*

Electronics industry (instrumentation)

Financial statistics
yearly - *AH, FD*

Electronics industry (semiconductors/components)

Financial statistics
yearly - *AH, FD*

Eligibility

Corporate bonds
monthly - *BG*

Employed

monthly - *Barron's*

Employees

Amex companies
number, average and median, yearly - *AmexFB*

Individual companies and industries
number, yearly - *FD*

Employment

Civilian
monthly and annual average - *SOSG*

Employment statistics

monthly - *Barron's*

English furniture—*see* Furniture

English silver—*see* Silver

Entertainment Index

Standard & Poor's
weekly, monthly, and yearly - *SPIR*
component companies, yearly - *SPIR*
range, yearly - *SPIR*

Entertainment industry

Financial statistics
yearly - *AH*

Environmental control revenue bonds—*see* Pollution and environmental control revenue bonds

Equipment, property and plant—*see* Property, plant and equipment

Equipment trust certificates

Ratings
Standard & Poor's, monthly - *BG*

Equipment trusts

NASDAQ
listings, monthly - *BQR*

Yield
individual trusts, monthly - *BQR*

Equity

After-tax return
individual companies and industries, yearly - *FD*

Common
and surplus, individual companies, yearly - *MHCS*
and surplus, percentage of capitalization, individual companies, yearly - *MHCS*
book value, individual companies and industries, yearly - *FD*
book value, per share, annual growth rate, individual companies and industries, latest year, 3 years, 5 years, and 10 years - *FD*
book value, percentage of invested capital, individual companies and industries, yearly - *FD*

individual companies, quarterly - *FD*
individual companies, yearly - *FD,
SPSR*
individual industries, yearly - *FD*
internal growth, individual companies
and industries, yearly - *FD*
per share, individual companies and
industries, amount and average,
yearly - *FD*
per share, ratio of price to, range,
individual companies and
industries, yearly - *FD*
percentage of assets, individual
companies, quarterly and yearly -
FD
percentage of assets, individual
industries, yearly - *FD*
percentage of current liabilities,
individual companies and
industries, yearly - *FD*
percentage of invested capital,
individual companies and
industries,
yearly - *FD*
pretax return, individual companies
and industries, yearly - *FD*
return, percentage of S&P 400 return,
individual companies and
industries, yearly - *FD*
return, percentage of S&P industry
relatives, individual companies,
yearly - *FD*

Earnings of unconsolidated subsidiaries
individual companies and industries,
yearly - *FD*

Percentage of capital
individual companies, quarterly - *VL*

Return on
individual companies, yearly - *MHCS,
SPSR*

Shareholders'
Amex companies, average and median,
yearly - *AmexFB*
Amex companies, 10 leading
companies, yearly - *AmexFB*

Equity options

Listings
by exchange, daily - *NYT, WSJ*
by exchange, weekly - *Barron's*

Equity status

Margin accounts
net, NYSE, one month each year -
NYSEFB

Equity trading

Value
selected foreign stock exchanges, yearly
- *NYSEFB*

Escudo, Chilean—*see* Chilean
escudo

Escudo, Portuguese—*see*
Portuguese escudo

Eurodollars

Futures spread
Treasury bill/Eurodollar, weekly -
Barron's

London Late
rate, daily - *WSJ*

Overnight
dollars, monthly - *Barron's*

Rates
weekly - *Barron's*

Term
dollars, monthly - *Barron's*

Time deposits
rate, daily - *NYT*

European currency units

Exchange rate
daily - *WSJ*
weekly - *Barron's*

European diversified industry

Financial statistics
yearly - *VL*

European paintings, 19th century—*see* Paintings

Excess reserves—*see* Reserves

Exchange

Corporate bonds
individual bonds, monthly - *BG*

Exchange distributions—*see*
Distributions

Exchange listings

New
monthly - *SOSG*

Exchange rates—*see* Foreign
exchange rates

Exchange seats

Number
monthly - *BQR*

Outstanding, number
by exchange, monthly - *BQR*

Prices
by exchange, monthly - *BQR*

Sales, NYSE
monthly - *Barron's, NYSEFB*
price range, monthly - *NYSEFB*

Ex-dividend

Stocks listed
daily - *WSJ*

Ex-dividend date

Calendar
yearly - *SPQDR*

Individual stocks
twice weekly - *MDR*
quarterly - *MHCS, SPQDR, SPSR*

Expenditures—*see* Capital
expenditures

Expense, nonoperating, and
income—*see* Nonoperating income
and expense

Expense margin

Cost of goods sold
change, effect on earnings per share,
individual companies and
industries, yearly - *FD*

Expenses

Accrued
individual industries, per share, yearly
- *AH*

Member organizations
yearly - *NYSEFB*

Expenses and costs—*see* Costs
and expenses

Expiration cycle

Options
Amex, individual securities, yearly -
AmexFB

Export-Import Bank

Debentures
ratings, Standard & Poor's, monthly -
BG

Extended credit

Federal Reserve banks
weekly - *Barron's, WSJ*

Extraordinary items

Individual companies and industries
yearly - *FD*

Extraordinary items and
discontinued operations

Change
effect on earnings per share, individual
companies and industries, yearly -
FD

Per share
individual companies and industries,
quarterly, moving 12 months, and
yearly - *FD*

F

Factory inventories—*see* Inventories

Factory operating rate
monthly - *Barron's*

Factory orders

Backlog
monthly - *Barron's*

New
monthly - *Barron's*

Factory shipments

monthly - *Barron's*

Failures, business—*see* Business failures

Fannie Mae—*see* Federal National Mortgage Association

Farm equipment

Barron's Group Stock Averages
weekly - *Barron's*
companies and weights, irregularly - *Barron's*
range, yearly - *Barron's*

Farmers Home Administration securities

Listings
weekly - *CFC*

Ratings
Standard & Poor's, monthly - *BG*

Yield
individual issues, weekly - *CFC*

Farmers Home Insured Notes

Listings
monthly - *BQR*

Yield
individual issues, monthly - *BQR*

Faz Index—*see* West Germany, Frankfurter Allgemeine Zeitung Stock Index

Federal agency bonds

Ratings
Standard & Poor's, monthly - *BG*

Federal agency issues

Bought outright
daily - *NYT*
weekly - *Barron's, WSJ*

Held under repurchase plan
weekly - *Barron's, WSJ*

Federal credit

Adjusted
weekly - *Barron's*

Federal Farm Credit Banks

Bonds
listings, monthly - *MBR*
yield, individual bonds, monthly - *MBR*

Securities
listings, daily - *NYT, WSJ*
listings, weekly - *Barron's, CFC*
listings, monthly - *BQR*
yield, individual securities, daily - *NYT, WSJ*
yield, individual securities, weekly - *Barron's, CFC*
yield, individual securities, monthly - *BQR*

Federal funds

Interest rates
daily - *NYT, WSJ*
daily, graph - *WSJ*
weekly - *Barron's, VL*
weekly, graph - *MBR, MBS, VL, WSJ*
last market bottom and last market top - *VL*
range, daily - *BQR*
range, 13-week and 50-week - *VL*

Federal Home Loan Bank

Bonds
listings, monthly - *MBR*
yield, individual bonds, monthly - *MBR*

Securities
listings, daily - *NYT, WSJ*
listings, weekly - *Barron's, CFC*
listings, monthly - *BQR*
yield, individual securities, daily - *NYT, WSJ*
yield, individual securities, weekly - *Barron's, CFC*
yield, individual securities, monthly - *BQR*

Federal Home Loan Mortgage Corporation

Bonds
listings, monthly - *MBR*
yield, individual bonds, current - *MBR*

Securities
listings, weekly - *Barron's, CFC*
yield, individual issues, weekly -
Barron's, CFC

Federal Home Mortgage Association securities

Listings
monthly - *BQR*

Yield
individual securities, monthly - *BQR*

Federal Intermediate Credit Banks securities

Debentures
listings, monthly - *MBR*
yield, individual issues, monthly -
MBR

Listings
daily - *NYT, WSJ*
weekly - *Barron's*
monthly - *BQR*

Yield
individual issues, daily - *NYT, WSJ*
individual issues, weekly - *Barron's*
individual issues, monthly - *BQR*

Federal Land Bank

Bonds
listings, monthly - *MBR*
yield, individual bonds, monthly -
MBR

Securities
listings, daily - *NYT, WSJ*
listings, weekly - *Barron's*
listings, monthly - *BQR*
yield, individual issues, daily - *NYT, WSJ*
yield, individual issues, weekly -
Barron's
yield, individual issues, monthly - *BQR*

Federal monetary and reserve aggregates

daily average of two-week period -
Barron's, WSJ

Federal National Mortgage Association

Bonds
listings, monthly - *MBR*
yield, individual bonds, monthly -
MBR

Debentures
listings, monthly - *BQR*
yield, individual securities, monthly -
BQR

Participating certificates
listings, monthly - *BQR*
yield, individual securities, monthly -
BQR

Rates
daily - *WSJ*

Securities
listings, daily - *NYT, WSJ*
listings, weekly - *Barron's, CFC*
yield, individual issues, daily - *NYT, WSJ*
yield, individual issues, weekly -
Barron's, CFC

Federal Reserve banks

Borrowings
daily average of two-week period -
Barron's, WSJ

Changes
weekly - *Barron's, WSJ*

Currency in circulation
weekly - *Barron's, WSJ*

Excess credit
daily average of two-week period -
Barron's, WSJ

Extended credit
weekly - *Barron's, WSJ*

Float
weekly - *Barron's, WSJ*

Foreign deposits
weekly - *WSJ*

Free reserves
daily average of two-week period -
Barron's, WSJ

Interest rates
weekly - *Barron's*

Loans and investments
weekly - *DSPR*

Monetary base
daily average of two-week period -
Barron's, WSJ

Nonborrowed reserves
daily average of two-week period -
Barron's, WSJ

Required reserves
daily average of two-week period -
Barron's, WSJ

Reserve bank credit
weekly - *Barron's, WSJ*

Reserves
daily average of two-week period -
Barron's, WSJ

Seasonal borrowings
weekly - *Barron's, WSJ*

Special Drawing Rights Certificate
Accounts
dollars, weekly - *Barron's, WSJ*

Statistics
daily - *WSJ*
weekly - *Barron's*

Treasury cash holdings
weekly - *WSJ*

Treasury deposits with
changes, weekly - *Barron's, WSJ*

Treasury gold stock
weekly - *Barron's, WSJ*

Federal tax status

Individual bonds
monthly - *MBR*

Fertilizers Index

Standard & Poor's
weekly, monthly, and yearly - *SPIR*
component companies, yearly - *SPIR*
range, yearly - *SPIR*

Fertilizers industry

Financial statistics
yearly - *AH*

Finance-bank-insurance
bonds—*see* Bank-finance-insurance
bonds

Finance company bonds

NASDAQ
listings, monthly - *BQR*
yield, individual bonds, monthly -
BQR

Finance industry (services)

Financial statistics
yearly - *FD*

Financial and real estate companies

Security issues
dollars, yearly - *MIM*

Financial companies

Commercial paper
amount outstanding, dollars, weekly -
WSJ
rates, daily - *NYT*

Financial futures

Prices
daily - *WSJ*

Volume
individual financial instruments, daily
- *WSJ*

Financial Index

Standard & Poor's
daily - *Barron's, DSPR, NYT, SPIR,*
WSJ
weekly - *Barron's, SPIR*
monthly and yearly - *SPIR, SPSR*
component companies, yearly - *SPIR*
dividends per share, monthly - *SPQDR*
price-earnings ratios, weekly - *SPIR*
range, weekly - *Barron's*
range, monthly, chart - *SOSG*
range, yearly - *SPIR, SPSR*

yield, weekly, monthly, and yearly - *SPIR*

Financial Index (banks outside New York City)

Standard & Poor's
weekly, monthly, and yearly - *SPIR*
component companies, yearly - *SPIR*
range, yearly - *SPIR*

Financial Index (life insurance companies)

Standard & Poor's
weekly, monthly, and yearly - *SPIR*
component companies, yearly - *SPIR*
range, yearly - *SPIR*

Financial Index (multiline insurance companies)

Standard & Poor's
weekly, monthly, and yearly - *SPIR*
component companies, yearly - *SPIR*
range, yearly - *SPIR*

Financial Index (New York City banks)

Standard & Poor's
weekly, monthly, and yearly - *SPIR*
component companies, yearly - *SPIR*
range, yearly - *SPIR*

Financial Index (personal loan companies)

Standard & Poor's
weekly, monthly, and yearly - *SPIR*
component companies, yearly - *SPIR*
range, yearly - *SPIR*

Financial Index (property-casualty insurance)

Standard & Poor's
weekly, monthly, and yearly - *SPIR*
component companies, yearly - *SPIR*
range, yearly - *SPIR*

Financial Index (savings and loan association holding companies)

Standard & Poor's
weekly, monthly, and yearly - *SPIR*
component companies, yearly - *SPIR*
range, yearly - *SPIR*

Financial Indicator

New York Stock Exchange
daily - *Barron's, BQR, DSPR, NYT, WSJ*
weekly - *Barron's*
monthly - *BQR*
range, weekly - *Barron's*
range, monthly - *Barron's, BQR, NYSEFB*

Financial industry

Financial statistics
yearly - *AH*

Financial ratios

Individual companies
quarterly - *FD, VL*
five-year average - *VL*

Individual industries
yearly - *AH*

Financial services companies stock price index

quarterly, graph - *MHCS*

Financial services industry

Financial statistics
yearly - *VL*

Financial strength

Individual companies
quarterly - *VL*

Financial Times 500 Stock Index—*see* United Kingdom, Financial Times 500 Stock Index

Financial Times Industrial Index—*see* United Kingdom, Financial Times Industrial Index

Financial Times Ordinary Share
Index—*see* United Kingdom, Financial Times Ordinary Share Index

Financial Times Stock Index—*see*
United Kingdom, Financial Times Stock Index

Financial Times 30 Stock
Index—*see* United Kingdom, Financial Times 30 Stock Index

Finished goods

Producer Price Index
monthly - *Barron's*

Finnish markka

Exchange rate
daily - *BQR, NYT, WSJ*
weekly - *Barron's*

Firm participation

Options
Amex, monthly and yearly - *AmexFB*
Amex, percentage of total options trading, monthly and yearly - *AmexFB*

Fiscal year

Dates
individual companies, monthly - *BG*
individual companies, quarterly - *VL*

Fixed charge coverage

Individual companies and industries
yearly - *FD*

Fixed charges, available for

Individual companies and industries
yearly - *FD*

Percentage of sales
individual companies and industries, yearly - *FD*

Fixed charges times earnings

Individual companies
yearly - *BG*
interim, monthly - *BG*

Fixed net asset value

Tax free money market funds
weekly - *Barron's*

Float

Federal Reserve banks
weekly - *Barron's, WSJ*

Floor traders

American Stock Exchange
purchases, weekly - *Barron's*
sales, weekly - *Barron's*
short sales, weekly - *Barron's*

New York Stock Exchange
purchases, weekly - *Barron's*
sales, weekly - *Barron's*
short sales, weekly - *Barron's*

Food

Wholesale Price Index
Dun and Bradstreet, weekly - *Barron's*

Food industry (canned)

Financial statistics
yearly - *FD*

Food industry (meat packers)

Financial statistics
yearly - *FD*

Food industry (packaged)

Financial statistics
yearly - *FD*

Food industry (processing)

Financial statistics
yearly - *VL*

Food industry (wholesalers)

Financial statistics
yearly - *VL*

Foods and beverages

Barron's Group Stock Averages
weekly - *Barron's*
companies and weights, irregularly -
  Barron's
range, yearly - *Barron's*

Foods Index

Standard & Poor's
weekly, monthly, and yearly - *SPIR*
component companies, yearly - *SPIR*
range, yearly - *SPIR*

Foods industry

Financial statistics
yearly - *AH*

Foreign bonds

Amount outstanding
individual bonds, monthly - *BG*

Call price
individual bonds, monthly - *BG*
sinking fund, individual bonds,
  monthly - *BG*

Interest rates
individual bonds, monthly - *BG*

Listings
weekly - *Barron's*

NASDAQ
listings, monthly - *BQR*

New York Stock Exchange
listings, daily - *NYT, WSJ*
volume, dollars, daily - *NYT, WSJ*
volume, dollars, year to date - *NYT*
volume, individual bonds, daily - *NYT,
  WSJ*
yield, individual bonds, daily - *NYT,
  WSJ*

Number of issues
weekly, six weeks, and projection -
  MBS

Price
individual bonds, monthly - *BG*

Price range
individual bonds, yearly - *BG*

Ratings
Standard & Poor's, individual bonds,
  monthly - *BG*

Sales
individual bonds, weekly - *Barron's*

Underwriter
individual bonds, monthly - *BG*

Volume
dollars, weekly, six weeks, and
  projection - *MBS*

Yield
individual bonds, weekly - *Barron's*
individual bonds, monthly - *BG, BQR*

Foreign bonds and corporate bonds—*see* Corporate bonds and foreign bonds

Foreign companies

NASDAQ
typical company profile, yearly -
  NASDAQFB

Foreign corporate bonds

New York Stock Exchange
market value, yearly - *NYSEFB*
market value, by geographic region,
  yearly - *NYSEFB*

Foreign currency options

Calls
open interest, by exchange, daily -
  WSJ
volume, by exchange, daily - *WSJ*

Listings
by exchange, daily - *WSJ*
by exchange, weekly - *Barron's*

Puts
open interest, by exchange, daily -
  WSJ
volume, by exchange, daily - *WSJ*

Foreign deposits

Federal Reserve banks
weekly - *WSJ*

Foreign exchange rates—*see also* specific currencies (e.g., Japanese yen)
daily - *BQR, NYT, WSJ*
weekly - *Barron's*

Foreign government bonds

New York Stock Exchange
issuers, number, yearly - *NYSEFB*
issues, number, yearly - *NYSEFB*
market value, yearly - *NYSEFB*
market value, by geographic region,
    yearly - *NYSEFB*
par value, yearly - *NYSEFB*

Foreign prime rates

daily - *WSJ*
weekly - *Barron's*

Foreign securities

American Stock Exchange
number, yearly - *AmexFB*
volume, yearly - *AmexFB*
volume, percentage of total share
    volume, yearly - *AmexFB*

Listed
daily - *WSJ*

NASDAQ
number, by originating country, yearly
    - *NASDAQFB*
typical security profile, yearly -
    NASDAQFB
volume leaders, yearly - *NASDAQFB*
volume leaders, dollar volume and
    closing price, yearly - *NASDAQFB*
volume leaders, share volume and
    closing price, yearly - *NASDAQFB*

New York Stock Exchange
listings, number, yearly - *NYSEFB*
listings, number, by geographic region,
    yearly - *NYSEFB*
market value, yearly - *NYSEFB*
market value, by geographic region,
    yearly - *NYSEFB*

Foreign stock exchanges—*see also* specific currencies (e.g., Japanese yen)

Listings
selected issues, daily - *NYT, WSJ*
selected issues, weekly - *Barron's*

Statistics
yearly - *NYSEFB*

Foreign stock indexes—*see also* specific currencies (e.g., Japanese yen)

daily - *NYT, WSJ*
weekly - *Barron's*

Foreign stocks—*see* Foreign securities

Foreigners

Purchases from Americans
foreign stocks, NYSE, quarterly and
    yearly - *NYSEFB*
US stocks, NYSE, quarterly and yearly
    - *NYSEFB*

Sales to Americans
foreign stocks, NYSE, quarterly and
    yearly - *NYSEFB*
US stocks, NYSE, quarterly and yearly
    - *NYSEFB*

Forest Products Index

Standard & Poor's
weekly, monthly, and yearly - *SPIR*
component companies, yearly - *SPIR*
range, yearly - *SPIR*

Forest products industry

Financial statistics
yearly - *AH*

Franc, Belgian—*see* Belgian franc

Franc, French—*see* French franc

Franc, Swiss—*see* Swiss franc

France, Agefi Stock Index

daily - *NYT*
weekly - *Barron's*

France, CAC General Index

yearly - *NYSEFB*

France, Paris Stock Exchange

Listings, selected stocks
daily - *NYT, WSJ*
weekly - *Barron's*

Statistics
yearly - *NYSEFB*

Frankfurt Stock Exchange—*see*
West Germany, Frankfort Stock
Exchange

Frankfurt Stock Index—*see* West
Germany, Commerzbank Index;
West Germany, Frankfurter
Allgemeine Zeitung Stock Index

**Frankfurter Allgemeine Zeitung
Stock Index**—*see* West Germany,
Frankfurter Allgemeine Zeitung
Stock Index

Freddie Mac—*see* Federal Home
Loan Mortgage Corporation

**Free credit balance cash
accounts**

New York Stock Exchange
monthly - *Barron's*

Free-flow cash generators

Biggest
stocks listed, weekly - *VL*

Free reserves

Federal Reserve banks
daily average of two-week period -
Barron's, WSJ

Freight car loadings

monthly and annual average - *SOSG*

**Freight transportation companies
stock price index**

quarterly, graph - *MHCS*

**French and Continental
Furniture**—*see* Furniture

French franc

Exchange rate
daily - *BQR, NYT, WSJ*
weekly - *Barron's*

Forward exchange rate
daily - *WSJ*
weekly - *Barron's*

French Stock Index—*see* France,
Agefi Stock Index; France, CAC
General Index

**Fully diluted earnings per
share**—*see* Earnings per share

Funded debt

Ratio to net property
individual companies, monthly - *BG*

Funds—*see* individual fund headings
(e.g., Mutual funds, Closed-end
bond funds, etc.)

Funds flow statement

Individual companies and industries
yearly - *FD*

Funds from operations

Individual companies and industries
yearly - *FD*

Furniture

American
Sotheby's Art Index, weekly - *Barron's*

English
Sotheby's Art Index, weekly - *Barron's*

French and Continental
Sotheby's Art Index, weekly - *Barron's*

**Furniture/home furnishings
industry**

Financial statistics
yearly - *VL*

Futures

Chicago Board of Trade—*see* entries
beginning Chicago Board of Trade

Commodity—*see* Commodity futures

International Monetary Market—*see*
headings beginning International
Monetary Market

Listings
daily - *NYT, WSJ*
weekly - *Barron's*

Open interest
individual commodities, daily - *NYT, WSJ*
individual commodities, weekly - *Barron's*
individual financial instruments, daily - *NYT, WSJ*
individual financial instruments, weekly - *Barron's*

Volume
individual commodities, daily - *NYT, WSJ*
individual commodities, weekly - *Barron's*
individual financial instruments, daily - *NYT, WSJ*
individual financial instruments, weekly - *Barron's*

Futures contracts

New York Futures Exchange Composite Index
basis, monthly, graph - *NYSEFB*
range and close, monthly, chart - *NYSEFB*

Futures options

Calls
open interest, by type of future, daily - *NYT, WSJ*
open interest, by type of future, weekly - *Barron's*
volume, by type of future, daily - *NYT, WSJ*
volume, by type of future, weekly - *Barron's*

Listings
daily - *NYT, WSJ*
by exchange, weekly - *Barron's*

New York Stock Exchange
volume, daily average, monthly - *NYSEFB*

Open interest
monthly - *NYSEFB*

Puts
open interest, by type of future, daily - *NYT, WSJ*
open interest, by type of future, weekly - *Barron's*

volume, by type of future, daily - *NYT, WSJ*
volume, by type of future, weekly - *Barron's*

Volume
by type of future, daily - *NYT, WSJ*
by type of future, weekly - *Barron's*

Futures Prices, Dow Jones Index
of—*see* Dow Jones Futures Index

Futures spread

Treasury bill/Eurodollar
weekly - *Barron's*

G

Gains, currency—*see* Currency gains

Gaming Companies Index

Standard & Poor's
weekly, monthly, and yearly - *SPIR*
component companies, yearly - *SPIR*
range, yearly - *SPIR*

Gaming/hotel industry—*see*
Hotel/gaming industry

Gasoline inventories—*see*
Inventories

General expenses—*see* Selling,
general and administrative expenses

General Motors Acceptance Corporation

Commercial paper
rates, daily - *WSJ*
rates, weekly - *Barron's*

General Services Administration securities

Listings
weekly - *CFC*
monthly - *BQR*

Ratings
Standard & Poor's, monthly - *BG*

Yield
individual securities, weekly - *CFC*
individual securities, monthly - *BQR*

Geographic distribution

Shareowners of public corporations
NYSE, yearly - *NYSEFB*

Geographic subindices

Market Value Index
Amex, close and composition, yearly -
AmexFB

Germany—*see* headings beginning
West Germany

Ginnie Mae—*see* Government
National Mortgage Association

GNMA—*see* Government National
Mortgage Association

Gold

Prices
daily - *NYT, WSJ*
weekly - *Barron's*

Gold coins

Prices
daily - *NYT, WSJ*
weekly - *Barron's*

Gold/diamond industry (South African)

Financial statistics
yearly - *VL*

Gold industry (North American)

Financial statistics
yearly - *VL*

Gold Mining

Barron's Group Stock Averages
weekly - *Barron's*
companies and weights, irregularly -
Barron's
range, yearly - *Barron's*

Gold Mining Index

Standard & Poor's
weekly, monthly, and yearly - *SPIR*
component companies, yearly - *SPIR*
range, yearly - *SPIR*

Gold mining industry

Financial statistics
yearly - *AH*

Gold options

American Stock Exchange
calls, number, monthly and yearly -
AmexFB
contracts traded, number and daily
average, monthly and yearly -
AmexFB
puts, number, monthly and yearly -
AmexFB

Gold/Silver Index

daily - *WSJ*

Gold stock—*see* Treasury gold stock

Federal Reserve banks
weekly - *Barron's, WSJ*

Goods

Durable
distribution, monthly - *Barron's*
new orders received, monthly -
Barron's

Finished
Producer Price Index, monthly -
Barron's

Nondurable
new orders received, monthly -
Barron's

Goods and services bought

Percentage of sales
individual companies and industries,
yearly - *FD*

Government agencies securities

Listings
daily - *NYT, WSJ*
weekly - *Barron's, CFC*

Government bonds

American Stock Exchange
volume, principal amount, yearly -
AmexFB

Foreign, NYSE
issuers, number, yearly - *NYSEFB*
issues, number, yearly - *NYSEFB*
market value, yearly - *NYSEFB*
market value, by geographic region,
yearly - *NYSEFB*
par value, yearly - *NYSEFB*

Long-term
yield, monthly, graph - *MBR*

New York Stock Exchange
issuers, number, yearly - *NYSEFB*
issues, number, yearly - *NYSEFB*
market value, yearly - *NYSEFB*
par value, yearly - *NYSEFB*
volume, dollars, daily and year to date
- *NYT*

Standard & Poor's Index
taxable issues, by length of maturity,
weekly, monthly, and yearly - *SPIR*
taxable issues, range, by length of
maturity, yearly - *SPIR*

Yield
monthly, graph - *MBR*
Standard & Poor's Index, by length of
term, weekly and monthly - *BG*
Standard & Poor's Index, by length of
term, range, weekly - *BG*
Standard & Poor's Index, taxable
issues, by length of maturity, weekly,
monthly, and yearly - *SPIR*
Standard & Poor's Index, taxable
issues, range, by length of maturity,
yearly - *SPIR*

Government/Corporate Yield Spread, Salomon—*see* Salomon Government/Corporate Yield Spread

Government mutual funds

Sales
monthly - *Barron's*

Government National Mortgage Association

Mutual funds
sales, monthly - *Barron's*

Securities
listings, daily - *NYT, WSJ*
listings, weekly - *Barron's, CFC*
listings, monthly - *BQR*
yield, individual issues, daily - *NYT,
WSJ*
yield, individual issues, weekly -
Barron's, CFC
yield, individual issues, monthly - *BQR*

Government securities

Bought outright
weekly - *Barron's, WSJ*

Held under repurchase plan
weekly - *Barron's, WSJ*

Listings
daily - *NYT, WSJ*
weekly - *Barron's*
monthly - *BQR*

Yield
monthly, graph - *MBR*
individual securities, daily - *NYT, WSJ*
individual securities, weekly - *Barron's*
individual securities, monthly - *BQR*

Greek drachma

Exchange rate
daily - *NYT, WSJ*
weekly - *Barron's*

Grocery chains

Barron's Group Stock Averages
weekly - *Barron's*
companies and weights, irregularly -
Barron's
range, yearly - *Barron's*

Grocery industry

Financial statistics
yearly - *VL*

Gross assets

Individual companies and industries
yearly - *FD*

Per employee
average, individual companies and
industries, yearly - *FD*

Percentage of invested capital
individual companies and industries,
yearly - *FD*

Gross for common percentage

Individual utilities
yearly - *MHCS*

Gross National Product

Adjusted annual rate
quarterly - *Barron's*

Deflator
quarterly - *Barron's*

Gross plant

Individual companies and industries
yearly - *FD*

Per employee
average, individual companies and
industries, yearly - *FD*

**Percentage equivalent to capital
expenditures**
individual companies and industries,
yearly - *FD*

**Percentage equivalent to depreciation,
depletion and amortization**
individual companies and industries,
yearly - *FD*

Percentage equivalent to net plant
individual companies and industries,
yearly - *FD*

Sales per dollar average
individual companies and industries,
yearly - *FD*

Gross revenues—*see* Revenues

Growth

High
stocks listed, weekly - *VL*

Internal
common equity, individual companies
and industries, yearly - *FD*
factors, individual companies and
industries, yearly - *FD*

Price
persistence, individual companies,
quarterly - *VL*

Growth and income mutual funds

Sales
monthly - *Barron's*

Growth mutual funds

Sales
monthly - *Barron's*

Growth rate

Compounded, volume
NYSE, yearly - *NYSEFB*

**New York Stock Exchange Common
Stock Index**
yearly - *NYSEFB*

Guarani, Paraguayan—*see*
Paraguayan guarani

Guilder, Dutch—*see* Dutch guilder

H

Hang Seng Stock Index—*see* Hong
Kong, Hang Seng Stock Index

Hardware and Tools Index

Standard & Poor's
weekly, monthly, and yearly - *SPIR*
component companies, yearly - *SPIR*
range, yearly - *SPIR*

Hardware and tools industry

Financial statistics
yearly - *AH*

Headquarters states

NASDAQ companies
yearly - *NASDAQFB*

High day

NASDAQ
volume and date, monthly and yearly -
NASDAQFB

High Dividend Series

Moody's Preferred Stock Yield Average
monthly and yearly - *MIM*

High grade bond prices

Composite Index, Standard & Poor's
weekly, monthly, and yearly - *SPIR*
range, yearly - *SPIR*

High grade commercial paper

Rates
weekly - *Barron's*

High Grade Common Stocks Index

Standard & Poor's
weekly, monthly, and yearly - *SPIR*
component companies, yearly - *SPIR*
range, yearly - *SPIR*

High Grade industrials

Moody's Preferred Stock Yield Averages
Low Dividend Series, monthly and
yearly - *MIM*

High grade public utilities

Moody's Preferred Stock Yield Averages
Low Dividend Series, monthly and
yearly - *MIM*

High-growth stocks

Listed
weekly - *VL*

High-yielding stocks

Listed
weekly - *VL*

Highest-yielding non-utility stocks

Listed
weekly - *VL*

Highs

American Stock Exchange
individual companies, yearly -
AmexFB

Highs, new

American Stock Exchange
number, daily - *Barron's, DSPR, NYT,
WSJ*
number, weekly - *Barron's*
stocks listed, weekly - *Barron's*

Bonds
Amex, number, daily - *Barron's, WSJ*
NYSE, number, daily - *Barron's, NYT,
WSJ*

Domestic bonds
NYSE, daily - *WSJ*

NASDAQ
number, daily - *Barron's, NYT, WSJ*
number, weekly - *Barron's*
stocks listed, weekly - *Barron's*

New York Stock Exchange
number, daily - *Barron's, DSPR, NYT,
WSJ*
number, weekly - *Barron's*
stocks listed, daily - *NYT, WSJ*
stocks listed, weekly - *Barron's*

Value Line stocks
number, weekly - *VL*
number, weekly, graph - *VL*

Home appliances industry

Financial statistics
yearly - *VL*

Home furnishings/furniture industry

Financial statistics
yearly - *VL*

Home Furnishings Index

Standard & Poor's
weekly, monthly, and yearly - *SPIR*
component companies, yearly - *SPIR*
range, yearly - *SPIR*

Homebuilding Index

Standard & Poor's
weekly, monthly, and yearly - *SPIR*
component companies, yearly - *SPIR*
range, yearly - *SPIR*

Homebuilding industry

Financial statistics
yearly - *AH*

Hong Kong, Hang Seng Stock Index

weekly - *Barron's*

Hong Kong dollar

Exchange rate
daily - *BQR, NYT, WSJ*
weekly - *Barron's*

Hong Kong Stock Exchange

Listings, selected stocks
daily - *NYT, WSJ*
weekly - *Barron's*

Hong Kong Stock Index

daily - *NYT*

Hospital Management Index

Standard & Poor's
weekly, monthly, and yearly - *SPIR*
component companies, yearly - *SPIR*
range, yearly - *SPIR*

Hospital management industry

Financial statistics
yearly - *AH*

Hospital Supplies Index

Standard & Poor's
weekly, monthly, and yearly - *SPIR*
component companies, yearly - *SPIR*
range, yearly - *SPIR*

Hospital supplies industry

Financial statistics
yearly - *AH*

Hotel/gaming industry

Financial statistics
yearly - *VL*

Hotel/Motel Index

Standard & Poor's
weekly, monthly, and yearly - *SPIR*
component companies, yearly - *SPIR*
range, yearly - *SPIR*

Hotel/motel industry

Financial statistics
yearly - *AH, FD*

Household Furnishings and Appliances Index

Standard & Poor's
weekly, monthly, and yearly - *SPIR*
component companies, yearly - *SPIR*
range, yearly - *SPIR*

Household furnishings and appliances industry

Financial statistics
yearly - *AH*

Household products industry

Financial statistics
yearly - *VL*

Housing starts

New
monthly - *Barron's*

I

Imports

Auto distribution
monthly - *Barron's*

Impressionist and Post-Impressionist paintings—*see* Paintings

Income

Before extraordinary items and discontinued operations
change, year to year, individual companies and industries, quarterly, moving 12 months, and yearly - *FD*
individual companies and industries, quarterly, moving 12 months, and yearly - *FD*
per dollar average gross plant, individual companies and industries, yearly - *FD*
per dollar average invested capital, individual companies and industries, yearly - *FD*
per employee, individual companies and industries, yearly - *FD*
per share, annual growth rate, individual companies and industries, latest year, 3 years, 5 years, and 10 years - *FD*
percentage of profit margin, individual companies, quarterly - *FD*
percentage of sales, individual companies and industries, quarterly, moving 12 months, and yearly - *FD*

Gross
sources, member organizations, NYSE, yearly - *NYSEFB*

Individual industries
per share, yearly - *AH*

Member organizations
NYSE, yearly - *NYSEFB*
NYSE, from securities commissions, yearly - *NYSEFB*

Income, net—*see* Net income

Income, nonoperating—*see* Nonoperating income

Income, nonoperating, and expense—*see* Nonoperating income and expense

Income, operating—*see* Operating income

Income, personal—*see* Personal income

Income, pretax—*see* Pretax income

Income data

Individual companies
yearly - *SPSR*

Income mutual funds

Sales
monthly - *Barron's*

Income statement

Individual companies
quarterly and yearly - *FD*

Individual industries
yearly - *FD*
per share, yearly - *AH*

Member organizations
NYSE, yearly - *NYSEFB*

Income tax

Deferred
and investment tax credit, individual companies and industries, yearly - *FD*
individual companies, yearly - *FD, MHCS*
individual industries, yearly - *FD*
individual industries, per share, yearly - *AH*

Standard & Poor's Index, by rating groups, range, weekly - *BG*
Standard & Poor's Index, by rating groups, range, yearly - *SPIR*

Industrial bonds and notes

Maturing
chronological list, yearly - *MIM*

Industrial Bonds Average, Dow Jones—*see* Dow Jones Industrial Bonds Average

Industrial convertible bond issues—*see* Convertible bonds

Industrial convertible stock issues

dollars, yearly - *MIM*

Industrial development revenue bonds

Listings
monthly - *MBR*

Ratings
Moody's, individual bonds, monthly - *MBR*

Industrial Index

NASDAQ
daily - *Barron's, DSPR, NYT, WSJ*

Industrial Indicator

New York Stock Exchange
daily - *Barron's, BQR, DSPR, NYT, WSJ*
weekly - *Barron's*
monthly - *BQR*
range, weekly - *Barron's*
range, monthly - *BQR, NYSEFB*

Industrial participating stocks

yearly - *MIM*

Industrial production

monthly - *Barron's*

Industrial production index

Including utilities
monthly and annual average - *SOSG*

Industrial revenue and pollution control bonds

Recent and prospective offerings
ratings, Moody's, individual bonds, weekly - *MBS*
statistics, individual bonds, weekly - *MBS*

Industrial services industry

Financial statistics
yearly - *VL*

Industrial stock purchase warrants—*see* Stock purchase warrants

Industrial stock splits—*see* Stock splits

Industrial subindices

Market Value Index, Amex
close and composition, yearly - *AmexFB*

Industrials, Dow Jones—*see* Dow Jones Industrial Average, Dow Jones Industrial Bonds Average

Industrials, Moody's—*see* Moody's Preferred Stock Yield Averages

Industrials, Standard & Poor's 400—*see* Standard & Poor's 400

Industry rank

Individual companies
weekly - *VL*

Initial margin requirements

New York Stock Exchange
historical - *NYSEFB*

Initial purchase

Individual mutual funds
minimum, monthly - *SOSG*

Insider decisions

Individual companies
monthly - *VL*

Insider transactions

Major
listed, weekly - *VL*

Installment financing

Barron's Group Stock Averages
weekly - *Barron's*
companies and weights, irregularly -
Barron's
range, yearly - *Barron's*

Instinet

Volume
weekly - *Barron's*
NYSE-listed stock, daily - *NYT, WSJ*
NYSE-listed stock, monthly and yearly
- *NYSEFB*
NYSE-listed stock, percentage of all
exchanges' trading in NYSE-listed
stock, yearly - *NYSEFB*

Institutional decisions

Individual companies
quarterly - *VL*

Institutional holdings

Individual companies
quarterly - *MHCS, VL*

Institutions
number, individual companies,
monthly - *SOSG*

NASDAQ NMS
10 most active stocks, percentage,
yearly, chart - *NASDAQFB*

Number of shares
individual companies, monthly - *SOSG*

Institutional investors

New York Stock Exchange
holdings, by type of institution, yearly
- *NYSEFB*

Number
individual companies, quarterly -
MHCS

Number of shares held
individual companies, quarterly -
MHCS

Percentage of stock held
individual companies, quarterly -
SPSR

Institutional money funds

dollars, monthly - *Barron's*

Insurance

Barron's Group Stock Averages
weekly - *Barron's*
companies and weights, irregularly -
Barron's
range, yearly - *Barron's*

Insurance-bank-finance
bonds—*see* Bank-finance-insurance
bonds

Insurance companies

Combined ratio
individual companies, yearly - *MHCS*

NASDAQ
listings, monthly - *BQR*
price-earnings ratios, current - *BQR*

Insurance company bonds

NASDAQ
listings, monthly - *BQR*
yield, individual bonds, monthly -
BQR

Insurance in force

Individual insurance companies
yearly - *MHCS*

Insurance Index—*see* NASDAQ
Insurance Index

Insurance industry (diversified)

Financial statistics
yearly - *VL*

Insurance industry (life)

Financial statistics
yearly - *VL*

Insurance industry (property/casualty)

Financial statistics
yearly - *VL*

Insurance sales

Individual insurance companies
yearly - *MHCS*

Intangibles

Individual companies and industries
yearly - *FD*

Individual industries
per share, yearly - *AH*

Percentage of assets
individual companies and industries,
  yearly - *FD*

Inter-American Development Bank securities

Listings
daily - *NYT, WSJ*
weekly - *Barron's, CFC*

Ratings
Standard & Poor's, monthly - *BG*

Yield
individual issues, daily - *NYT, WSJ*
individual issues, weekly - *CFC*

Interest

Long-term
individual companies, quarterly - *VL*

Minority
deferred taxes and investment tax
  credit, percentage of invested
  capital, individual companies and
  industries, yearly - *FD*

individual companies, yearly - *FD,
  MHCS*
individual industries, yearly - *FD*
Open—*see* Open interest
Short—*see* Short interest

Short-term debt
average, individual companies and
  industries, yearly - *FD*

Interest coverage

Individual companies
quarterly - *VL*

Pretax
individual companies and industries,
  yearly - *FD*

Interest dates

Bonds
individual bonds, monthly - *MBR*

Convertible bonds
individual bonds, monthly - *BG*

Corporate bonds
individual bonds, monthly - *BG*

Foreign bonds
individual bonds, monthly - *BG*

Interest earned

Long-term
individual companies, quarterly - *VL*

Interest expense

Individual companies
quarterly and yearly - *FD*

Individual industries
yearly - *FD*

Percentage of sales
individual companies and industries,
  yearly - *FD*

Percentage of value added
individual companies and industries,
  yearly - *FD*

Interest paid

Individual industries
per share, yearly - *AH*

Interest periods

Bonds
Amex, individual bonds, weekly - *CFC*
Amex, individual bonds, monthly - *BQR*
NYSE, individual bonds, weekly - *CFC*
NYSE, individual bonds, monthly - *BQR*

Interest rates—*see* specific categories (e.g., Commercial paper, Certificates of deposit, etc.)

Interest rate options

American Stock Exchange
calls, number, yearly - *AmexFB*
contracts traded, number, yearly - *AmexFB*
puts, number, yearly - *AmexFB*

Listings
by exchange, daily - *NYT, WSJ*
by exchange, weekly - *Barron's*

Interim dividends—*see* Dividends

Interim earnings—*see* Earnings

Intermarket Trading System

Activity
monthly and yearly - *NYSEFB*

Executed share volume
total and daily average, monthly and yearly - *NYSEFB*

Executed trades
total and daily average, monthly and yearly - *NYSEFB*

Issues eligible
monthly and yearly - *NYSEFB*

Size of trade
average, monthly and yearly - *NYSEFB*

Intermediate grade bonds

Volume
percentage of NYSE volume, weekly - *Barron's*

Yield
weekly - *Barron's*

Intermediate Grade Bonds
Index—*see* Barron's Intermediate Grade Bonds Index

Intermediate-term promissory notes

Listings
monthly - *MBR*

Ratings
Moody's, monthly - *MBR*

Intermountain Stock Exchange

Seat prices
monthly - *BQR*

Seats outstanding
number, monthly - *BQR*

Internal growth

Common equity
individual companies and industries, yearly - *FD*

Internal growth factors

Individual companies and industries
yearly - *FD*

International Bank for Reconstruction and Development securities

Listings
weekly - *Barron's, CFC*
monthly - *BQR*

Ratings
Standard & Poor's, monthly - *BG*

Yield
individual securities, weekly - *Barron's, CFC*
individual securities, monthly - *BQR*

International contribution

Individual companies
yearly - *FD*

International Monetary Market

Listings
weekly - *Barron's*

Seat prices
monthly - *BQR*

Seats outstanding
number, monthly - *BQR*

International mutual funds

Sales
monthly - *Barron's*

International operating income—*see* Operating income

International sales—*see* Sales

International transactions

New York Stock Exchange
dollars, quarterly and yearly - *NYSEFB*

Interrogation devices

New York Stock Exchange
number, yearly - *NYSEFB*

Inti, Peruvian—*see* Peruvian inti

Inventories

Business
monthly - *Barron's*

Domestic crude oil
weekly - *Barron's*

Factory
monthly - *Barron's*

Gasoline
weekly - *Barron's*

Individual companies
quarterly - *VL*
yearly - *FD, VL*

Individual industries
yearly - *FD*
per share, yearly - *AH*

Manufacturers
monthly and annual average - *SOSG*

Merchant wholesalers
monthly and annual average - *SOSG*

Newsprint
US and Canada, monthly - *Barron's*

Percentage of assets
individual companies and industries,
yearly - *FD*

Percentage of current assets
individual companies and industries,
yearly - *FD*

Percentage of sales
individual companies and industries,
yearly - *FD*

Retailers
monthly and annual average - *SOSG*

Statistics
monthly - *Barron's*

Inventory accounting method

Individual companies
quarterly - *VL*

Inventory-to-sales ratio

monthly - *Barron's*

Inventory turnover

Individual companies
quarterly and yearly - *FD*

Individual industries
yearly - *AH, FD*

Invested capital

After-tax return
change, effect on earnings per share,
individual companies and
industries, yearly - *FD*
individual companies and industries,
yearly - *FD*

Individual companies and industries
yearly - *FD*

Per employee
average, individual companies and
industries, yearly - *FD*

Per share
annual growth rate, individual
companies and industries, latest

year, 3 years, 5 years, and 10 years - *FD*

Percentage equivalent to common equity (book value)
individual companies and industries, yearly - *FD*

Percentage equivalent to long-term debt
individual companies and industries, yearly - *FD*

Percentage equivalent to minority interest, deferred taxes and investment tax credit
individual companies and industries, yearly - *FD*

Percentage equivalent to non-redeemable preferred stock
individual companies and industries, yearly - *FD*

Percentage equivalent to redeemable preferred stock
individual companies and industries, yearly - *FD*

Pretax return
change, effect on earnings per share, individual companies and industries, yearly - *FD*
individual companies and industries, yearly - *FD*

Investment Companies Index (bond fund)

Standard & Poor's
weekly, monthly, and yearly - *SPIR*
component companies, yearly - *SPIR*
range, yearly - *SPIR*

Investment Companies Index (closed-end)

Standard & Poor's
weekly, monthly, and yearly - *SPIR*
component companies, yearly - *SPIR*
range, yearly - *SPIR*

Investment income

Distributions per share from
individual mutual funds, yearly - *SOSG*

Yield from
individual mutual funds, monthly - *SOSG*

Investment industry

Financial statistics
yearly - *VL*

Investment industry (foreign)

Financial statistics
yearly - *VL*

Investment tax credit

Individual companies and industries
quarterly, moving 12 months, and yearly - *FD*

Per share
change, individual companies and industries, yearly - *FD*
individual companies and industries, yearly - *FD*

Percentage of earnings per share primary, excluding extraordinary items and discontinued operations
individual companies and industries, quarterly, moving 12 months, yearly - *FD*

Investment tax credit and deferred taxes

Individual companies and industries
yearly - *FD*

Investment tax credit, minority interest and deferred taxes

Percentage of invested capital
individual companies and industries, yearly - *FD*

Investments, short-term, and cash—*see* Cash and short-term investments

Investments and advances

Individual companies and industries
yearly - *FD*

Percentage of assets
individual companies and industries, yearly - *FD*

Investments and advances to unconsolidated subsidiaries

Individual industries
per share, yearly - *AH*

Investments and loans

Federal Reserve banks
weekly - *DSPR*

Iranian rial

Exchange rate
daily - *BQR*

Irish pound

Exchange rate
daily - *BQR*

Irish punt

Exchange rate
daily - *NYT, WSJ*
weekly - *Barron's*

Israeli shekel

Exchange rate
daily - *NYT, WSJ*
weekly - *Barron's*

Issue date

Individual bonds
monthly - *MBR*

Issues

American Stock Exchange
number, yearly - *AmexFB, NASDAQFB*

Canadian
Amex, number, yearly - *AmexFB*
Amex, volume, yearly - *AmexFB*
Amex, volume, percentage of total volume, yearly - *AmexFB*

Common stock and warrants
Amex, number, yearly - AmexFB

Corporate bonds
dollars, yearly - *MIM*
publicly offered, dollars, yearly - *MIM*

Yield, Moody's Average, composite and by rating group, monthly - *MIM*

Corporate common stock
dollars, yearly - *MIM*

Corporate preferred stock
dollars, yearly - *MIM*

Eligible for trading
Intermarket Trading System, monthly and yearly - *NYSEFB*

Federal agency
bought outright, weekly - *Barron's, WSJ*
held under repurchase plan, weekly - *Barron's, WSJ*

Foreign
Amex, number, yearly - *AmexFB*
Amex, volume, yearly - *AmexFB*
Amex, volume, percentage of total volume, yearly - *AmexFB*

Industrial convertible bonds
dollars, yearly - *MIM*

NASDAQ
market value, average, by number of market makers, yearly - *NASDAQFB*
number, yearly - *NASDAQFB*
number, by number of market makers, yearly - *NASDAQFB*
number, percentage increase, latest 10 years - *NASDAQFB*

NASDAQ NMS
market value, by number of market makers, average, yearly - *NASDAQFB*
number, by number of market makers, yearly - *NASDAQFB*

New York Stock Exchange
common stock, number listed, by industry, yearly - *NYSEFB*
number, yearly - *NASDAQFB, NYSEFB*
number, by industry, yearly - *NYSEFB*

Securities
commercial and miscellaneous companies, dollars, yearly - *MIM*
communications companies, dollars, yearly - *MIM*
corporate, dollars, yearly - *MIM*
dollars, yearly - *MIM*
financial and real estate companies, dollars, yearly - *MIM*

manufacturing companies, dollars,
yearly - *MIM*
public utilities, dollars, yearly - *MIM*
real estate and financial companies,
dollars, yearly - *MIM*
transportation companies, dollars,
yearly - *MIM*

Stock
industrial convertible, dollars, yearly -
MIM

Warrant, and common stock
Amex, number, yearly - *AmexFB*

Issues traded

American Stock Exchange
number, daily - *NYT, WSJ*

Bonds
NYSE, number, daily - *NYT, WSJ*

Domestic bonds
NYSE, number, daily - *WSJ*

NASDAQ
number, daily - *NYT, WSJ*

New York Stock Exchange
number, daily - *NYT, WSJ*

Value Line stocks
number, weekly - *VL*

Italian lira

Exchange rate
daily - *BQR, NYT, WSJ*
weekly - *Barron's*

Italy, MIB Historical Index

yearly - *NYSEFB*

Italy, Milan Stock Exchange

Listings, selected stocks
daily - *NYT, WSJ*
weekly - *Barron's*

Statistics
yearly - *NYSEFB*

Italy, Milan Stock Index

daily - *NYT*
weekly - *Barron's*

J

Japan, Nikkei Dow Jones Stock Index

daily - *NYT*

Japan, Nikkei Stock Average

daily - *WSJ*

Japan, Nikkei 225 Stock Index

weekly - *Barron's*

Japan, Tokyo Stock Exchange

Listings, selected stocks
weekly - *Barron's*

Statistics
yearly - *NYSEFB*

Volume
dollars, yearly, chart - *NASDAQFB*

Japan, TSE Stock Price Index

yearly - *NYSEFB*

Japanese American Depository Receipts

Listings
daily - *WSJ*

Japanese/Australian diversified industry

Financial statistics
yearly - *VL*

Japanese prime rate

daily - *WSJ*
weekly - *Barron's*

Japanese yen

Exchange rate
daily - *BQR, NYT, WSJ*
weekly - *Barron's*

Forward exchange rates
daily - *NYT, WSJ*
weekly - *Barron's*

Japo Industrial Index—*see* Sweden,
Japo Industrial Index

**Johannesburg Stock
Exchange**—*see* South Africa,
Johannesburg Stock Exchange

Jordanian dinar

Exchange rate
daily - *NYT, WSJ*
weekly - *Barron's*

Junk bonds

Yield spread
vs. Treasury bonds, weekly, graph -
Barron's

K

Kansas City Board of Trade

Listings
weekly - *Barron's*

Seat prices
Class A, monthly - *BQR*

Seats outstanding
Class A, number, monthly - *BQR*

Koruna, Czechoslovakian—*see*
Czechoslovakian koruna

Krona, Swedish—*see* Swedish Krona

Krone, Danish—*see* Danish krone

Krone, Norwegian—*see* Norwegian
krone

Kuwaiti dinar

Exchange rate
daily - *NYT, WSJ*
weekly - *Barron's*

L

Labor and related expense

Individual companies and industries
yearly - *FD*

Percentage of sales
individual companies and industries,
quarterly, moving 12 months, and
yearly - *FD*

Labor costs

Change, effect on earnings per share
individual companies and industries,
yearly - *FD*

Per employee
individual companies and industries,
yearly - *FD*

Percentage of value added
individual companies and industries,
yearly - *FD*

Labor force

Civil
monthly - *Barron's*

Large block transactions

American Stock Exchange
number, daily - *Barron's, WSJ*
volume, yearly - *AmexFB*
volume, dollars, yearly - *AmexFB*
volume, dollars, percentage of total
dollar volume, yearly - *AmexFB*
volume, percentage of total volume,
yearly - *AmexFB*

NASDAQ
number, daily - *WSJ*

NASDAQ NMS
block size, average, yearly -
NASDAQFB
volume, number of block trades,
monthly and yearly - *NASDAQFB*
volume, number of shares, monthly
and yearly - *NASDAQFB*
volume, percentage of total volume,
monthly and yearly - *NASDAQFB*
volume, percentage of total volume,
yearly, chart - *NASDAQFB*

New York Stock Exchange
down ticks, number, daily - *Barron's*
no change, number, daily - *Barron's*
number, daily - *Barron's, WSJ*
number and daily average, monthly
    and yearly - *NYSEFB*
number of shares, monthly and yearly
    - *NYSEFB*
percentage of reported volume,
    monthly and yearly - *NYSEFB*
percentage of reported volume, yearly,
    chart - *NASDAQFB*
percentage of reported volume,
    records, yearly - *NYSEFB*
10 largest, name of stock and volume,
    yearly - *NYSEFB*
up ticks, number, daily - *Barron's*
volume, records, yearly - *NYSEFB*

Last-sale devices

New York Stock Exchange
number, yearly - *NYSEFB*

Leading Indicators Composite Index

monthly - *Barron's*

Leases

Capitalized
individual companies, yearly - *FD,
    MHCS*
individual industries, yearly - *FD*
percentage of capitalization, individual
    companies, yearly - *MHCS*

Uncapitalized
individual companies, quarterly - *VL*

Lebanese pound

Exchange rate
daily - *BQR, NYT, WSJ*
weekly - *Barron's*

Legal status

Individual bonds
monthly - *MBR*

Leisure Time Index

Standard & Poor's
weekly, monthly, and yearly - *SPIR*
component companies, yearly - *SPIR*

range, yearly - *SPIR*

Leisure time industry

Financial statistics
yearly - *AH*

Leverage

Balance sheet
change, effect on earnings per share,
    individual companies and
    industries, yearly - *FD*
individual companies and industries,
    yearly - *FD*

Individual companies and industries
yearly - *FD*

Liabilities

Banks
10 leading, New York City, weekly -
    WSJ

Current
individual companies, monthly - *BG*
individual companies, quarterly - *FD,
    VL*
individual companies, yearly - *FD,
    SPSR, VL*
individual industries, yearly - *FD*
individual industries, per share, yearly
    - *AH*

Individual industries
per share, yearly - *AH*

Member organizations
NYSE, yearly - *NYSEFB*

LIBOR—*see* London interbank offered
    rates

Life accounts

Variable
listings, weekly - *Barron's*

Life insurance industry

Financial statistics
yearly - *AH*

Lipper Mutual Fund Indexes

weekly - *Barron's*

Lipper Mutual Fund Investment Performance Averages

weekly - *Barron's*

Liquid asset ratio (equity and balanced) for mutual funds

monthly - *Barron's*

Liquidating value

Stocks at discount from
listed, weekly - *VL*

Liquor

Barron's Group Stock Averages
weekly - *Barron's*
companies and weights, irregularly - *Barron's*
range, yearly - *Barron's*

Lira, Italian—*see* Italian lira

Lira, Maltese—*see* Maltese lira

Lira, Turkish—*see* Turkish lira

Listing applications

weekly - *Barron's*

Listing date

Options
Amex, individual companies, yearly - *AmexFB*

Listing requirements

American Stock Exchange
yearly - *AmexFB*

NASDAQ
yearly - *NASDAQFB*

NASDAQ NMS
yearly - *NASDAQFB*

New York Stock Exchange
yearly - *NYSEFB*

Listings, new—*see* New listings

Loadings

Freight car
monthly and annual average - *SOSG*

Loans

Call—*see* Call loans

Individual bank corporations
yearly - *MHCS*

Short-term—*see* Short-term loans

Loans and investments

Federal Reserve banks
weekly - *DSPR*

London interbank offered rates

daily - *NYT, WSJ*
weekly - *Barron's*

London Late Eurodollars

Rates
daily - *WSJ*

London Metal Exchange

Prices
daily - *NYT, WSJ*

London Stock Exchange

Bonds
listings, selected bonds, daily - *NYT*

Listings, selected stocks
daily - *NYT, WSJ*
weekly - *Barron's*

Statistics
yearly - *NYSEFB*

Volume
dollars, yearly, chart - *NASDAQFB*

London Stock Index—*see* headings beginning United Kingdom, Financial Times

Long-term debt—*see* Debt

Long-term government bonds

Yield
monthly, graph - *MBR*

Long-term interest—*see* Interest

Long-term interest earned—*see* Interest earned

Long-term price score, Moody's—*see* Moody's long-term price score

Long-term Treasury bonds—*see* Treasury bonds

Losses, currency—*see* Currency losses

Low

American Stock Exchange
individual companies, yearly - *AmexFB*

Low day

NASDAQ
volume and date, monthly and yearly - *NASDAQFB*

Low Dividend Series

Moody's Preferred Stock Yield Averages
monthly and yearly - *MIM*

Low-Priced Index—*see* Barron's Low-Priced Index

Low-Priced Common Stocks Index

Standard & Poor's
weekly, monthly, and yearly - *SPIR*
component companies, yearly - *SPIR*
range, yearly - *SPIR*

Lows, new

American Stock Exchange
number, daily - *Barron's, DSPR, NYT, WSJ*

number, weekly - *Barron's*
stocks listed, weekly - *Barron's*

Bonds
Amex, number, daily - *Barron's, WSJ*
NYSE, number, daily - *Barron's, NYT, WSJ*

Domestic bonds
NYSE, daily - *WSJ*

NASDAQ
number, daily - *Barron's, NYT, WSJ*
number, weekly - *Barron's*

New York Stock Exchange
number, daily - *Barron's, DSPR, NYT, WSJ*
number, weekly - *Barron's*
stocks listed, daily - *NYT, WSJ*
stocks listed, weekly - *Barron's*

Value Line stocks
number, weekly - *VL*
number, weekly, graph - *VL*

Lumber production

monthly - *Barron's*

Lumber shipments

monthly - *Barron's*

M

M1—*see* Money supply

M2—*see* Money supply

M3—*see* Money supply

Machine tools

Barron's Group Stock Averages
weekly - *Barron's*
companies and weights, irregularly - *Barron's*
range, yearly - *Barron's*

Distribution
monthly - *Barron's*

New orders received
monthly - *Barron's*

Machine Tools Index

Standard & Poor's
weekly, monthly, and yearly - *SPIR*
component companies, yearly - *SPIR*
range, yearly - *SPIR*

Machine tools industry

Financial statistics
yearly - *AH, VL*

Machinery (heavy)

Barron's Group Stock Averages
weekly - *Barron's*
companies and weights, irregularly -
  Barron's
range, yearly - *Barron's*

Machinery Index (agricultural)

Standard & Poor's
weekly, monthly, and yearly - *SPIR*
component companies, yearly - *SPIR*
range, yearly - *SPIR*

Machinery Index (construction and material handling)

Standard & Poor's
weekly, monthly, and yearly - *SPIR*
component companies, yearly - *SPIR*
range, yearly - *SPIR*

Machinery Index (industrial/specialty)

Standard & Poor's
weekly, monthly, and yearly - *SPIR*
component companies, yearly - *SPIR*
range, yearly - *SPIR*

Machinery industry

Financial statistics
yearly - *VL*

Machinery industry (agricultural)

Financial statistics
yearly - *AH*

Machinery industry (construction and material handling)

Financial statistics
yearly - *AH*

Machinery industry (construction and mining)

Financial statistics
yearly - *VL*

Machinery industry (diversified)

Financial statistics
yearly - *AH*

Madrid Stock Index—*see* Spain,
  Madrid Stock Index

Maintenance

Utilities
per share, yearly - *AH*

Major Market Index

daily - *WSJ*

Amex, stock index options
calls, number, yearly - *AmexFB*
close, monthly and yearly - *AmexFB*
contracts, number and daily average,
  yearly - *AmexFB*
puts, number, yearly - *AmexFB*

Malaysian dollar

Exchange rate
daily - *BQR*

Malaysian ringgit

Exchange rate
daily - *WSJ*
weekly - *Barron's*

Maltese lira

Exchange rate
daily - *WSJ*
weekly - *Barron's*

Market Value Index

American Stock Exchange
close, monthly - *AmexFB*
geographic subindices, close and
    composition, yearly - *AmexFB*
industrial subindices, close and
    composition, yearly - *AmexFB*
range, daily - *NYT*
range, monthly, chart - *MHCS*
range, monthly, graph - *MIM*
stock index options, calls, number,
    yearly - *AmexFB*
stock index options, close, monthly
    and yearly - *AmexFB*
stock index options, contracts, number
    and daily average, yearly - *AmexFB*
stock index options, puts, number,
    yearly - *AmexFB*

Market value leaders

NASDAQ
listed, yearly - *NASDAQFB*
market value, individual companies,
    yearly - *NASDAQFB*
shares outstanding, individual
    companies, yearly - *NASDAQFB*

Markka, Finnish—*see* Finnish markka

Maturing industrial bonds and notes

Chronological list
yearly - *MIM*

Maturity

Money market funds
weekly - *Barron's*

Tax-free money market funds
listings, weekly - *Barron's*

Maturity range

Interest rates
medium-term notes, individual issues,
    monthly - *MBR*

McCarthy, Crisanti & Maffei, Inc.

Bond rating changes
weekly - *Barron's*

Medical services industry

Financial services
yearly - *VL*

Medical supplies industry

Financial services
yearly - *VL*

Medium Grade Industrials

**Moody's Preferred Stock Yield
    Averages**
High Dividend Series, monthly and
    yearly - *MIM*
Low Dividend Series, monthly and
    yearly - *MIM*

Medium Grade Public Utilities

**Moody's Preferred Stock Yield
    Averages**
Low Dividend Series, monthly and
    yearly - *MIM*

Medium-term notes

Interest rates
effective date, individual issues,
    monthly - *MBR*
maturity range, individual issues,
    monthly - *MBR*

Listings
monthly - *MBR*

Principal amount
individual issues, monthly - *MBR*

Ratings
Moody's, effective date, monthly -
    MBR
Moody's, individual issues, monthly -
    MBR
Standard & Poor's, monthly - *BG*

Member buy volume

New York Stock Exchange
weekly - *Barron's*

Member net buy/sell

New York Stock Exchange
weekly - *Barron's*

Member organizations

New York Stock Exchange
assets, yearly - *NYSEFB*
balance sheet, yearly - *NYSEFB*
capital, yearly - *NYSEFB*
corporations, number, yearly - *NYSEFB*
expenses, yearly - *NYSEFB*
gross income, sources, yearly - *NYSEFB*
income, yearly - *NYSEFB*
income, from securities commissions, yearly - *NYSEFB*
income statement, yearly - *NYSEFB*
liabilities, yearly - *NYSEFB*
number, yearly - *NYSEFB*
number, by type, yearly - *NYSEFB*
offices, number, yearly - *NYSEFB*
partnerships, number, yearly - *NYSEFB*
profit, net, after taxes, estimated, yearly - *NYSEFB*
profit, net, before taxes, yearly - *NYSEFB*
registered personnel, number, yearly - *NYSEFB*
registered representatives, number, by state, yearly - *NYSEFB*
sales offices, number, by state, yearly - *NYSEFB*

Members

American Stock Exchange
buy/sell, net, weekly - *Barron's*
options principal, sales, range and last, yearly - *AmexFB*
purchases, weekly - *Barron's*
purchases plus sales, yearly - *AmexFB*
purchases plus sales, percentage of total purchases plus sales, yearly - *AmexFB*
sales, weekly - *Barron's*
sales, range and last, yearly - *AmexFB*
short sales, weekly - *Barron's*
volume, percentage of total volume, weekly - *Barron's*

New York Stock Exchange
buy/sell, net, weekly - *Barron's*
participation rate, yearly - *NYSEFB*
participation rate, trades originating off the floor, yearly - *NYSEFB*
participation rate, trades originating on the floor, yearly - *NYSEFB*
purchases, weekly - *Barron's*

purchases, round lots, monthly - *NYSEFB*
purchases, round lots, originating off the floor, monthly - *NYSEFB*
purchases, round lots, originating on the floor, monthly - *NYSEFB*
purchases and sales, round lots, number of shares, yearly - *NYSEFB*
purchases and sales, round lots, originating off the floor, number of shares, yearly - *NYSEFB*
purchases and sales, round lots, originating on the floor, number of shares, yearly - *NYSEFB*
purchases and sales, round lots, records, yearly - *NYSEFB*
records, yearly - *NYSEFB*
sales, weekly - *Barron's*
sales, round lots, monthly - *NYSEFB*
sales, round lots, originating off the floor, monthly - *NYSEFB*
sales, round lots, originating on the floor, monthly - *NYSEFB*
short sales, weekly - *Barron's*
short sales, records, yearly - *NYSEFB*
short sales, round lots, number of shares, yearly - *NYSEFB*
volume, weekly - *Barron's*
volume, percentage of total volume, weekly - *Barron's*

Membership prices

New York Stock Exchange
range, yearly - *NYSEFB*
records, yearly - *NYSEFB*

Merchant wholesalers

Inventories
monthly and annual average - *SOSG*

Sales
monthly and yearly - *SOSG*

Mergers and consolidations—*see*
Consolidations and mergers

Merrill Lynch 500

Municipal bond index
weekly - *WSJ*

Merrill Lynch Ready Assets Trust

Rate
daily - *WSJ*
weekly - *Barron's*

Metal fabricating industry

Financial statistics
yearly - *VL*

Metals—*see also* Precious metals,
Non-ferrous metals

Metals and mining industry (general)

Financial statistics
yearly - VL

Metals and mining industry (industrial)

Financial statistics
yearly - *VL*

Metals Index (miscellaneous)

Standard & Poor's
weekly, monthly, and yearly - *SPIR*
component companies, yearly - *SPIR*
range, yearly - *SPIR*

Metals industry (miscellaneous)

Financial statistics
yearly - *AH*

Metals industry (steel)

Financial statistics
yearly - *FD*

Metals industry (steel products)

Financial statistics
yearly - *FD*

Mexican American Depository Receipts

Listings
daily - *WSJ*

Mexican peso

Exchange rate
daily - *BQR, NYT, WSJ*
weekly - *Barron's*

MIB Historical Index—*see* Italy, MIB Historical Index

Midwest Stock Exchange

Dividends, indicated annual
individual stocks, weekly - *CFC*
individual stocks, monthly - *BQR*

Listings
daily - *CFC, NYT, WSJ*
weekly - *Barron's*
monthly - *BQR*

Price-earnings ratio
individual stocks, weekly - *CFC*
individual stocks, monthly - *BQR*

Price range
individual stocks, year to date - *CFC*

Sale price range
individual stocks, monthly and year to date - *BQR*

Sales
daily - *NYT, WSJ*
individual stocks, weekly - *CFC*
individual stocks, monthly and year to date - *BQR*
selected individual stocks, daily - *NYT, WSJ*

Seat prices
monthly - *BQR*

Seats outstanding
number - *BQR*

Volume
monthly - *BQR, NYSEFB*
year to date - *BQR*
yearly - *NYSEFB*
NYSE-listed stocks, daily - *NYT, WSJ*
NYSE-listed stock, weekly - *Barron's*
NYSE-listed stock, monthly and yearly - *NYSEFB*
NYSE-listed stock, percentage of total NYSE-listed stock volume, monthly and yearly - *NYSEFB*
percentage of all exchanges' trading, yearly - *NYSEFB*

Yield
individual stocks, weekly - *CFC*
individual stocks, monthly - *BQR*

Milan Stock Exchange—*see* Italy,
Milan Stock Exchange

Milan Stock Index—*see* Italy, Milan
Stock Index

Mining production

monthly - *Barron's*

Minneapolis Grain Exchange

Listings
weekly - *Barron's*

Seat prices
monthly - *BQR*

Seats outstanding
number, monthly - *BQR*

Minority interest

Individual companies
yearly - *FD, MHCS*

Individual industries
yearly - *FD*
per share, yearly - *AH*

Percentage of capitalization
individual companies, yearly - *MHCS*

Percentage of invested capital
individual companies, yearly - *FD*
individual industries, yearly - *FD*

**Minority interest, deferred taxes
and investment tax credit**

Percentage of invested capital
individual companies and industries,
yearly - *FD*

**Mobile homes and builders
industry**

Financial statistics
yearly - *FD*

Mobile Homes Index

Standard & Poor's
weekly, monthly, and yearly - *SPIR*
component companies, yearly - *SPIR*
range, yearly - *SPIR*

**Modern paintings
(1900–1950)**—*see* Paintings

**Monetary and reserve
aggregates**

Federal Reserve banks
daily average of two-week period -
Barron's, WSJ

Monetary base

Federal Reserve banks
daily average of two-week period -
Barron's, WSJ

Money funds

Independent
dollars, monthly - *Barron's*

Institutional
dollars, monthly - *Barron's*

Money market deposit accounts

dollars, monthly - *Barron's*

Rates
average, weekly - *Barron's*

Top savings deposit yields
weekly - *Barron's*

Money market funds

Assets
weekly - *Barron's*

Listings
weekly - *Barron's*

Tax-free
listings, weekly - *Barron's*

Money market rates

weekly, graph - *MBR*

Money rates

daily - *NYT, WSJ*
weekly - *Barron's*

Money supply

M1
daily average, weekly - *Barron's, MBS, WSJ*
daily average of four-week period - *WSJ*
daily average, monthly - *Barron's, WSJ*

M2
daily average, monthly - *Barron's, WSJ*

M3
daily average, monthly - *Barron's, WSJ*

Montreal Stock Exchange—*see*
Canada, Montreal Stock Exchange

Moody's Aaa Corporate Bond Yield

weekly, last market bottom, and last market top - *VL*

Range
13-week and 50-week - *VL*

Moody's Average of Yields on Corporate Bonds—*see* Moody's Corporate Bond Yield Averages

Moody's Average of Yields on Industrial Bonds—*see* Moody's Industrial Bond Yield Averages

Moody's Average of Yields on Newly Issued Corporate Bonds

composite and by rating groups, monthly - *MIM*

Moody's Average of Yields on Newly Issued Industrial Bonds

composite and by rating groups, monthly - *MIM*

Moody's Bond Yields

by rating groups, monthly and yearly - *MIM*

Moody's Composite Average of Yields on Corporate Bonds—*see* Moody's Corporate Bond Yield Averages

Moody's Composite Average of Yields on Industrial Bonds—*see* Moody's Industrial Bond Yield Averages

Moody's Corporate Bond Yield Averages

monthly - *MBR*
by rating groups and industry categories, monthly - *MBR*
composite and by rating groups, daily - *MBS*
composite and by rating groups, monthly and yearly - *MIM*
composite and by rating groups, range, yearly - *MBS*

Moody's Daily Commodity Price Index

monthly and yearly - *MIM*

Component companies and weights
yearly - *MIM*

Range
monthly - *MIM*
monthly, graph - *MIM*
yearly - *MIM*

Moody's Index of Scrap Commodities Prices

weekly - *MBS*
monthly - *MIM*
monthly, graph - *MIM*
yearly - *MIM*

Component commodities and weights
yearly - *MIM*

Range
yearly - *MBS*

Moody's Industrial Bond Yield Averages

composite and by rating groups, daily - *MBS*
composite and by rating groups, monthly - *MBR, MIM*

composite and by rating groups, yearly
- *MIM*
composite and by rating groups, range,
yearly - *MBS*

Moody's long-term price score

Individual companies
quarterly - *MHCS*

Moody's Municipal Bond Yield Averages

composite and by rating groups,
weekly and monthly - *MBS*
composite and by rating groups,
monthly - *MBR*
composite and by rating groups, range,
yearly - *MBS*

Moody's Preferred Stock Yield Averages

High Dividend Series
monthly and yearly - *MIM*
component companies, yearly - *MIM*

Low Dividend Series
monthly and yearly - *MIM*
component companies, yearly - *MIM*
High Grade Industrials, monthly,
graph - *MIM*
High Grade Public Utilities, monthly,
graph - *MIM*
Medium Grade Industrials, monthly,
graph - *MIM*
Medium Grade Public Utilities,
monthly, graph - *MIM*
Public Utilities, by rating group,
monthly, graph - *MIM*

Moody's Public Utility Bond Yield Averages

composite and by rating groups, daily -
MBS
composite and by rating groups,
monthly - *MBR*
composite and by rating groups, range,
yearly - *MBS*

Moody's Public Utility Common Stock Yield Averages

weekly - *MBS*

Range
yearly - *MBS*

Moody's Public Utility Preferred Stock Yield Averages

by rating groups, weekly - *MBS*
by rating groups, monthly - *MBR,
MIM*
by rating groups, range, yearly - *MBS*

Component companies
yearly - *MIM*

Moody's Railroad Bond Yield Averages

composite and by rating groups, daily -
MBS
composite and by rating groups,
monthly - *MBR*
composite and by rating groups, range,
yearly - *MBS*

Moody's ratings

Adjusted rate revenue bonds
changes, individual bonds, monthly -
MBR

Bank deposits
changes, individual banks, monthly -
MBR

Bonds
changes, weekly - *Barron's*
explanation and key, monthly - *MBR*
monthly - *MBR*

Commercial paper
changes, individual issues, monthly -
MBR
explanation and key, monthly - *MBR*
individual issues, monthly - *MBR*

Corporate bonds
explanation and key, monthly - *MBR*

Corporate securities
changes, individual securities, monthly
- *MBR*

Industrial development revenue bonds
changes, individual bonds, monthly -
MBR

Industrial revenue and pollution control bonds
recent and prospective offerings,
individual bonds,
weekly - *MBS*

Municipal bonds
explanation and key, monthly - *MBR*
individual bonds, monthly - *MBR*
new offerings, weekly - *MBS*

Municipal securities
changes, individual securities, monthly
- *MBR*

Municipal short-term loans
new offerings, individual loans, weekly
- *MBS*

**Pollution and environmental control
   revenue bonds**
individual bonds, monthly - *MBR*
recent and prospective offerings,
   weekly - *MBS*

Preferred stock
changes, individual stocks, monthly -
   MBR
explanation, monthly - *MBR*
individual stocks, monthly - *MBR*
new and prospective offerings,
   individual stocks, weekly - *MBS*

Railroad equipment trust certificates
individual certificates, monthly - *MBR*

Shelf registrations
prospective, individual issues, weekly -
   MBS

Short-term loans
explanation, monthly - *MBR*
individual loans, monthly - *MBR*

Short-term securities
changes, individual securities, monthly
- *MBR*

Moody's Scrap Commodities
   Prices Index—*see* Moody's Index
   of Scrap Commodities Prices

Moody's short-term price score

Individual companies
quarterly - *MHCS*

Moody's Spot Commodity Prices
   Index

weekly - *MBS*

Range
yearly - *MBS*

Moody's Treasury Bill Yield
   Averages

weekly and monthly - *MBS*

Range
yearly - *MBS*

Moody's Treasury Bond Yield
   Averages

daily and monthly - *MBS*

Range
yearly - *MBS*

Moody's Treasury Issues Yield
   Averages

daily, weekly, and monthly - *MBS*

Range
yearly - *MBS*

Moody's Treasury Note Yield
   Averages

daily and monthly - *MBS*

Range
yearly - *MBS*

Moody's utility stocks

Dividends per share
monthly, graph - *MHCS*

Earnings per share
monthly, graph - *MHCS*

Prices
monthly, graph - *MHCS*

Moody's Weighted Averages of
   Yields

Newly Issued Domestic Bonds
yearly - *MIM*

**Newly Issued Domestic Industrial
   Company Bonds**
yearly - *MIM*

**Newly Issued Domestic Railroad
   Company Bonds**
yearly - *MIM*

**Newly Issued Domestic Utility
   Company Bonds**
yearly - *MIM*

Morgan Guaranty Index

daily, graph - *WSJ*
weekly, graph - *Barron's, WSJ*

Mortgage certificates

Pass-through
rates, individual certificates, monthly -
    BG
ratings, Standard & Poor's, monthly -
    BG

Mortgage rates

Adjustable rate mortgages base rates
weekly - *Barron's*

Mortgage-related securities

Listings
weekly - *Barron's*

Yield
individual issues, weekly - *Barron's*

Most active bonds

New York Stock Exchange
yearly - *NYSEFB*
par value of reported volume, yearly -
    NYSEFB

Most active equity options

Calls
listed, by exchange, weekly - *Barron's*

Puts
listed, by exchange, weekly - *Barron's*

Most active options

American Stock Exchange
yearly - *AmexFB*
contracts traded, number, yearly -
    AmexFB

Listed, by exchange
daily - *NYT, WSJ*

Sales
individual options, by exchange, daily -
    NYT, WSJ

Most active stocks

American Stock Exchange
daily - *NYT, WSJ*
weekly - *Barron's*
price, average and 10-day average,
    daily - *DSPR*

Dow Jones companies
closing, average, daily - *Barron's*
ratio to total trading, daily - *Barron's*

NASDAQ
daily - *NYT, WSJ*
weekly - *Barron's*
yearly - *NASDAQFB*
volume and closing price, individual
    companies, yearly - *NASDAQFB*

NASDAQ NMS
block volume, percentage of total
    volume, individual stocks, yearly,
    chart - *NASDAQFB*
institutional holdings, percentage,
    yearly, chart - *NASDAQFB*

New York Stock Exchange
daily - *NYT, WSJ*
weekly - *Barron's*
yearly - *NYSEFB*
price, average, daily - *DSPR*
price, average, weekly - *Barron's,
    DSPR*
volume, yearly - *NYSEFB*
volume, percentage of total volume,
    weekly - *Barron's, DSPR*

Motel/hotel industry—*see*
Hotel/motel industry

Motion Pictures

Barron's Group Stock Averages
weekly - *Barron's*
companies and weights, irregularly -
    Barron's
range, yearly - *Barron's*

Multiform industry

Financial statistics
yearly - *VL*

Multiline insurance industry

Financial statistics
yearly - *AH*

Municipal Bond Index

Bond Buyers
weekly - *Barron's*

Merrill Lynch 500
weekly - *WSJ*

Municipal bond offerings

weekly - *Barron's*

Municipal Bond Price Index

Standard & Poor's
weekly, monthly, and yearly - *SPIR*
component bonds, yearly - *SPIR*
range, yearly - *SPIR*

Municipal bonds

Canadian
statistics, individual bonds, monthly -
    MBR

Competitive offerings
number of issues, weekly, six weeks,
    and projection - *MBS*
volume, dollars, weekly, six weeks, and
    projection - *MBS*

NASDAQ
listings, monthly - *BQR*

Negotiated offerings
number of issues, weekly, six weeks,
    and projection - *MBS*
volume, dollars, weekly, six weeks, and
    projection - *MBS*

New offerings
ratings, Moody's, individual bonds,
    weekly - *MBS*
statistics, individual bonds, weekly -
    MBS

Rates
daily - *NYT*

Ratings
Moody's, explanation and key,
    monthly - *MBR*
Moody's, individual bonds, monthly -
    MBR
Standard & Poor's, definitions,
    monthly - *BG*
Standard & Poor's, individual bonds,
    monthly - *BG*

Yield
monthly, graph - *MBR*
by rating groups, weekly and monthly,
    graph - *MBR*
individual bonds, monthly - *BQR*
Moody's Averages, composite and by
    rating groups, weekly - *MBS*
Moody's Averages, composite and by
    rating groups, weekly, graph - *MBS*
Moody's Averages, composite and by
    rating groups, monthly - *MBR, MBS*
Moody's Averages, composite and by
    rating groups, range, yearly - *MBS*
Standard & Poor's Index, weekly,
    monthly, and yearly - *BG, SPIR*
Standard & Poor's Index, range,
    weekly - *BG*
Standard & Poor's Index, range, yearly
    - *SPIR*

Yield spread
among rating groups, weekly, graph -
    MBS
vs. Treasury bonds, weekly, graph -
    MBS

Municipal issues

New
long-term, NYSE, yearly - *NYSEFB*
NYSE, yearly - *NYSEFB*
short-term, NYSE, yearly - *NYSEFB*

Municipal securities

Ratings
Moody's, changes, individual
    securities, monthly - *MBR*
Moody's, new, weekly - *MBS*
Moody's, reviewed and confirmed,
    weekly - *MBS*
Moody's, reviewed and revised, weekly
    - *MBS*
Moody's, unchanged, weekly - *MBS*
Moody's, withdrawn, weekly - *MBS*

Municipal short-term loans

New offerings
ratings, Moody's, individual loans,
    weekly - *MBS*
statistics, individual loans, weekly -
    MBS

Mutual fund indicators

monthly - *Barron's*

Mutual funds

Aggressive growth
sales, monthly - *Barron's*

Assets
monthly - *Barron's*
net, yearly - *SOSG*

Assets per share
net, percentage change, yearly - *SOSG*

Cash and equivalent
yearly - *SOSG*

Distributions per share from investment income
yearly - *SOSG*

Distributions per share from security profits
yearly - *SOSG*

Dividend, indicated annual
individual funds, monthly - *BQR*

Holdings of cash and short-term securities
monthly - *Barron's*

Liquid asset ratio (equity and balanced)
monthly - *Barron's*

Listings
daily - *NYT, WSJ*
weekly - *Barron's, CFC*
monthly - *BQR, SOSG*

Maximum sales charge
percentage, monthly - *SOSG*

Minimum initial purchase
monthly - *SOSG*

Money market
assets, monthly - *Barron's*

NASDAQ
dividends, indicated annual, individual funds, weekly - *CFC*
listings, weekly - *CFC*
listings, monthly - *BQR*

Net asset value
individual funds, daily - *NYT, WSJ*
individual funds, weekly - *Barron's*
individual funds, yearly - *SOSG*

Net assets
yearly - *SOSG*

Net assets per share
percentage change, yearly - *SOSG*

Purchases of common stock for
monthly - *Barron's*

Purchases of securities other than common stock for
monthly - *Barron's*

Redemption of shares held
monthly - *Barron's*

Sales
monthly - *Barron's*
common stock, monthly - *Barron's*
other securities (not including common stock), monthly - *Barron's*

Year formed
monthly - *SOSG*

Yield from investment income
yearly - *SOSG*

N

Name changes, company—*see* Changes

Name changes, mutual funds—*see* Changes

NASDAQ

Advance volume
daily - *WSJ*

Advances
leaders, stocks listed, daily - *NYT, WSJ*
number, daily - *Barron's, NYT, WSJ*
number, weekly - *Barron's*

American Depository Receipts
number, by originating country, yearly - *NASDAQFB*
volume leaders, yearly - *NASDAQFB*
volume leaders, dollar volume and closing price, yearly - *NASDAQFB*
volume leaders, share volume and closing price, yearly - *NASDAQFB*

Bid and asked quotations
individual stocks, daily - *WSJ*

Decline volume
daily - *WSJ*

Declines
leaders, stocks listed, daily - *NYT, WSJ*
number, daily - *Barron's, NYT, WSJ*
number, weekly - *Barron's*

Foreign companies
typical company profile, yearly - *NASDAQFB*

Foreign securities
number, by originating country, yearly - *NASDAQFB*
typical security profile, yearly - *NASDAQFB*
volume leaders, yearly - *NASDAQFB*
volume leaders, dollar volume and closing price, yearly - *NASDAQFB*
securities, volume leaders, share volume and closing price, yearly - *NASDAQFB*

Highs, new
number, daily - *Barron's, NYT, WSJ*
number, weekly - *Barron's*
stocks listed, weekly - *Barron's*

Issues
market value, average, by number of market makers, yearly - *NASDAQFB*
number, yearly - *NASDAQFB*
number, by number of market makers, yearly - *NASDAQFB*
number, percentage increase, latest 10 years - *NASDAQFB*

Issues traded
number, daily - *NYT, WSJ*

Large block transactions
number, daily - *WSJ*

Listing requirements
yearly - *NASDAQFB*

Listings
daily - *NYT, WSJ*
weekly - *Barron's, CFC*
monthly - *BQR*

Lows, new
number, daily - *Barron's, NYT, WSJ*
number, weekly - *Barron's*
stocks listed, weekly - *Barron's*

Market makers
listed, yearly - *NASDAQFB*
number, yearly - *NASDAQFB*
number, by state, yearly - *NASDAQFB*

number, per security, average, yearly - *NASDAQFB*

Market-making positions
number, yearly - *NASDAQFB*

Market value leaders
yearly - *NASDAQFB*
market value, individual companies, yearly - *NASDAQFB*
shares outstanding, individual companies, yearly - *NASDAQFB*

Most active stocks
yearly - *NASDAQFB*
listed, daily - *NYT, WSJ*
listed, weekly - *Barron's*
volume and closing price, individual companies, yearly - *NASDAQFB*

Mutual funds
dividends, indicated annual, individual funds, weekly - *CFC*
listings, weekly - *CFC*

Number
stocks available, daily - *Barron's*
stocks listed, weekly - *Barron's*

Price-earnings ratio
individual stocks, weekly - *CFC*

Price range
individual stocks, daily - *NYT, WSJ*
individual stocks, weekly - *Barron's*

Securities
number, yearly - *NASDAQFB*
number, by index classification, yearly - *NASDAQFB*
number, by type, yearly - *NASDAQFB*

Short interest
listings, weekly - *Barron's*

Stock price
average share traded, monthly and yearly - *NASDAQFB*
change, net, individual stocks, yearly - *NASDAQFB*
change, percentage, individual stocks, yearly - *NASDAQFB*
final adjusted inside, individual stocks, yearly - *NASDAQFB*
individual stocks, daily - *DSPR*
range, individual stocks, yearly - *NASDAQFB*

Ticker symbols
weekly - *CFC*
yearly - *NASDAQFB*

Trading days
number, monthly and yearly -
  NASDAQFB
10 highest, dates and volume -
  NASDAQFB

Unchanged stock prices
number, daily - *Barron's, NYT, WSJ*
number, weekly - *Barron's*

Volume
daily - *NYT, WSJ*
weekly and 10-week average - *VL*
total and daily average, monthly -
  NASDAQFB
total and daily average, yearly -
  NASDAQFB
dollars, monthly and yearly -
  NASDAQFB
dollars, percentage increase, latest 10
  years - *NASDAQFB*
dollars, percentage of all exchanges'
  dollar volume, yearly - *NASDAQFB*
individual stocks, yearly - *NASDAQFB*
NYSE-listed stock, daily - *NYT, WSJ*
NYSE-listed stock, weekly - *Barron's*
NYSE-listed stock, monthly and yearly
  - *NYSEFB*
NYSE-listed stock, percentage of all
  exchanges' trading in NYSE-listed
  stock, yearly - *NYSEFB*
percentage increase, total and daily
  average, latest 10 years -
  NASDAQFB
percentage of all exchanges' volume,
  yearly - *NASDAQFB*
percentage of NYSE volume, weekly
  and 10-week average - *VL*
records, yearly - *NASDAQFB*

Volume leaders
yearly - *NASDAQFB*
number of shares traded and price,
  average, yearly - *NASDAQFB*
number of shares traded and price,
  individual companies, yearly -
  NASDAQFB

NASDAQ Bank Index

daily - *Barron's, DSPR, WSJ*
weekly - *Barron's*
monthly and yearly - *NASDAQFB*

Change
percentage, yearly - *NASDAQFB*
10-year, yearly - *NASDAQFB*

Range
weekly - *Barron's*
yearly - *NASDAQFB*

Records
yearly - *NASDAQFB*

NASDAQ companies

Headquarters states
number of companies per state, yearly
  - *NASDAQFB*

Number
yearly - *NASDAQFB*
percentage increase, latest 10 years -
  NASDAQFB

NASDAQ Composite Index

daily - *Barron's, DSPR, NYT, WSJ*
weekly - *Barron's*
monthly - *NASDAQFB*
monthly, graph - *NASDAQFB*
yearly - *NASDAQFB*

Change
percentage, yearly - *NASDAQFB*
10-year, yearly - *NASDAQFB*

Range
weekly - *Barron's*
yearly - *NASDAQFB*

Records
yearly - *NASDAQFB*

NASDAQ Industrial Index

daily - *Barron's, DSPR, NYT, WSJ*
weekly - *Barron's*
monthly and yearly - *NASDAQFB*

Change
percentage, yearly - *NASDAQFB*
10-year, yearly - *NASDAQFB*

Range
weekly - *Barron's*
yearly - *NASDAQFB*

Records
yearly - *NASDAQFB*

NASDAQ Insurance Index

daily - *Barron's, DSPR, WSJ*
weekly - *Barron's*
monthly and yearly - *NASDAQFB*

Yield
individual stocks, weekly - *Barron's*

NASDAQ NMS companies

Typical company profile
yearly - *NASDAQFB*

NASDAQ NMS Composite Index

daily - *Barron's, NYT, WSJ*
weekly - *Barron's*
monthly - *NASDAQFB*

Range
weekly - *Barron's*

Records
yearly - *NASDAQFB*

NASDAQ NMS Industrial Index

daily - *Barron's, NYT, WSJ*
weekly - *Barron's*
monthly - *NASDAQFB*

Range
weekly - *Barron's*

Records
yearly - *NASDAQFB*

NASDAQ OTC

Banks and trust companies stocks
listings, monthly - *BQR*
price-earnings ratios, individual stocks,
  monthly - *BQR*

Industrial and miscellaneous stocks
listings, monthly - *BQR*
price-earnings ratios, individual stocks,
  monthly - *BQR*

Insurance companies stocks
listings, monthly - *BQR*
price-earnings ratios, individual stocks,
  monthly - *BQR*

Listings
daily - *NYT, WSJ*
weekly - *Barron's, CFC*
monthly - *BQR*

Price range
individual stocks, daily - *NYT, WSJ*
individual stocks, weekly - *Barron's*

Sales
daily - *Barron's*
individual stocks, daily - *NYT, WSJ*

individual stocks, weekly - *Barron's*

Volume
yearly - *NASDAQFB*
dollars, yearly - *NASDAQFB*
dollars, percentage of all exchanges'
  dollar volume, yearly - *NASDAQFB*
percentage of all exchanges' volume,
  yearly - *NASDAQFB*

NASDAQ Other Finance Index

monthly and yearly - *NASDAQFB*

Change
percentage, yearly - *NASDAQFB*
10-year, yearly - *NASDAQFB*

Range
yearly - *NASDAQFB*

Records
yearly - *NASDAQFB*

NASDAQ Over-the-Counter—*see* NASDAQ OTC

NASDAQ Supplemental Stock Listing

Listings
daily - *NYT*
weekly - *Barron's*

Sales
individual stocks, weekly - *Barron's*

NASDAQ Transportation Index

monthly and yearly - *NASDAQFB*

Change
percentage, yearly - *NASDAQFB*
10-year, yearly - *NASDAQFB*

Range
yearly - *NASDAQFB*

Records
yearly - *NASDAQFB*

NASDAQ Utility Index

monthly and yearly - *NASDAQFB*

Change
percentage, yearly - *NASDAQFB*
10-year, yearly - *NASDAQFB*

Range
yearly - *NASDAQFB*

Records
yearly - *NASDAQFB*

National Association of Securities Dealers Automated Quotations
—*see* NASDAQ

National List, NASDAQ—*see* NASDAQ National List

National Market System, NASDAQ—*see* NASDAQ NMS

National Market System Composite Index—*see* NASDAQ NMS Composite Index

National Market System Industrial Index—*see* NASDAQ NMS Industrial Index

National OTC Index

daily - *WSJ*

Natural gas distributors and pipelines

Financial statistics
yearly - *AH*

Natural gas industry (distribution)

Financial statistics
yearly - *VL*

Natural gas industry (diversified)

Financial statistics
yearly - *VL*

Natural gas industry (transmission)

Financial statistics
yearly - *FD*

Negotiated municipal bonds—*see* Municipal bonds

Net asset value

Closed-end bond funds
weekly - *Barron's*

Mutual funds
individual funds, daily - *NYT, WSJ*
individual funds, weekly - *Barron's*
per share, yearly - *SOSG*

Tax-free money market funds
weekly - *Barron's*

Net assets—*see* Assets

Net buy/sell—*see* Buy/sell

Net capital flow

International transactions
foreign stocks, NYSE, quarterly and
    yearly - *NYSEFB*
US stocks, NYSE, quarterly and yearly
    - *NYSEFB*

Net capital ratio

Individual securities brokerage
    companies
yearly - *MHCS, SPSR*

Net equity status—*see* Equity status

Net income

Before taxes
individual companies, yearly - *SPSR*

Companies
Amex, average and median, yearly -
    AmexFB
Amex, 10 leading companies, yearly -
    AmexFB
NYSE, aggregate, yearly - *NYSEFB*
NYSE, aggregate, percentage of all US
    companies' net income, yearly -
    NYSEFB
US, aggregate, yearly - *NYSEFB*

From operations
percentage of value added, individual
    companies and industries, yearly -
    FD

Individual companies
yearly - *FD, MHCS, SPSR*

Individual industries
yearly - *FD*
per share, yearly - *AH*

Percentage of revenues
individual companies, yearly - *SPSR*

Net operating assets—*see* Assets

Net operating income—*see*
Operating income

Net plant

Individual companies and industries
yearly - *FD*

Percentage of assets
individual companies and industries,
yearly - *FD*

Percentage of gross plant
individual companies and industries,
yearly - *FD*

Percentage operating income to
individual utilities, yearly - *MHCS*

Net profit

Individual companies and industries
yearly and projection - *VL*

Member organizations, NYSE
after taxes, estimated, yearly -
NYSEFB
before taxes, estimated, yearly -
NYSEFB

Net profit margin—*see* Profit margin

**Net property, plant and
equipment**—*see* Property, plant
and equipment

Net worth

Individual companies and industries
yearly and projection - *VL*

Percent earned on
individual securities brokerage
companies, yearly - *MHCS*

Netherlands guilder

Exchange rate
daily - *BQR, WSJ*
weekly - *Barron's*

Netherlands Stock Index

weekly - *Barron's*

New capital

Average price
individual companies, yearly - *MIM*

New common listings

American Stock Exchange
weekly - *Barron's*
yearly - *AmexFB*

NASDAQ
weekly - *Barron's*

New York Stock Exchange
weekly - *Barron's*
companies and dates, yearly - *NYSEFB*
number, yearly - *NYSEFB*

New issues

Bonds
NYSE, dollars, quarterly and yearly -
NYSEFB

Common stock
NYSE, dollars, quarterly and yearly -
NYSEFB

Stock
NYSE, dollars, quarterly and yearly -
NYSEFB

New listings

monthly - *SOSG*

Pending
monthly - *SOSG*

Resulting in increase in stock list
NYSE, number, yearly - *NYSEFB*

Technical
NYSE, companies and dates, yearly -
NYSEFB

New offerings

Calendar
monthly - *BG*

New privately placed corporate bond issues

dollars, yearly - *MIM*

New securities offered for cash sale

dollars, yearly - *MIM*

New York City banks

Assets
10 leading banks, weekly - *WSJ*

Liabilities
10 leading banks, weekly - *WSJ*

Primary offerings
rates, daily - *NYT*

New York Commodity Exchange

Listings
weekly - *Barron's*

New York Cotton Exchange

Listings
weekly - *Barron's*

Seat prices
monthly - *BQR*

Seats outstanding
number, monthly - *BQR*

New York Futures Exchange

Contract specifications
for NYSE stock index futures, yearly - *NYSEFB*
for NYSE stock index options on futures, yearly - *NYSEFB*

Listings
weekly - *Barron's*

New York Futures Exchange Composite Index

Futures
range and close, monthly, chart - *NYSEFB*

Futures contracts
basis, monthly, graph - *NYSEFB*

New York Mercantile Exchange

Listings
weekly—*Barron's*

Seat prices
monthly - *BQR*

Seats outstanding
number, monthly - *BQR*

New York Society of Financial Analysts

Schedule of companies to be discussed
by date and place, weekly - *Barron's*

New York Stock Exchange

Advance-decline line
daily and 10-day total, daily - *DSPR*

Advance volume
daily - *NYT, WSJ*

Advances
leaders, stocks listed, daily - *NYT, WSJ*
number, daily - *Barron's, DSPR, NYT, WSJ*
number, weekly - *Barron's*

Bid/ask services
number, yearly - *NYSEFB*

Bonds
advances, number, daily - *Barron's, NYT, WSJ*
banks, international, market value, yearly - *NYSEFB*
banks, international, number of issuers, yearly - *NYSEFB*
banks, international, number of issues, yearly - *NYSEFB*
banks, international, par value, yearly - *NYSEFB*
declines, number, daily - *Barron's, NYT, WSJ*
highs, new, number, daily - *Barron's, NYT, WSJ*

interest period, individual bonds,
weekly - *CFC*
interest period, individual bonds,
monthly - *BQR*
issues traded, number, daily - *NYT,
WSJ*
listings, daily - *NYT, WSJ*
listings, weekly - *Barron's, CFC*
listings, monthly - *BQR*
lows, new, number, daily - *Barron's,
NYT, WSJ*
market value, all listed bonds, yearly -
NYSEFB
new issues, dollars, quarterly and
yearly - *NYSEFB*
number available, weekly - *Barron's*
number of issues, yearly - *NYSEFB*
number of issuers, yearly - *NYSEFB*
par value, all listed bonds, yearly -
NYSEFB
par value, all traded bonds, total and
daily average, yearly - *NYSEFB*
par value, all traded bonds, records,
yearly - *NYSEFB*
price, average, yearly - *NYSEFB*
price range, individual bonds, daily -
NYT, WSJ
price range, individual bonds, weekly -
Barron's, CFC
price range, individual bonds, year to
date - *CFC*
price range, individual bonds, 52
weeks - *Barron's*
private placements, yearly - *NYSEFB*
ratings, individual bonds, weekly -
CFC
ratings, individual bonds, monthly -
BQR
sale price range, individual bonds,
monthly and year to date - *BQR*
sales, daily and weekly - *Barron's*
sales, monthly - *BQR*
sales, year to date - *WSJ*
sales, individual bonds, daily - *NYT*
sales, individual bonds, weekly -
Barron's, CFC
sales, individual bonds, monthly and
year to date - *BQR*
sales, par value, monthly - *SPIR*
unchanged bond prices, number, daily
- *Barron's, NYT, WSJ*
volume, weekly and monthly - *Barron's*
volume, dollars, daily - *NYT, WSJ*
volume, dollars, monthly - *BQR*
volume, dollars, year to date - *BQR,
NYT, WSJ*
volume, dollars, yearly - *NYT*

volume, individual bonds, daily and
year to date - *WSJ*
volume, par value, daily average,
yearly - *NYSEFB*
volume, par value, records, yearly -
NYSEFB
volume, par value, total reported,
yearly - *NYSEFB*
yield, individual bonds, daily - *NYT,
WSJ*
yield, individual bonds, weekly -
Barron's, CFC
yield, individual bonds, monthly -
BQR

Buy/sell
members, net, weekly - *Barron's*

Calls
open interest, daily - *NYT, WSJ*
open interest, weekly - *Barron's*
volume, daily - *NYT, WSJ*
volume, weekly - *Barron's*

Collateral
ratio to debt, monthly - *Barron's*

Collateral securing debt
monthly and quarterly - *NYSEFB*
records, yearly - *NYSEFB*

Common stock
advances, number, daily - *Barron's*
declines, number, daily - *Barron's*
dividend records, longevity, by number
of years, yearly - *NYSEFB*
market value, by industry, yearly -
NYSEFB
new issues, dollars, quarterly and
yearly - *NYSEFB*
new listings, companies and date,
yearly - *NYSEFB*
new listings, number, yearly - *NYSEFB*
number of issues available, daily -
Barron's
number of issues listed, yearly -
NYSEFB
number of issues listed, by industry,
yearly - *NYSEFB*
number of shares listed, by industry,
yearly - *NYSEFB*
number paying cash dividends during
year, yearly - *NYSEFB*
removals, number, yearly - *NYSEFB*
splits, yearly - *NYSEFB*
unchanged stock prices, number, daily
- *Barron's*
yield, median, yearly - *NYSEFB*
yield, number of issues by percentage
ranges, yearly - *NYSEFB*

yield, records, yearly - *NYSEFB*

Consolidations and mergers
companies and dates, yearly - *NYSEFB*

Contract specifications
for NYSE Composite Index and NYSE
   Double Index options, yearly -
   NYSEFB

Corporate bonds
foreign, market value, yearly -
   NYSEFB
foreign, number of issuers, yearly -
   NYSEFB
foreign, number of issues, yearly -
   NYSEFB
foreign, par value, yearly - *NYSEFB*
US, market value, yearly - *NYSEFB*
US, number of issuers, yearly -
   NYSEFB
US, number of issues, yearly -
   NYSEFB
US, par value, yearly - *NYSEFB*
volume, dollars, daily - *WSJ*

Credit balance
cash accounts, quarterly - *NYSEFB*
margin accounts, monthly and
   quarterly - *NYSEFB*

Customers
credit balance, monthly - *Barron's*
credit balance, records, yearly -
   NYSEFB
margin debt, monthly - *Barron's*
margin debt, records, yearly - *NYSEFB*
purchases, odd lots, daily - *WSJ*
purchases, odd lots, weekly - *Barron's*
purchases, odd lots, volume, number
   of shares and value, monthly -
   NYSEFB
sales, odd lots, volume, number of
   shares and value, monthly -
   NYSEFB
short sales, odd lots, weekly - *Barron's*
short sales, odd lots, monthly and
   yearly - *NYSEFB*

Dates
significant historical, yearly - *NYSEFB*

Decline volume
daily - *NYT, WSJ*

Declines
leaders, stocks listed, daily - *NYT,
   WSJ*
number, daily - *Barron's, DSPR, NYT,
   WSJ*
number, weekly - *Barron's*

Disbursements for customer assistance
yearly - *NYSEFB*

Distribution
institutional/intermediary share
   volume, yearly - *NYSEFB*
most active stocks volume, yearly -
   NYSEFB

Dividends
estimated aggregate cash payments,
   yearly - *NYSEFB*
indicated annual, individual stocks,
   weekly - *CFC*
indicated annual, individual stocks,
   monthly - *BQR*
individual stocks, daily - *NYT, WSJ*
individual stocks, weekly - *Barron's*

Dollar value of trading
records, yearly - *NYSEFB*

Domestic bonds
advances, number, daily - *WSJ*
declines, number, daily - *WSJ*
highs, new, number, daily - *WSJ*
issues traded, number, daily - *WSJ*
lows, new, number, daily - *WSJ*
unchanged bond prices, number, daily
   - *WSJ*
volume, dollars, daily and year to date
   - *NYT*

Earnings
individual stocks, yearly - *Barron's*

Foreign bonds
listings, daily - *WSJ*
volume, dollars, daily - *NYT, WSJ*
volume, dollars, year to date - *NYT*

Foreign securities
market value, yearly - *NYSEFB*
market value, total and by geographic
   region, yearly - *NYSEFB*
number of listings, total and by
   geographic region, yearly - *NYSEFB*

Foreign stocks
market value, total and by geographic
   region, yearly - *NYSEFB*
number of listings, total and by
   geographic region, yearly - *NYSEFB*

Foreigners' purchases from Americans
foreign stocks, quarterly and yearly -
   NYSEFB
US stocks, quarterly and yearly -
   NYSEFB

Foreigners' sales to Americans
foreign stocks, quarterly and yearly -
    NYSEFB
US stocks, quarterly and yearly -
    NYSEFB

Free credit balance cash accounts
monthly - *Barron's*

Geographic distribution of shareowners
yearly - *NYSEFB*

Government bonds
foreign, market value, total and by
    geographic region, yearly - *NYSEFB*
foreign, number of issuers, yearly -
    NYSEFB
foreign, number of issues, yearly -
    NYSEFB
foreign, par value, yearly - *NYSEFB*
US, market value, yearly - *NYSEFB*
US, number of issuers, yearly -
    NYSEFB
US, number of issues, yearly -
    NYSEFB
US, par value, yearly - *NYSEFB*
volume, dollars, daily and year to date
    - *NYT*

Highs, new
number, daily - *Barron's, DSPR, NYT,
    WSJ*
number, weekly - *Barron's*
stocks listed, daily - *NYT, WSJ*
stocks listed, weekly - *Barron's*

Initial margin requirement
yearly - *NYSEFB*

Institutional investors
holdings by type of institution, yearly -
    NYSEFB

International transactions
number, quarterly and yearly -
    NYSEFB

Interrogation devices
number, yearly - *NYSEFB*

Issues
number, yearly - *NASDAQFB,
    NYSEFB*
number, by industry, yearly - *NYSEFB*

Issues traded
number, daily - *NYT, WSJ*

Large block transactions
down ticks, number, daily - *Barron's*
no change, daily - *Barron's*
number, daily - *Barron's, WSJ*

number and daily average, monthly
    and yearly - *NYSEFB*
number of shares, monthly and yearly
    - *NYSEFB*
percentage of reported volume,
    monthly and yearly - *NYSEFB*
percentage of reported volume, yearly,
    chart - *NASDAQFB*
percentage of reported volume,
    records, yearly - *NYSEFB*
10 largest, name of stock and volume,
    yearly - *NYSEFB*
up ticks, number, daily - *Barron's*
volume, records, yearly - *NYSEFB*

Last sale devices
number, yearly - *NYSEFB*

Listing requirements
yearly - *NYSEFB*

Listings
daily - *CFC, NYT, WSJ*
weekly - *Barron's*
monthly - *BQR*

Lows, new
number, daily - *Barron's, DSPR, NYT,
    WSJ*
number, weekly - *Barron's*
stocks listed, daily - *NYT, WSJ*
stocks listed, weekly - *Barron's*

Margin accounts
number, monthly - *Barron's, NYSEFB*
number, quarterly - *NYSEFB*
number, records, yearly - *NYSEFB*
number in debit status, quarterly -
    NYSEFB
number in debit status, records, yearly
    - *NYSEFB*

Margin debt
monthly - *DSPR, NYSEFB*
quarterly - *NYSEFB*

Market depth
yearly - *NYSEFB*

Market quality
yearly - *NYSEFB*

Market value
all shares listed, total and by industry,
    yearly - *NYSEFB*
leading stocks, yearly - *NYSEFB*

Member buy volume
weekly - *Barron's*

Member organizations
assets, yearly - *NYSEFB*
balance sheet, yearly - *NYSEFB*
capital, yearly - *NYSEFB*
corporations, number, yearly -
  NYSEFB
expenses, yearly - *NYSEFB*
gross income, sources, yearly -
  NYSEFB
income, yearly - *NYSEFB*
income, from securities commissions,
  yearly - *NYSEFB*
income statement, yearly - *NYSEFB*
liabilities, yearly - *NYSEFB*
number, yearly - *NYSEFB*
number, by type, yearly - *NYSEFB*
offices, number, yearly - *NYSEFB*
partnerships, number, yearly -
  NYSEFB
profit, net, after taxes, estimated,
  yearly - *NYSEFB*
profit, net, before taxes, yearly -
  NYSEFB
registered personnel, number, yearly -
  NYSEFB
registered representatives, number, by
  state, yearly - *NYSEFB*
sales offices, number, by state, yearly -
  NYSEFB

Member trading
weekly - *Barron's*
records, yearly - *NYSEFB*

Members
buy/sell, net, weekly - *Barron's*
floor traders, purchases, weekly -
  Barron's
floor traders, sales, weekly - *Barron's*
floor traders, short sales, weekly -
  Barron's
participation rate, yearly - *NYSEFB*
participation rate, trades originating off
  the floor, yearly - *NYSEFB*
participation rate, trades originating on
  the floor, yearly - *NYSEFB*
purchases, weekly - *Barron's*
purchases, round lots, monthly -
  NYSEFB
purchases, round lots, originating off
  the floor, monthly - *NYSEFB*
purchases, round lots, originating on
  the floor, monthly - *NYSEFB*
purchases and sales, records, yearly -
  NYSEFB
purchases and sales, round lots,
  number of shares, yearly - *NYSEFB*

purchases and sales, round lots,
  originating off the floor, number of
  shares, yearly - *NYSEFB*
purchases and sales, round lots,
  originating on the floor, number of
  shares, yearly - *NYSEFB*
sales, total and daily average, weekly -
  Barron's
sales, round lots, monthly - *NYSEFB*
sales, round lots, originating off the
  floor, monthly - *NYSEFB*
sales, round lots, originating on the
  floor, monthly - *NYSEFB*
sell volume, weekly - *Barron's*
short sales, weekly - *Barron's*
short sales, records, yearly - *NYSEFB*
short sales, round lots, monthly and
  yearly - *NYSEFB*
specialists, purchases, weekly - *Barron's*
specialists, sales, weekly - *Barron's*
volume, first round, shares and
  warrants, weekly - *Barron's*
volume, percentage of total volume,
  weekly - *Barron's*

Membership prices
range, yearly - *NYSEFB*
records, yearly - *NYSEFB*

Mergers and consolidations
companies and dates, yearly - *NYSEFB*

Most active bonds
listed, yearly - *NYSEFB*
par value of reported volume, yearly -
  NYSEFB

Most active equity options
calls, listed, weekly - *Barron's*
puts, listed, weekly - *Barron's*

Most active options
listed, daily - *WSJ*
sales, individual options, daily - *WSJ*

Most active stocks
listed, daily - *NYT, WSJ*
listed, weekly - *Barron's*
listed, yearly - *NYSEFB*
price, average, daily - *DSPR*
price, average, weekly - *Barron's,
  DSPR*
volume, individual stocks, yearly -
  NYSEFB
volume, percentage of total volume,
  weekly - *Barron's, DSPR*

Municipal issues
new, yearly - *NYSEFB*
new, long-term, yearly - *NYSEFB*
new, short-term, yearly - *NYSEFB*

Net capital flow
international transactions, foreign
 stocks, quarterly and yearly -
 NYSEFB
international transactions, US stocks,
 quarterly and yearly - *NYSEFB*

Net equity status of margin accounts
yearly - *NYSEFB*

New common listings
weekly - *Barron's*

New listings
resulting in increase in stock list,
 number, yearly - *NYSEFB*

Nonmembers
short sales, round lots, monthly and
 yearly - *NYSEFB*

Number of companies
by industry, yearly - *NYSEFB*

Number of shares listed
total and average, yearly - *NYSEFB*
by industry, yearly - *NYSEFB*
records, yearly - *NYSEFB*

Number of shares per reported trade
records, yearly - *NYSEFB*

Number of stocks available
daily - *Barron's*

Number of stocks listed
weekly - *Barron's*

Odd-lot dealers
purchases and sales, round lots,
 number of shares, yearly - *NYSEFB*

Odd lots
activity, weekly - *Barron's*
prices, average, yearly - *NYSEFB*
purchases, daily - *DSPR, NYT*
ratios, daily and 10-day, daily - *DSPR*
sales, daily - *Barron's, DSPR, NYT,
 WSJ*
sales, compared to odd-lot purchases,
 weekly, last market bottom, and last
 market top - *VL*
sales, compared to odd-lot purchases,
 range, 13-week and 50-week - *VL*
short sales, daily - *Barron's, DSPR,
 WSJ*
volume, number of shares, yearly -
 NYSEFB
volume, number of shares, records,
 yearly - *NYSEFB*
volume, purchases, daily - *NYT*
volume, purchases, yearly - *NYSEFB*

volume, purchases, value, yearly -
 NYSEFB
volume, sales, daily - *NYT*
volume, sales, yearly - *NYSEFB*
volume, sales, value, yearly - *NYSEFB*
volume, value, yearly - *NYSEFB*
volume, value, records, yearly -
 NYSEFB

Off-floor short sales
records, yearly - *NYSEFB*

Off-floor trading
records, yearly - *NYSEFB*

Options
listings, daily - *NYT, WSJ*
listings, weekly - *Barron's*

Percent leaders
winners and losers, weekly - *Barron's*

Percentage gainers and losers
daily - *WSJ*

Potential purchasing power
monthly - *DSPR*
quarterly - *NYSEFB*
records, yearly - *NYSEFB*
securities market credit, monthly -
 NYSEFB

Preferred stock
dividends, estimated aggregate cash
 payments, yearly - *NYSEFB*
dividends, number paying cash, yearly
 - *NYSEFB*
number of issues listed at year end,
 yearly - *NYSEFB*
yield, median, yearly - *NYSEFB*

Price continuity
yearly - *NYSEFB*

Price-earnings ratio
individual stocks, daily - *NYT, WSJ*
individual stocks, weekly - *Barron's,
 CFC*
individual stocks, monthly - *BQR*

Price range
individual stocks, daily - *NYT, WSJ*
individual stocks, weekly - *Barron's,
 CFC*
individual stocks, year to date - *CFC*
individual stocks, 52 weeks - *Barron's,
 NYT, WSJ*

Price-volume accumulation line
daily and 10-day total, daily - *DSPR*

Private placements
yearly - *NYSEFB*
bonds, yearly - *NYSEFB*
stocks, yearly - *NYSEFB*

Public
short sales, weekly - *Barron's*
short sales, percentage of total short
   sales, weekly, last market bottom,
   and last market top - *VL*
short sales, percentage of total short
   sales, range, 13-week and 50-week -
   VL
volume, quarterly - *NYSEFB*

Public Transaction Study
yearly - *NYSEFB*

Puts
open interest, daily - *NYT, WSJ*
open interest, weekly - *Barron's*
volume, daily - *NYT, WSJ*
volume, weekly - *Barron's*

Quality of security credit
monthly, graph - *NYSEFB*

Quotation spreads
yearly - *NYSEFB*

Removals
yearly - *NYSEFB*

Sale price range
individual stocks, monthly and year to
   date - *BQR*

Sales
individual stocks, daily - *NYT, WSJ*
individual stocks, weekly - *Barron's,
   CFC*
individual stocks, monthly and year to
   date - *BQR*
market value, yearly - *NYSEFB*
market value, percentage of all
   exchanges' sales
   yearly - *NYSEFB*
number, daily - *SPIR*
number, weekly - *Barron's*
number, monthly - *BQR*
number, yearly - *NYSEFB*
percentage of all exchanges' sales,
   yearly - *NYSEFB*

Seat prices
monthly - *BQR*

Seat sales
number, monthly - *Barron's, NYSEFB*
price range, monthly - *NYSEFB*

Seats outstanding
number, monthly - *BQR*

Securities market credit
records, yearly - *NYSEFB*

Shareowners
characteristics, yearly - *NYSEFB*

Short interest
monthly - *Barron's, DSPR, NYSEFB*
compared to average daily volume
   (5-week), weekly, last market
   bottom, and last market top - *VL*
compared to average daily volume
   (5-week), range, 13-week and
   50-week - *VL*
number of shares, year end, yearly -
   NYSEFB
records, yearly - *NYSEFB*

Short-interest ratio
weekly - *Barron's*
monthly - *Barron's, DSPR*

Short issues
weekly - *Barron's*
volume, weekly - *Barron's*

Short ratio
members/public, weekly - *Barron's*
specialists/public, weekly - *Barron's*

Short sales
weekly - *Barron's*
percentage of total volume, weekly, last
   market bottom, and last market top
   - *VL*
percentage of total volume, range,
   13-week and 50-week - *VL*
round lots, number of shares, monthly
   and yearly - *NYSEFB*

Short-term trading index
daily - *Barron's*

Specialist stabilization
yearly - *NYSEFB*

Specialists
participation rate, yearly - *NYSEFB*
purchases, round lots, monthly -
   NYSEFB
purchases and sales, round lots,
   number of shares, yearly - *NYSEFB*
records, yearly - *NYSEFB*
sales, round lots, monthly - *NYSEFB*
short sales, weekly - *Barron's*
short sales, percentage of total short
   sales, weekly, last market bottom,
   and last market top - *VL*

purchases, odd lots, number of shares,
   yearly - *NYSEFB*
records, yearly - *NYSEFB*
round lots and odd lots, number of
   shares, yearly - *NYSEFB*
round lots and odd lots, number of
   shares, records, yearly - *NYSEFB*
round lots and odd lots, value of
   shares, yearly - *NYSEFB*
round lots and odd lots, value of
   shares, records, yearly - *NYSEFB*
sources, quarterly - *NYSEFB*

Volume leaders
yearly - *NASDAQFB*
number of shares traded and price,
   average, yearly - *NASDAQFB*
number of shares traded and price,
   individual companies, yearly -
   NASDAQFB

Volume on margin
public individuals, percentage,
   quarterly - *NYSEFB*

Warrants
number, yearly - *NYSEFB*
number of companies, yearly -
   NYSEFB
number of issues, yearly - *NYSEFB*
value, yearly - *NYSEFB*
volume, total and daily average, yearly
   - *NYSEFB*
volume, records, yearly - *NYSEFB*

Yield
individual stocks, daily - *NYT, WSJ*
individual stocks, weekly - *Barron's,
   CFC*

**New York Stock Exchange Beta
Index**

daily - *WSJ*

**New York Stock Exchange
Common Stock Index**

daily - *DSPR, NYSEFB, NYT, WSJ*
daily, chart - *NYT*
weekly - *Barron's*
weekly, graph - *VL*
monthly and yearly - *NYSEFB*

Futures
contract specifications, New York
   Futures Exchange, yearly - *NYSEFB*
options, contract specifications, New
   York Futures Exchange, yearly -
   NYSEFB

Growth rates
yearly - *NYSEFB*

Options
contract specifications, NYSE, yearly -
   NYSEFB
open interest, monthly - *NYSEFB*
open interest, monthly, graph -
   NYSEFB
volume, daily average, monthly -
   NYSEFB
volume, daily average, monthly, graph
   - *NYSEFB*

Price-earnings ratio
quarterly - *NYSEFB*

Range
weekly - *Barron's*
monthly - *NYSEFB*
monthly, chart - *MHCS*
monthly, graph - *MIM*

Records
yearly - *NYSEFB*

Yield
quarterly - *NYSEFB*

**New York Stock Exchange
companies**

Assets
aggregate, yearly - *NYSEFB*
aggregate, percentage of all US
   companies' assets, yearly - *NYSEFB*

Common stockholders-of-record
largest number, name and number,
   yearly - *NYSEFB*

Dividend reinvestment plans
listed, yearly - *SPQDR*

Name changes
weekly - *Barron's*
monthly - *SOSG*
quarterly - *MHCS*
year to date - *BQR*
yearly - *NYSEFB*

Net income
aggregate, yearly - *NYSEFB*
aggregate, percentage of all US
   companies' net income, yearly -
   NYSEFB

Number
yearly - *NASDAQFB, NYSEFB*
percentage of all US companies, yearly
   - *NYSEFB*

Number with listed stocks
yearly - *NYSEFB*

Revenues
aggregate, yearly - *NYSEFB*
aggregate, percentage of all US
   companies' revenues, yearly -
   NYSEFB

Sales
aggregate, yearly - *NYSEFB*
aggregate, percentage of all US
   companies' sales, yearly - *NYSEFB*

New York Stock Exchange
Composite Indicator—*see* New
York Stock Exchange Common
Stock Index

New York Stock Exchange
Double Index

daily - *WSJ*

Options
contract specifications, NYSE, yearly -
   NYSEFB
open interest, monthly - *NYSEFB*
open interest, monthly, graph -
   NYSEFB
volume, daily average, monthly -
   NYSEFB
volume, daily average, monthly, graph
   - *NYSEFB*

New York Stock Exchange
Financial Indicator

daily - *Barron's, BQR, DSPR, NYT,
   WSJ*
weekly - *Barron's*
monthly - *BQR*

Range
weekly - *Barron's*
monthly - *Barron's, BQR, NYSEFB*

New York Stock Exchange
Industrial Indicator

daily - *BQR, DSPR, NYT, WSJ*
weekly - *Barron's*
monthly - *BQR*

Range
weekly - *Barron's*
monthly - *BQR, NYSEFB*

NYSE-listed stock

Volume
by exchange, daily - *NYT, WSJ*
by exchange, monthly and yearly -
   NYSEFB
Amex, percentage of Amex volume,
   yearly - *NYSEFB*
Boston Stock Exchange, percentage of
   Boston Stock Exchange volume,
   yearly - *NYSEFB*
Cincinnati Stock Exchange, percentage
   of Cincinnati Stock Exchange
   volume, yearly - *NYSEFB*
Instinet, percentage of Instinet volume,
   yearly - *NYSEFB*
Midwest Stock Exchange, percentage of
   Midwest Stock Exchange volume,
   yearly - *NYSEFB*
NASDAQ, percentage of NASDAQ
   volume, yearly - *NYSEFB*
NYSE, percentage of total volume,
   yearly - *NYSEFB*
Pacific Stock Exchange, percentage of
   Pacific Stock Exchange volume,
   yearly - *NYSEFB*
percentage of NYSE-listed stock
   volume, by exchange, yearly -
   NYSEFB
Philadelphia Stock Exchange,
   percentage of Philadelphia Stock
   Exchange volume, yearly - *NYSEFB*

New York Stock Exchange
Transportation Indicator

daily - *BQR, DSPR, NYT, WSJ*
weekly - *Barron's*
monthly - *BQR*

Range
weekly - *Barron's*
monthly - *BQR, NYSEFB*

New York Stock Exchange
Utilities Indicator

daily - *BQR, DSPR, NYT, WSJ*
weekly - *Barron's*
monthly - *BQR*

Range
monthly - *BQR, NYSEFB*

New Zealand dollar

Exchange rate
daily - *BQR, NYT, WSJ*
weekly - *Barron's*

Newly issued corporate bonds—*see* Corporate bonds

Newly issued domestic industrial bonds—*see* Domestic industrial bonds

Newly issued domestic railroad bonds—*see* Domestic railroad bonds

Newly issued domestic utility bonds—*see* Domestic utility bonds

Newly issued industrial bonds—*see* heading Industrial bonds

Newly issued public utility bonds—*see* heading Public utility bonds

Newly issued railroad bonds—*see* heading Railroad bonds

Newspaper industry

Financial statistics
yearly - *VL*

Newsprint

Inventories
US and Canada, monthly - *Barron's*

Production
US and Canada, monthly - *Barron's*

Nikkei Dow Jones Stock Index—*see* Japan, Nikkei Dow Jones Stock Index

Nikkei Stock Average—*see* Japan, Nikkei Stock Average

Nikkei 225 Stock Index—*see* Japan, Nikkei 225 Stock Index

Nineteenth-century European paintings—*see* Paintings

Nonborrowed reserves

Federal Reserve banks
daily average of two-week period - *Barron's, WSJ*

Nondurable goods

New orders received
dollars, monthly - *Barron's*

Nondurable manufacturing production

monthly - *Barron's*

Non-ferrous metals

Barron's Group Stock Averages
weekly - *Barron's*
companies and weights, irregularly - *Barron's*
range, yearly - *Barron's*

Nonfinancial companies

Commercial paper
amount outstanding, dollars, weekly - *WSJ*

Nonoperating income

Percentage of gross assets
individual companies and industries, yearly - *FD*

Nonoperating income and expense

Individual companies
quarterly and yearly - *FD*

Individual industries
yearly - *FD*

Nonredeemable preferred stock

Individual companies and industries
yearly - *FD*

Percentage of invested capital
individual companies and industries, yearly - *FD*

Norwegian krone

Exchange rate
daily - *BQR, NYT, WSJ*
weekly - *Barron's*

Notes

Chronological list classified according to Moody's ratings
yearly - *MIM*

Industrial
maturing, chronological list, yearly - *MIM*

Medium-term—*see* Medium-term notes

Treasury—*see* Treasury notes

Notes payable

Individual companies and industries
yearly - *FD*

Individual industries
per share, yearly - *AH*

Novo cruzeiro, Brazilian—*see* Brazilian novo cruzeiro

NOWs and SuperNOWs

dollars, monthly - *Barron's*

O

Odd-lot dealers

New York Stock Exchange
purchases and sales, round lots, number of shares, yearly - *NYSEFB*

Odd lots

American Stock Exchange
customers, short sales, weekly - *Barron's*
purchases plus sales, yearly - *AmexFB*
purchases plus sales, percentage of total purchases plus sales, yearly - *AmexFB*

New York Stock Exchange
customers, purchases, daily - *WSJ*
customers, purchases, weekly - *Barron's*
customers, purchases, volume, number of shares and value, monthly - *NYSEFB*
customers, sales, weekly - *Barron's*
customers, sales, volume, number of shares and value, monthly - *NYSEFB*
customers, short sales, weekly - *Barron's*
prices, average, yearly - *NYSEFB*
purchases, compared to odd-lot sales, weekly, last market bottom, and last market top - *VL*
purchases, compared to odd-lot sales, range, 13-week and 50-week - *VL*
purchases, volume, daily - *Barron's, DSPR, NYT*
purchases, volume, yearly - *NYSEFB*
purchases, volume, value, yearly - *NYSEFB*
ratios, daily and 10-day, daily - *DSPR*
sales, daily - *WSJ*
sales, compared to odd-lot purchases, weekly, last market bottom, and last market top - *VL*
sales, compared to odd-lot purchases, range, 13-week and 50-week - *VL*
sales, volume, daily - *Barron's, DSPR, NYT*
sales, volume, yearly - *NYSEFB*
sales, volume, value, yearly - *NYSEFB*
short sales, daily - *Barron's, DSPR, WSJ*
volume, weekly - *Barron's*
volume, number of shares, yearly - *NYSEFB*
volume, records, yearly - *NYSEFB*
volume, value, yearly - *NYSEFB*

Short sales
weekly - *Barron's*

Off-floor short sales

New York Stock Exchange
records, yearly - *NYSEFB*

Off-floor trading

New York Stock Exchange
records, yearly - *NYSEFB*

Offerings—*see also* Convertible
offerings, Corporate offerings

Bonds
weekly - *Barron's*

New
calendar, monthly - *BG*

New securities
for cash sale, dollars, yearly - *MIM*

Newly filed
weekly - *Barron's*

Primary
New York City banks, rates, daily -
NYT

Special
number and total shares, yearly -
NYSEFB

Stock
weekly - *Barron's*

Office and business equipment industry

Financial statistics
yearly - *FD*

Office equipment

Barron's Group Stock Averages
weekly - *Barron's*
companies and weights, irregularly -
Barron's
range, yearly - *Barron's*

Office equipment and supplies industry

Financial statistics
yearly - *VL*

Offices, member organizations

New York Stock Exchange
number, yearly - *NYSEFB*

Offshore Drilling Index

Standard & Poor's
weekly, monthly, and yearly - *SPIR*
companies listed, yearly - *SPIR*
range, yearly - *SPIR*

Offshore drilling industry

Financial statistics
yearly - *AH*

Oil

Barron's Group Stock Averages
weekly - *Barron's*
companies and weights, irregularly -
Barron's
range, yearly - *Barron's*

Inventories
domestic crude, weekly - *Barron's*

Price
daily - *NYT, WSJ*

Oil and Gas Index

American Stock Exchange
stock index options, close, monthly
and yearly - *AmexFB*

Oil Index

daily - *WSJ*

American Stock Exchange
stock index options, calls, number,
yearly - *AmexFB*
stock index options, close, monthly
and yearly - *AmexFB*
stock index options, contracts, number
and daily average, yearly - *AmexFB*
stock index options, puts, number,
yearly - *AmexFB*

Oil Index (composite)

Standard & Poor's
weekly, monthly, and yearly - *SPIR*
component companies yearly - *SPIR*
range, yearly - *SPIR*

Oil Index (crude producers)

Standard & Poor's
weekly, monthly, and yearly - *SPIR*
component companies, yearly - *SPIR*
range, yearly - *SPIR*

Oil Index (integrated domestic)

Standard & Poor's
weekly, monthly, and yearly - *SPIR*
component companies, yearly - *SPIR*

range, yearly - *SPIR*

Oil Index (integrated international)

Standard & Poor's
weekly, monthly, and yearly - *SPIR*
component companies, yearly - *SPIR*
range, yearly - *SPIR*

Oil industry (composite)

Financial statistics
yearly - *AH*

Oil industry (crude producers)

Financial statistics
yearly - *AH*

Oil industry (integrated domestic)

Financial statistics
yearly - *AH, FD*

Oil industry (integrated international)

Financial statistics
yearly - *AH*

Oil Well Equipment and Services Index

Standard & Poor's
weekly, monthly, and yearly - *SPIR*
component companies, yearly - *SPIR*
range, yearly - *SPIR*

Oil well equipment and services industry

Financial statistics
yearly - *AH*

Oilfield services/equipment industry

Financial statistics
yearly - *VL*

Old Master paintings—*see* Paintings

Open interest

American Stock Exchange
daily - *NYT, WSJ*
weekly - *Barron's*
monthly - *AmexFB*
calls, monthly and yearly - *AmexFB*
puts, monthly and yearly - *AmexFB*

By exchange
monthly - *BQR*

Calls
by exchange and type of option, daily - *NYT, WSJ*
by exchange and type of option, weekly - *Barron's*

Futures
individual commodities, daily - *NYT, WSJ*
individual commodities, weekly - *Barron's*

New York Futures Exchange
futures contracts, monthly - *NYSEFB*
options contracts, monthly - *NYSEFB*

New York Stock Exchange Common Stock Index
options, monthly - *NYSEFB*
options, monthly, graph - *NYSEFB*

New York Stock Exchange Double Index
options, monthly - *NYSEFB*
options, monthly, graph - *NYSEFB*

Puts
by exchange and type of option, daily - *WSJ*

Operating assets—*see* Assets

Operating income

After depreciation
individual companies and industries, yearly - *FD*
per dollar average gross plant, individual companies and industries, yearly - *FD*
per dollar average invested capital, individual companies and industries, yearly - *FD*
percentage of sales, individual companies and industries, quarterly, moving 12 months, and yearly - *FD*

Before depreciation

change, year to year, individual
   companies and industries, quarterly,
   moving 12 months, and yearly - *FD*
individual companies and industries,
   quarterly, moving 12 months, and
   yearly - *FD*
per dollar average gross plant,
   individual companies and
   industries, yearly - *FD*
per dollar average invested capital,
   individual companies and
   industries, yearly - *FD*
per employee, individual companies
   and industries, yearly - *FD*
per share, annual growth rate,
   individual companies and
   industries, latest year, 3 years, 5
   years, and 10 years - *FD*
per share, change, individual
   companies and industries, yearly -
   FD
per share, individual companies and
   industries, yearly - *FD*
per share, least squares growth rate
   and coefficient of determination,
   individual companies and
   industries, 5-year and 10-year - *FD*
percentage of industry operating
   income before depreciation,
   individual companies, yearly - *FD*
percentage of sales, individual
   companies and industries, quarterly,
   moving 12 months, and yearly - *FD*

By segment

change, individual companies, yearly -
   FD
individual companies, yearly - *FD*
percentage of total operating income,
   individual companies, yearly - *FD*

Individual companies
yearly - *SPSR*

International
percentage of total operating income,
   individual companies, yearly - *FD*

Margin
by segment, individual companies,
   yearly - *FD*

Net, utilities
per share, yearly - *AH*

Percentage of revenues
individual companies, yearly - *SPSR*

Percentage to net plant
individual utilities, yearly - *MHCS*

Operating income margin

By segment
individual companies, yearly - *FD*

Operating margin

Individual companies and industries
yearly and projection - *VL*

Operating profit

Individual industries
per share, yearly - *AH*

Operating profit margin—*see* Profit
margin

Operating rate—*see* Factory
operating rate

Operating ratio

Utilities
yearly - *AH*

Operating revenues

Utilities
per share, yearly - *AH*

Operations, funds from

Individual companies and industries
yearly - *FD*

Option/income mutual funds

Sales
monthly - *Barron's*

Option leaders

Calls down
weekly - *Barron's*

Calls up
weekly - *Barron's*

Puts down
weekly - *Barron's*

Puts up
weekly - *Barron's*

price range, monthly and since issue -
BQR
sales, monthly - *BQR*

Trading

Amex, number and daily average,
   monthly and yearly - *AmexFB*
Amex, number of underlying
   companies, monthly and yearly -
   AmexFB

Options principal members

American Stock Exchange
sales, range and last, yearly - *AmexFB*

Order backlog

Individual companies and industries
yearly - *FD*

Orders, factory—*see* Factory orders

Orders received, new

monthly - *Barron's*

Durable goods
monthly - *Barron's*

Machine tools
monthly - *Barron's*

Nondurable goods
monthly - *Barron's*

Orders statistics

Unfilled
monthly - *Barron's*

OTC—*see* NASDAQ OTC

OTC Bank Index—*see* NASDAQ
Bank Index

OTC Composite Index—*see*
NASDAQ Composite Index

OTC Industrial Index—*see*
NASDAQ Industrial Index

OTC Insurance Index—*see*
NASDAQ Insurance Index

OTC Other Finance Index—*see*
NASDAQ Other Finance Index

OTC Transportation Index—*see*
NASDAQ Transportation Index

OTC Utility Index—*see* NASDAQ
Utility Index

Outstanding shares

Number, individual companies
yearly - *MHCS*

Over-the-counter—*see* NASDAQ
OTC

Overnight Eurodollars

dollars, monthly - *Barron's*

Overnight repurchase agreements

dollars, monthly - *Barron's*

P

Pacific Stock Exchange

Bonds
listings, selected bonds, daily - *NYT,
   WSJ*
listings, selected bonds, weekly -
   Barron's
sales, selected individual bonds, daily -
   NYT, WSJ

Calls
open interest, daily - *NYT, WSJ*
open interest, weekly - *Barron's*
volume, daily - *NYT, WSJ*
volume, weekly - *Barron's*

Dividends, indicated annual
individual stocks, weekly - *CFC*
individual stocks, monthly - *BQR*

Listings
daily - *CFC, NYT, WSJ*
weekly - *Barron's*
monthly - *BQR*

Most active equity options
calls, listed, weekly - *Barron's*
puts, listed, weekly - *Barron's*

Most active options
listed, daily - *NYT, WSJ*
sales, individual options, daily - *NYT, WSJ*
sales, individual options, weekly - *Barron's*

NYSE-listed stock
volume, daily - *NYT, WSJ*
volume, weekly - *Barron's*
volume, monthly and yearly - *NYSEFB*
volume, percentage of all exchanges' trading in NYSE-listed stock, yearly - *NYSEFB*

Options
listings, daily - *NYT, WSJ*
listings, weekly - *Barron's*
listings, monthly - *BQR*
open interest, monthly - *BQR*
price range, monthly and since issue - *BQR*
sales, monthly - *BQR*

Price-earnings ratio
individual stocks, weekly - *CFC*
individual stocks, monthly - *BQR*

Price range
individual stocks, year to date - *CFC*

Puts
open interest, daily - *NYT, WSJ*
open interest, weekly - *Barron's*
volume, daily - *NYT, WSJ*
volume, weekly - *Barron's*

Sale price range
individual stocks, monthly and year to date - *BQR*

Sales
daily - *NYT, WSJ*
individual selected stocks, daily - *NYT, WSJ*
individual stocks, weekly - *CFC*
individual stocks, monthly and year to date - *BQR*

Seat prices
monthly - *BQR*

Seats outstanding
number, monthly - *BQR*

Short interest ratio
weekly - *Barron's*

Short issues
volume, weekly - *Barron's*

Stocks
volume, year to date - *BQR*

Volume
monthly and year to date - *BQR*

Yield
individual stocks, weekly - *CFC*
individual stocks, monthly - *BQR*

Packaging and container industry

Financial statistics
yearly - *VL*

Packing

Barron's Group Stock Averages
weekly - *Barron's*
companies and weights, irregularly - *Barron's*
range, yearly - *Barron's*

Paintings

American, 1800-pre-World War II
Sotheby's Art Index, weekly - *Barron's*

Impressionist and post-Impressionist
Sotheby's Art Index, weekly - *Barron's*

Modern
Sotheby's Art Index, weekly - *Barron's*

Nineteenth-century European
Sotheby's Art Index, weekly - *Barron's*

Old Master
Sotheby's Art Index, weekly - *Barron's*

Pakistani rupee

Exchange rate
daily - *BQR, NYT, WSJ*
weekly - *Barron's*

Paper

Barron's Group Stock Averages
weekly - *Barron's*
companies and weights, irregularly - *Barron's*
range, yearly - *Barron's*

Production
weekly - *Barron's*

Paper and forest products industry

Financial statistics
yearly - *VL*

Paper Index

Standard & Poor's
weekly, monthly, and yearly - *SPIR*
companies listed, yearly - *SPIR*
range, yearly - *SPIR*

Paper industry

Financial statistics
yearly - *AH, FD*

Paperboard

Production
weekly - *Barron's*

Par value

Bonds, NYSE
all listed bonds, yearly - *NYSEFB*
traded, total and daily average,
   monthly and yearly - *NYSEFB*
traded, records, yearly - *NYSEFB*
volume, total and daily average, yearly
  - *NYSEFB*
volume, records, yearly - *NYSEFB*

Domestic bonds
selected foreign stock exchanges, yearly
  - *NYSEFB*

Individual stocks
monthly - *SOSG*

Most active bonds, NYSE
volume, yearly - *NYSEFB*

Paraguayan guarani

Exchange rate
daily - *BQR*

Paris Stock Exchange—*see* France, Paris Stock Exchange

Paris Stock Index—*see* France, Agefi Stock Index; France, CAC General Index

Participating stocks

Industrial
dollars, yearly - *MIM*

Participation rate

Members
NYSE, yearly - *NYSEFB*
NYSE, trades originating off the floor,
  yearly - *NYSEFB*
NYSE, trades originating on the floor,
  yearly - *NYSEFB*

Specialists
Amex, yearly - *AmexFB*
Amex, by type of option, yearly -
  AmexFB
NYSE, yearly - *NYSEFB*

Partnerships

Member organizations
NYSE, number, yearly - *NYSEFB*

Pass-through mortgage certificates

Rates
individual certificates, monthly - *BG*

Ratings
Standard & Poor's, monthly - *BG*

Payable

Notes
individual companies and industries,
  yearly - *FD*

Payable date

Dividends
individual stocks, weekly - *Barron's*
individual stocks, quarterly - *MHCS,
  SPQDR, SPSR*

Payment

Dividends, boosts
weekly - *Barron's*

Payout

Dividend
individual companies, yearly - *MHCS*

Payout ratio

Dow Jones Industrial Average
quarterly - *Barron's*

Dow Jones Transportation Average
quarterly - *Barron's*

Dow Jones Utilities Average
quarterly - *Barron's*

Individual companies
yearly - *SPSR*

Pension and retirement expense

Individual companies and industries
yearly - *FD*

Percentage of sales
individual companies and industries,
yearly - *FD*

Pension liability

Individual companies
quarterly - *VL*

Percentage leaders

American Stock Exchange
winners and losers, weekly - *Barron's*

NASDAQ
winners and losers, weekly - *Barron's*

New York Stock Exchange
winners and losers, weekly - *Barron's*

Options
winners and losers, weekly - *Barron's*

Performance

Best
last 13 weeks, stocks listed, weekly -
VL

Price
best, individual industries, most recent
six weeks - *VL*
worst, individual industries, most
recent six weeks - *VL*

Worst
stocks listed, most recent 13 weeks -
VL

Persistence

Price growth
individual companies, quarterly - *VL*

Personal income

annual rate, monthly - *SOSG*

Personal loans industry

Financial statistics
yearly - *AH*

Personnel

Registered
member organizations, NYSE, number,
yearly - *NYSEFB*

Securities industry
New York City, number, yearly -
NYSEFB
New York State, number, yearly -
NYSEFB
US, number, yearly - *NYSEFB*

Peruvian inti

Exchange rate
daily - *NYT, WSJ*

Peruvian sol

Exchange rate
daily - *BQR*
weekly - *Barron's*

Peseta, Spanish—*see* Spanish
peseta

Peso, Argentine—*see* Argentine
peso

Peso, Chilean—*see* Chilean peso

Peso, Colombian—*see* Colombian
peso

Peso, Mexican—*see* Mexican peso

Peso, Philippine—*see* Philippine
peso

Peso, Uruguayan—*see* Uruguayan
peso

Petroleum

Production
weekly - *Barron's*
rated capacity, weekly - *Barron's*

Petroleum industry (integrated)

Financial statistics
yearly - *VL*

Petroleum industry (producing)

Financial statistics
yearly - *VL*

Philadelphia Stock Exchange

Bonds
listings, selected bonds, daily - *NYT*
sales, individual selected bonds, daily -
  NYT

Calls
open interest, daily - *NYT, WSJ*
open interest, weekly - *Barron's*
volume, daily - *NYT, WSJ*
volume, weekly - *Barron's*

Listings
weekly - *Barron's*
monthly - *BQR*
selected stocks, daily - *NYT, WSJ*

Most active equity options
calls, listed, weekly - *Barron's*
puts, listed, weekly - *Barron's*

Most active options
listed, daily - *NYT, WSJ*
sales, individual options, daily - *NYT,
  WSJ*

NYSE-listed stock
volume, weekly - *Barron's*
volume, monthly and yearly - *NYSEFB*
volume, yearly - *NYSEFB*
volume, percentage of all exchanges'
  trading in NYSE-listed stock, yearly
  - *NYSEFB*

Option membership
seat prices, monthly - *BQR*
seats outstanding, number, monthly -
  BQR

Options
listings, daily - *NYT, WSJ*
listings, weekly - *Barron's*
listings, monthly - *BQR*
open interest, monthly - *BQR*
price range, monthly and since issue -
  BQR
sales, monthly - *BQR*

Puts
open interest, daily - *NYT, WSJ*
open interest, weekly - *Barron's*
volume, daily - *NYT, WSJ*
volume, weekly - *Barron's*

Sale price range
individual stocks, monthly and year to
  date - *BQR*

Sales
daily - *NYT, WSJ*
individual selected stocks, daily - *NYT,
  WSJ*
individual stocks, monthly and year to
  date - *BQR*

Seat prices
monthly - *BQR*

Seats outstanding
number, monthly - *BQR*

Volume
NYSE-listed stocks, daily - *WSJ*

Philippine peso

Exchange rate
daily - *BQR, NYT, WSJ*
weekly - *Barron's*

Plant, gross—*see* Gross plant

Plant, net—*see* Net plant

**Plant, property and
  equipment**—*see* Property, plant
and equipment

Pollution and environmental
control revenue bonds

Listings
monthly - *MBR*

Ratings
Moody's, individual bonds, monthly -
  MBR

Recent and prospective offerings
ratings, Moody's, weekly - *MBS*
statistics, individual bonds, weekly -
MBS

Pollution Control Index

Standard & Poor's
weekly, monthly, and yearly - *SPIR*
component companies, yearly - *SPIR*
range, yearly - *SPIR*

Pollution control industry

Financial statistics
yearly - *AH, FD*

Pollution control revenue bonds

Ratings
Moody's, changes, weekly - *MBS*
Moody's, new, weekly - *MBS*

Portuguese escudo

Exchange rate
daily - *BQR, NYT, WSJ*
weekly - *Barron's*

Post-impressionist (Impressionist) paintings—*see* Paintings

Postal Service, United States—*see* United States Postal Service

Potential, appreciation—*see* Appreciation potential

Potential purchasing power

New York Stock Exchange
monthly - *DSPR*
quarterly - *NYSEFB*
records, yearly - *NYSEFB*

Securities market credit
NYSE, monthly - *NYSEFB*

Pound, British—*see* British pound

Pound, Egyptian—*see* Egyptian pound

Pound, Irish—*see* Irish pound

Pound, Lebanese—*see* Lebanese pound

Power, electric—*see* Electric power production

Precious metals

Mutual funds
sales, monthly - *Barron's*

Precision instrument industry

Financial statistics
yearly - *VL*

Predictability

Earnings
individual companies, quarterly - *VL*

Preferred dividend factor

Individual companies and industries
yearly - *FD*

Preferred dividends

Individual companies and industries
yearly - *FD*

Individual industries
per share, yearly - *AH*

Preferred stock

Amount outstanding
individual companies, quarterly - *VL*

Book value
individual industries, per share, yearly
- *AH*

Call price
individual stocks, monthly - *MBR*

Corporate
issues, dollars, yearly - *MIM*

Dividend dates
individual stocks, monthly - *MBR*

New money preferred
monthly - *MBR*

New offerings
ratings, Moody's, weekly - *MBS*
statistics, individual stocks, weekly -
MBS

New York Stock Exchange
dividends, estimated aggregate cash
   payments, yearly - *NYSEFB*
dividends, number paying cash
   dividends, yearly - *NYSEFB*
issues, number listed, yearly - *NYSEFB*
yield, median, yearly - *NYSEFB*

Nonredeemable
individual companies and industries,
   yearly - *FD*
percentage of invested capital,
   individual companies and
   industries, yearly - *FD*

Number of issues
weekly, six weeks, and projection -
   MBS

Percentage of capitalization
individual companies, yearly - *MHCS*

Percentage of invested capital
individual companies and industries,
   yearly - *FD*

Prospective offerings
ratings, Moody's, weekly - *MBS*
statistics, individual stocks, weekly -
   MBS

Public utilities
NASDAQ, monthly - *BQR*
ratings, Standard & Poor's, monthly -
   BG, SOSG
yield, Moody's Averages, by rating
   groups, weekly - *MBS*
yield, Moody's Averages, by rating
   groups, monthly - *MIM*
yield, Moody's Averages, by rating
   groups, range, yearly - *MBS*

Ratings
Moody's, changes, individual stocks,
   monthly - *MBR*
Moody's, explanation, monthly - *MBR*
Moody's, individual stocks, monthly -
   MBR
Moody's, new, weekly - *MBS*
Moody's, reviewed and confirmed,
   weekly - *MBS*
Moody's, reviewed and revised, weekly
   - *MBS*
Moody's, withdrawn, weekly - *MBS*
Standard & Poor's, monthly - *SOSG*
Standard & Poor's, changes, monthly -
   SOSG
Standard & Poor's, definitions,
   monthly - *SOSG*

Redeemable
individual companies and industries,
   yearly - *FD*
percentage of invested capital,
   individual companies and
   industries, yearly - *FD*

Shares outstanding
individual stocks, monthly - *MBR*

Sinking fund
monthly - *MBR*

Value
individual companies, monthly - *MBR*
individual companies, yearly - *MHCS*

Volume
dollars, weekly, six weeks, and
   projection - *MBS*

Yield
Moody's Averages, High Dividend
   Series, monthly and yearly - *MIM*
Moody's Averages, Low Dividend
   Series, monthly and yearly - *MIM*
Moody's Averages, Low Dividend
   Series, High Grade Industrials,
   monthly, graph - *MIM*
Moody's Averages, Low Dividend
   Series, High Grade Public Utilities,
   monthly, graph - *MIM*
Moody's Averages, Low Dividend
   Series, Medium Grade Industrials,
   monthly, graph - *MIM*
Moody's Averages, Low Dividend
   Series, Medium Grade Public
   Utilities, monthly, graph - *MIM*
Moody's Averages, Low Dividend
   Series, Public Utilities, by rating
   groups, monthly, graph - *MIM*
Moody's Averages, Public Utilities, by
   rating groups, monthly - *MBR*
Standard & Poor's Indexes, weekly,
   monthly, and yearly - *SPIR*
Standard & Poor's Indexes, component
   companies, yearly - *SPIR*
Standard & Poor's Indexes, range,
   yearly - *SPIR*

Preferred stock and bonds

Number of issues
weekly, six weeks, and projection -
   MBS

Volume
dollars, weekly, six weeks, and
   projection - *MBS*

Preferred Stock Price Indexes

Standard & Poor's
weekly, monthly, and yearly - *SPIR*
component stocks, yearly - *SPIR*
range, yearly - *SPIR*

Premium per contract

American Stock Exchange
options, average, yearly - *AmexFB*

Pretax cash flow—*see* Cash flow

Pretax income

Change
year to year, individual companies and
industries, quarterly, moving 12
months, and yearly - *FD*

From operations
percentage of value added, individual
companies and industries, yearly -
FD

Individual companies and industries
quarterly, moving 12 months, and
yearly - *FD*

Per dollar average gross plant
individual companies and industries,
yearly - *FD*

Per dollar average invested capital
individual companies and industries,
yearly - *FD*

Per employee
individual companies and industries,
yearly - *FD*

Per share
annual growth rate, individual
companies and industries, latest
year, 3 years, 5 years, and 10 years -
FD
change, individual companies and
industries, yearly - *FD*
individual companies and industries,
yearly - *FD*
least squares growth rate and
coefficient of determination,
individual companies and
industries, 5-year and 10-year - *FD*

Percentage increase in sales carried to
individual companies, yearly - *FD*

Percentage of industry pretax income
individual companies, yearly - *FD*

Percentage of profit margin
individual companies, quarterly - *FD*

Percentage of sales
individual companies and industries,
quarterly, moving 12 months, and
yearly - *FD*

Pretax interest coverage—*see*
Interest coverage

Pretax margin—*see* Margin

Pretax return—*see* Return

Price

Bonds
individual bonds, monthly and when
issued - *MBR*

Commodity—*see* Moody's Daily
Commodity Price Index

Common stock and warrant issues
Amex, average, yearly - *AmexFB*

Corporate bonds
Amex, average, yearly - *AmexFB*

Most active stocks
Amex, average and 10-day average,
daily - *DSPR*
NYSE, average, daily - *DSPR*
NYSE, average, weekly - *Barron's,*
DSPR

New capital
average, yearly - *MIM*

Odd lots
NYSE, average, yearly - *NYSEFB*

Oil
daily - *NYT, WSJ*

Round lots
NYSE, average, yearly - *NYSEFB*

Round lots and odd lots combined
NYSE, average, yearly - *NYSEFB*

Share
NASDAQ, average, monthly and
yearly - *NASDAQFB*
NYSE, average, monthly and yearly -
NYSEFB

Stock

Amex, average, yearly - *AmexFB*
individual industries, range, yearly -
  AH
NASDAQ, final adjusted inside,
  individual stocks, yearly -
  NASDAQFB
NASDAQ, net change, individual
  stocks, yearly - *NASDAQFB*
NASDAQ, percentage change,
  individual stocks, yearly -
  NASDAQFB
NASDAQ, range and close, individual
  stocks, yearly - *NASDAQFB*
NASDAQ NMS, final adjusted inside,
  individual stocks, yearly -
  NASDAQFB
NASDAQ NMS, net change,
  individual stocks, yearly -
  NASDAQFB
NASDAQ NMS, percentage change,
  individual stocks, yearly -
  NASDAQFB
NASDAQ NMS, range and close,
  individual stocks, yearly -
  NASDAQFB
utilities, range, yearly - *AH*

Warrant issues and common stock
Amex, average, yearly - *AmexFB*

Price continuity

New York Stock Exchange
yearly - *NYSEFB*

Price-earnings ratio

American Stock Exchange
individual stocks, daily - *NYT, WSJ*
individual stocks, weekly - *Barron's,
  CFC*
individual stocks, monthly - *BQR*

Barron's 50-Stock Average
actual year end, weekly - *Barron's*
five-year average, weekly - *Barron's*
annualized projected, weekly - *Barron's*

Dow Jones Industrial Average
weekly - *Barron's, VL*
monthly and quarterly - *Barron's*
yearly - *Barron's*
last market bottom and last market top
  - *VL*
range, 13-week and 50-week - *VL*

Dow Jones Transportation Average
weekly, monthly, and quarterly -
  Barron's

Dow Jones Utility Average
weekly, monthly, and quarterly -
  Barron's

Earnings, all stocks with
median, weekly, last market high, and
  last market low - *VL*
median, 26 weeks ago - *VL*

High as percentage of low
individual companies and industries,
  yearly - *FD*

Highest
stocks listed, weekly - *VL*

Individual companies
quarterly - *SPSR, VL*
yearly - *FD, MHCS, SPSR*
average annual, yearly - *VL*
average annual, yearly, projection - *VL*
average monthly, percentage of S&P
  400 average monthly price-earnings
  ratio, yearly - *FD*
highest monthly, percentage of S&P
  400 highest monthly price-earnings
  ratio, yearly - *FD*
lowest monthly, percentage of S&P 400
  lowest monthly price-earnings ratio,
  yearly - *FD*
percentage of S&P Industrial
  price-earnings ratio, range, yearly -
  FD
companies, range, yearly - *FD*
companies, standard deviation,
  monthly, percentage of S&P 400
  standard deviation of monthly
  price-earnings ratio, yearly - *FD*

Individual industries
yearly - *FD*
average annual, yearly - *VL*
average annual, yearly, projection - *VL*
percentage of S&P 400 price-earnings
  ratio, range, yearly - *FD*
range, yearly - *AH, FD*

Lowest
stocks listed, weekly - *VL*

Midwest Stock Exchange
individual stocks, weekly - *CFC*
individual stocks, monthly - *BQR*

NASDAQ
individual stocks, weekly - *Barron's,
  CFC*

individual stocks, monthly - *BQR*

NASDAQ NMS
individual stocks, weekly - *Barron's*

New York Stock Exchange
individual stocks, daily - *NYT, WSJ*
individual stocks, weekly - *Barron's, CFC*
individual stocks, monthly - *BQR*

New York Stock Exchange Common Stock Index
quarterly - *NYSEFB*

Pacific Stock Exchange
individual stocks, weekly - *CFC*
individual stocks, monthly - *BQR*

Relative
individual companies, quarterly - *VL*
individual companies and industries, yearly and projection - *VL*

Standard & Poor's Financial Index
weekly - *SPIR*

Standard & Poor's 500
weekly and quarterly - *SPIR*
range, yearly - *AH*

Standard & Poor's 400
weekly - *Barron's, SPIR*
quarterly - *SPIR*
range, yearly - *AH*

Standard & Poor's Railroad Index
weekly - *SPIR*

Standard & Poor's Transportation Index
weekly - *SPIR*

Standard & Poor's Utilities Index
weekly - *SPIR*

Toronto Stock Exchange
individual stocks, weekly - *CFC*
individual stocks, monthly - *BQR*

Trailing
individual companies, quarterly - *VL*
median, weekly - *VL*

Utilities
range, yearly - *AH*

Value Line stocks
median, weekly, last market bottom, and last market top - *VL*
median, range, 13-week and 50-week - *VL*

Price gain

American Stock Exchange
individual companies, 10 leading companies, yearly - *AmexFB*

Individual companies
percentage, projection - *VL*

Price growth persistence

Individual companies
quarterly - *VL*

Price Level Index

American Stock Exchange Index System
daily - *BQR*

Price performance

Best
individual industries, last six weeks - *VL*

Worst
individual industries, last six weeks - *VL*

Price range

Bonds
Amex, individual bonds, weekly and year to date - *CFC*
Amex, individual bonds, 52 weeks - *Barron's*
individual bonds, year to date and since issue - *MBR*
NYSE, individual bonds, weekly and year to date - *CFC*
NYSE, individual bonds, 52 weeks - *Barron's*

Convertible bonds
individual bonds, year to date - *BG*

Corporate bonds
individual bonds, yearly - *BG*

Foreign bonds
individual bonds, yearly - *BG*

Stocks
Amex, individual stocks, daily - *NYT, WSJ*
Amex, individual stocks, weekly - *Barron's, CFC*

Amex, individual stocks, year to date - *CFC*

Amex, individual stocks, 52 weeks - *Barron's, NYT, WSJ*

Amex, individual stocks, yearly - *AmexFB*

Boston Stock Exchange, individual stocks, year to date - *Barron's*

individual stocks, monthly, chart - *SPSR*

individual stocks, year to date - *SPSR*

individual stocks, latest 52 weeks and yearly - *MHCS*

Midwest Stock Exchange, individual stocks, year to date - *Barron's, CFC*

Montreal Stock Exchange, individual stocks, year to date - *Barron's*

NYSE, individual stocks, daily - *NYT, WSJ*

NYSE, individual stocks, weekly - *Barron's, CFC*

NYSE, individual stocks, year to date - *CFC*

NYSE, individual stocks, 52 weeks - *Barron's, NYT, WSJ*

Pacific Stock Exchange, individual stocks, year to date - *Barron's, CFC*

Philadelphia Stock Exchange, individual stocks, year to date - *Barron's*

Toronto Stock Exchange, individual stocks, year to date - *Barron's, CFC*

Price ratios

Individual companies and industries
quarterly, moving 12 months, and yearly - *FD*

Price score

Moody's long-term
individual companies, quarterly - *MHCS*

Moody's short-term
individual companies, quarterly - *MHCS*

Price strength

Relative
individual companies, monthly, graph - *VL*

Price-to-cash-flow ratio

Range
individual companies and industries, yearly - *FD*

Price to common equity per share

Range
individual companies and industries, yearly - *FD*

Price variations

Trade-to-trade
specialists, Amex, yearly - *AmexFB*
specialists, Amex, options, by type of options, yearly - *AmexFB*

Price-Volume Accumulation Line

New York Stock Exchange
daily and 10-day total, daily - *DSPR*

Prices—*see* entries beginning Price

Primary offerings

New York City banks
rates, daily - *NYT*

Prime bankers acceptances

Rates
daily - *BQR*

Prime rate

daily - *NYT, WSJ*
weekly - *Barron's, VL*
weekly, graph - *MBR, MBS, VL*
last market bottom and last market top - *VL*

Range
13-week and 50-week - *VL*

Rate spread
vs. commercial paper rate, weekly - *MBS*

Prime rates, foreign

daily - *WSJ*
weekly - *Barron's*

Principal amount

Medium-term notes
individual issues, monthly - *MBR*

Private construction spending

monthly - *Barron's*

Private exempt funding securities

weekly - *Barron's*

Private Export Funding Corporation securities

Listings
daily - *WSJ*
weekly - *Barron's*
monthly - *BQR*

Ratings
Standard & Poor's, monthly - *BG*

Yield
individual issues, daily - *WSJ*
individual issues, weekly - *Barron's*
individual issues, monthly - *BQR*

Private placements

Bonds, NYSE
yearly - *NYSEFB*

New York Stock Exchange
yearly - *NYSEFB*

Stocks, NYSE
yearly - *NYSEFB*

Privately placed corporate bonds—*see* Corporate bonds

Producer Price Index Finished Goods

monthly - *Barron's*

Production

Auto
US domestic units, weekly - *Barron's*

Durable manufacturing
monthly - *Barron's*

Electric power
weekly - *Barron's*
quarterly and yearly - *SOSG*

Industrial
monthly - *Barron's*
including utilities, index, monthly and
    yearly - *SOSG*

Lumber
monthly - *Barron's*

Manufacturing
monthly - *Barron's*

Mining
monthly - *Barron's*

Newsprint
US and Canada, monthly - *Barron's*

Nondurable manufacturing
monthly - *Barron's*

Paper
weekly - *Barron's*

Paperboard
weekly - *Barron's*

Petroleum
daily runs, weekly - *Barron's*
rated capacity, weekly - *Barron's*

Statistics
weekly and monthly - *Barron's*

Steel
weekly - *Barron's*
rated capacity, weekly - *Barron's*
raw, monthly and yearly - *SOSG*

Utilities
monthly - *Barron's*

Profit, net—*see* Net profit

Profit, operating—*see* Operating profit

Profit margin

Individual industries
per share, yearly - *AH*

Net
individual companies and industries,
    yearly and projection - *VL*

Operating
before depreciation, individual
    companies and industries, yearly -
    FD
individual companies, yearly - *MHCS*

Percentage of pretax income
individual companies, quarterly - *FD*

Promissory notes

Intermediate-term
listings, monthly - *MBR*
ratings, Moody's, monthly - *MBR*

Property, net—*see* Net property

Property, plant and equipment

Net
individual industries, per share, yearly
- *AH*

Percentage earned on
utilities, per share, yearly - *AH*

Ratio of funded debt to
individual companies, monthly - *BG*

Sale
individual companies and industries,
yearly - *FD*

Utilities
per share, yearly - *AH*

Property-casualty insurance industry

Financial statistics
yearly - *AH*

Public construction spending

monthly - *Barron's*

Public debt

Outstanding
weekly - *Barron's*

Subject to limit
weekly - *Barron's*

Public offerings

Initial
selected, listed, weekly - *Barron's*

Public short sales—*see* Short sales

Public Transaction Study

New York Stock Exchange
yearly - *NYSEFB*

Public utilities

Dow Jones Averages—*see* Dow Jones
Public Utilities Average

**High Grade, Moody's Preferred Stock
Yield Averages**
Low Dividend Series, monthly and
yearly - *MIM*

**Medium Grade, Moody's Preferred
Stock Yield Averages**
Low Dividend Series, monthly and
yearly - *MIM*

Preferred stock
listings, NASDAQ, monthly - *BQR*
yield, individual stocks, monthly -
BQR

Security issues
dollars, yearly - *MIM*

Public utility bonds

Distributed
yield, composite and by rating groups,
monthly - *MBS*

Listings
NASDAQ, monthly - *BQR*

Newly issued
amount, composite and by rating
groups, monthly - *MBS*
yield, Moody's Averages, composite
and by rating groups, monthly -
MBS

Yield
by rating groups, weekly, graph - *MBR*
by rating groups, monthly, graph -
MBR
individual bonds, monthly - *BQR*
Moody's Averages, composite and by
rating groups, daily - *MBS*
Moody's Averages, composite and by
rating groups, range, yearly - *MBS*
Standard & Poor's Index, by rating
groups, weekly and monthly - *BG,
SPIR*
Standard & Poor's Index, by rating
groups, yearly - *SPIR*
Standard & Poor's Index, range, by
rating groups, weekly - *BG*

Standard & Poor's Index, range, by
rating groups, yearly - *SPIR*

Public utility common stock

Yield
Moody's Averages, weekly - *MBS*
Moody's Averages, range, yearly - *MBS*

Public utility preferred stock

Yield
Moody's Averages, by rating groups,
weekly - *MBS*
Moody's Averages, by rating groups,
monthly - *MIM*
Moody's Averages, by rating groups,
range, yearly - *MBS*

Public volume

All markets
quarterly - *NYSEFB*

New York Stock Exchange
quarterly - *NYSEFB*

Publicly offered corporate bond

issues—*see* Corporate bonds
dollars, yearly - *MBR, MIM*

Publishing Index

Standard & Poor's
weekly, monthly, and yearly - *SPIR*
component companies, yearly - *SPIR*
range, yearly - *SPIR*

Publishing Index (newspapers)

Standard & Poor's
weekly, monthly, and yearly - *SPIR*
component companies, yearly - *SPIR*
range, yearly - *SPIR*

Publishing industry

Financial statistics
yearly - *AH, VL*

Publishing industry (newspapers)

Financial statistics
yearly - *AH*

Punt, Irish—*see* Irish punt

Purchase

Minimum initial
mutual funds, monthly - *SOSG*

Purchase warrants

Stock
industrial, yearly - *MIM*

Purchases

Customers
Amex, odd lots, weekly - *Barron's*
NYSE, odd lots, weekly - *Barron's*
NYSE, odd lots, number of shares and
value, monthly - *NYSEFB*

Floor traders
Amex, weekly - *Barron's*
NYSE, weekly - *Barron's*

Foreigners
from Americans, NYSE, foreign stocks,
quarterly and yearly - *NYSEFB*
from Americans, NYSE, US stocks,
quarterly - *NYSEFB*
from Americans, NYSE, US stocks,
yearly - *NYSEFB*

Members, Amex
weekly - *Barron's*

Members, NYSE
weekly - *Barron's*
round lots, monthly - *NYSEFB*
round lots, trades originating off the
floor, monthly - *NYSEFB*
round lots, trades originating on the
floor, monthly - *NYSEFB*

New York Stock Exchange
odd lots, daily - *Barron's, DSPR, NYT*

Odd lots
weekly - *Barron's*

Other securities
for mutual funds (other than common
stocks), monthly - *Barron's*

Specialists
Amex, weekly - *Barron's*
NYSE, weekly - *Barron's*
NYSE, round lots, monthly - *NYSEFB*

Purchases plus sales

American Stock Exchange
members, yearly - *AmexFB*
members, percentage of total purchases
  plus sales, yearly - *AmexFB*
odd lots, yearly - *AmexFB*
odd lots, percentage of total purchases
  plus sales, yearly - *AmexFB*
specialists, yearly - *AmexFB*

Purchasing power statistics

monthly - *Barron's*

Purchasing power, potential—*see*
Potential purchasing power

Put-call ratio

**Chicago Board Options Exchange
  Equity Index**
weekly - *Barron's*

Standard & Poor's 100
weekly - *Barron's*

Puts—*see also* Options

American Stock Exchange
contracts exercised, yearly - *AmexFB*
exercises, number, monthly and yearly
  - *AmexFB*
gold options, number, monthly and
  yearly - *AmexFB*
interest rate options, number, yearly -
  AmexFB
number, total and daily average,
  monthly and yearly - *AmexFB*
open interest, monthly and yearly -
  AmexFB
options, number traded, total and daily
  average, yearly - *AmexFB*
stock index options, by index, number,
  yearly - *AmexFB*

Chicago Board Options Exchange
volume, compared to call volume,
  weekly, last market bottom, and last
  market top - *VL*
volume, compared to call volume,
  range, 13-week and 50-week - *VL*

Most active equity options
listed, by exchange, weekly - *Barron's*

Open interest
by exchange, daily - *NYT, WSJ*
by exchange, weekly - *Barron's*

Volume
by exchange, daily - *NYT, WSJ*
by exchange, weekly - *Barron's*

Q

Quality

Market
NYSE, yearly - *NYSEFB*

Security credit
NYSE, monthly, graph - *NYSEFB*

Quick ratio

Individual companies
yearly - *FD*

Individual industries
yearly - *AH, FD*

Quotation spreads

New York Stock Exchange
yearly - *NYSEFB*

R

Radio-TV Broadcasters Index

Standard & Poor's
weekly, monthly, and yearly - *SPIR*
component companies, yearly - *SPIR*
range, yearly - *SPIR*

Radio-TV broadcasting industry

Financial statistics
yearly - *FD*

Railroad bonds

Distributed
yield, composite and by rating groups,
  monthly - *MBS*

Domestic
Newly Issued, Moody's Weighted
   Averages of Yields, yearly - *MIM*

Newly issued
amount, composite and by rating
   groups, monthly - *MBS*
yield, Moody's Averages, composite
   and by rating groups, monthly -
   MBS

Yield
by rating groups, weekly and monthly,
   graph - *MBR*
Moody's Averages, composite and by
   rating groups, daily - *MBS*
Moody's Averages, composite and by
   rating groups, range, yearly - *MBS*

Railroad equipment

Barron's Group Stock Averages
weekly - *Barron's*
companies and weights, irregularly -
   Barron's
range, yearly - *Barron's*

Railroad Equipment Index

Standard & Poor's
weekly, monthly, and yearly - *SPIR*
component companies, yearly - *SPIR*
range, yearly - *SPIR*

Railroad equipment trust certificates

Moody's ratings
individual certificates, monthly - *MBR*

Railroad Index, Standard & Poor's—*see* Standard & Poor's Railroad Index; Transportation Index

Railroad industry

Financial statistics
yearly - *AH, FD, VL*

Rand, South African—*see* South African rand

Range

Stock prices
individual companies, daily - *NYT,
   WSJ*
individual companies, weekly -
   Barron's
individual companies, year to date -
   CFC
individual companies, yearly - *MHCS,
   SOSG*
individual companies, latest 52 weeks -
   Barron's, MHCS, NYT, WSJ

Rank for safety

Individual stocks
weekly - *VL*

Rankings—*see* Ratings

Rate spread

Commercial paper rate vs. prime rate
weekly - *MBS*

Ratings

Bonds
Amex, individual bonds, weekly - *CFC*
Amex, individual bonds, monthly -
   BQR
changes, weekly - *Barron's*
Moody's, explanation and key,
   monthly - *MBR*
Moody's, individual bonds, monthly -
   MBR
NYSE, individual bonds, weekly -
   CFC
individual bonds, monthly - *BQR*
Standard & Poor's, changes, individual
   bonds, monthly - *BG*
Standard & Poor's, changes, potential,
   individual bonds, monthly - *BG*

Commercial paper
Moody's, explanation and key,
   monthly - *MBR*
Moody's, individual issues, monthly -
   MBR
Standard & Poor's, definitions,
   monthly - *BG*
Standard & Poor's, individual issues,
   yearly - *FD*

Common stock
Standard & Poor's, monthly - *SOSG*
Standard & Poor's, changes, monthly - *SOSG*
Standard & Poor's, definitions, monthly - *SOSG*

Companies
Standard & Poor's, individual companies, quarterly - *SPSR*

Convertible bonds
Standard & Poor's, individual bonds, monthly - *BG*

Corporate bonds
Moody's, explanation and key, monthly - *MBR*
Standard & Poor's, by class of debt, individual companies, yearly - *FD*
Standard & Poor's, definitions, monthly - *BG*
Standard & Poor's, individual bonds, monthly - *BG*

Equipment trust certificates
Standard & Poor's, individual issues, monthly - *BG*

Federal agency bonds
Standard & Poor's, individual bonds, monthly - *BG*

Foreign bonds
Standard & Poor's, individual bonds, monthly - *BG*

Medium-term notes
Moody's, individual issues, monthly - *MBR*
Moody's, individual issues, effective date, monthly - *MBR*
Standard & Poor's, individual issues, monthly - *BG*

Municipal bonds
Moody's, explanation and key, monthly - *MBR*
Standard & Poor's, definitions, monthly - *BG*
Standard & Poor's, individual bonds, monthly - *BG*

Pass-through mortgage certificates
Standard & Poor's, individual issues, monthly - *BG*

Preferred stock
Moody's, explanation, monthly - *MBR*
Standard & Poor's, changes, individual stocks, monthly - *SOSG*

Standard & Poor's, definitions, monthly - *SOSG*
Standard & Poor's, individual stocks, monthly - *SOSG*

Toll revenue bonds
Standard & Poor's, individual bonds, monthly - *BG*

Utility preferred stocks
Standard & Poor's, individual stocks, monthly - *BG, SOSG*

Ratio

Bond yields/stock yields
Barron's 50-Stock Averages, weekly - *Barron's*

Combined
individual insurance companies, yearly - *MHCS*

Current
individual companies, yearly - *FD, SPSR*
individual industries, yearly - *FD*

Net capital
individual securities brokerage companies, yearly - *MHCS*

Payout
individual companies, yearly - *SPSR*

10 most active stocks (composite) to total trading
Dow Jones stocks, daily - *Barron's*

Ratios

Financial
individual companies, quarterly - *FD*
individual industries, yearly - *AH*

Price
individual companies and industries, quarterly, moving 12 months, and yearly - *FD*

Raw steel—*see* Steel

Real estate and financial companies

Security issues
dollars, yearly - *MIM*

Real estate industry

Financial statistics
yearly - *VL*

Real Estate Investment Trust Index

Standard & Poor's
weekly, monthly, and yearly - *SPIR*
component companies, yearly - *SPIR*
range, yearly - *SPIR*

Real Estate Investment Trust industry

Financial statistics
yearly - *VL*

Receivables

Individual companies
quarterly and yearly - *FD, VL*

Individual industries
yearly - *FD*
per share, yearly - *AH*

Percentage of assets
individual companies and industries,
    yearly - *FD*

Percentage of sales
individual companies and industries,
    yearly - *FD*

Receivables outstanding

Days'
individual companies and industries,
    yearly - *FD*

Record date

Dividends
individual companies, twice weekly -
    MDR
individual companies, weekly -
    Barron's
individual companies, quarterly -
    MHCS

Records set

New York Stock Exchange
yearly - *NYSEFB*

Recreation industry

Financial statistics
yearly - *VL*

Recreational vehicles/ manufactured housing industry—*see* Manufactured housing/recreational vehicles industry

Redeemable preferred stock

Individual companies and industries
yearly - *FD*

Percentage of invested capital
individual companies and industries,
    yearly - *FD*

Redemption provisions

Corporate bonds
individual bonds, monthly - *BG*

Redemptions

Shares held by mutual funds
monthly - *Barron's*

Reduction of long-term debt

Individual companies and industries
yearly - *FD*

Regional exchanges—*see also* specific exchanges

Volume
yearly - *NASDAQFB*
dollars, yearly - *NASDAQFB*
dollars, percentage of all exchanges'
    dollar volume, yearly - *NASDAQFB*
percentage of all exchanges' volume,
    yearly - *NASDAQFB*

REIT—*see* Real Estate Investment
    Trust headings

Relative price-earnings ratio

Individual companies
quarterly and yearly - *VL*
yearly, projection - *VL*

Individual industries
yearly and projection - *VL*

Relative strength

Stock prices
individual industries, monthly, graph -
   VL
individual stocks, weekly - *DSPR*
individual stocks, monthly, graph - *VL*
Value Line Composite vs. Dow Jones
   Industrial Average, weekly and
   monthly, graph - *VL*

Removals

Common stock
NYSE, number, yearly - *NYSEFB*

New York Stock Exchange
yearly - *NYSEFB*

Rental expense

Individual companies and industries
yearly - *FD*

Reported share volume

New York Stock Exchange
yearly - *NYSEFB*

Reported trades

New York Stock Exchange
yearly - *NYSEFB*

Representatives

Registered
member organizations, NYSE, number,
   by state, yearly - *NYSEFB*

Repurchase agreements

Overnight
dollars, monthly - *Barron's*

Term
dollars, monthly - *Barron's*

Required reserves

Federal Reserve banks
daily average of two-week period -
   Barron's, WSJ

Research and development expense

Individual companies and industries
yearly - *FD*

Percentage of sales
individual companies and industries,
   yearly - *FD*

Reserve bank credit

Federal Reserve banks
weekly - *Barron's, WSJ*

Reserves

Excess
Federal Reserve banks, daily average
   of two-week period - *Barron's, WSJ*

Federal Reserve banks
daily average of two-week period -
   Barron's, WSJ

Free
Federal Reserve banks, daily average
   of two-week period - *Barron's, WSJ*

Nonborrowed
Federal Reserve banks, daily average
   of two-week period - *Barron's, WSJ*

Required
Federal Reserve banks, daily average
   of two-week period - *Barron's, WSJ*

Residual change

Earnings per share
individual companies and industries,
   yearly - *FD*

Restaurant industry

Financial statistics
yearly - *AH, VL*

Restaurants Index

Standard & Poor's
weekly, monthly, and yearly - *SPIR*
component companies, yearly - *SPIR*
range, yearly - *SPIR*

Retail companies stock price index

Department stores
quarterly, graph - *MHCS*

Discount and variety stores
quarterly, graph - *MHCS*

Retail industry

Composite
financial statistics, yearly - *VL*

Department stores
financial statistics, yearly - *FD*

Drug stores
financial statistics, yearly - *FD*

Food chains
financial statistics, yearly - *FD*

Miscellaneous
financial statistics, yearly - *FD*

Specialty
financial statistics, yearly - *FD, VL*

Retail merchandise

Barron's Group Stock Averages
weekly - *Barron's*
companies and weights, irregularly - *Barron's*
range, yearly - *Barron's*

Retail store sales

monthly - *Barron's*

Retail Stores Index (composite)

Standard & Poor's
weekly, monthly, and yearly - *SPIR*
component companies, yearly - *SPIR*
range, yearly - *SPIR*

Retail Stores Index (department stores)

Standard & Poor's
weekly, monthly, and yearly - *SPIR*
component companies, yearly - *SPIR*
range, yearly - *SPIR*

Retail Stores Index (discount stores)

Standard & Poor's
weekly, monthly, and yearly - *SPIR*
component companies, yearly - *SPIR*
range, yearly - *SPIR*

Retail Stores Index (drugstores)

Standard & Poor's
weekly, monthly, and yearly - *SPIR*
component companies, yearly - *SPIR*
range, yearly - *SPIR*

Retail Stores Index (food chains)

Standard & Poor's
weekly, monthly, and yearly - *SPIR*
component companies, yearly - *SPIR*
range, yearly - *SPIR*

Retail Stores Index (general merchandise chains)

Standard & Poor's
weekly, monthly, and yearly - *SPIR*
component companies, yearly - *SPIR*
range, yearly - *SPIR*

Retail stores industry (composite)

Financial statistics
yearly - *AH*

Retail stores industry (department stores)

Financial statistics
yearly - *AH*

Retail stores industry (drugstores)

Financial statistics
yearly - *AH*

Retail stores industry (food chains)

Financial statistics
yearly - *AH*

Retail stores industry (general merchandise chains)

Financial statistics
yearly - *AH*

Retailers

Inventories
monthly and annual average - *SOSG*

Sales
monthly and yearly - *SOSG*

Retained earnings

Individual industries
per share, yearly - *AH*

Percentage of common equity
individual companies and industries, yearly and projection - *VL*

Retention

Earnings
individual companies and industries, yearly - *FD*

Retention rate

Individual companies and industries
yearly - *FD*

Retirement and pension expense—*see* Pension and retirement expense

Return

After-tax
on average invested capital, individual companies and industries, yearly - *FD*
on average total assets, individual companies and industries, yearly - *FD*
on equity, individual companies and industries, yearly - *FD*
on invested capital, change, effect on earnings per share, individual companies and industries, yearly - *FD*
on invested capital, individual companies and industries, yearly - *FD*

Common equity
percentage of S&P 400 return, individual companies and industries, yearly - *FD*
percentage of S&P industry category return, individual companies, yearly - *FD*

Highest annual
3–5 years, stocks listed, weekly - *VL*

Individual companies
yearly, projection - *VL*

Pretax
on average common equity, individual companies and industries, yearly - *FD*
on average invested capital, individual companies and industries, yearly - *FD*
on average total assets, individual companies and industries, yearly - *FD*
on average total operating assets, individual companies and industries, yearly - *FD*
on invested capital, change, effect on earnings per share, individual companies and industries, yearly - *FD*

Return differential

Change
effect on earnings per share, individual companies and industries, yearly - *FD*

Individual companies and industries
yearly - *FD*

Return on assets—*see* Assets

Return on equity—*see* Equity

Reuter United Kingdom Commodities Index

daily - *WSJ*

Revenues

Companies
NYSE, aggregate, yearly - *NYSEFB*
NYSE, aggregate, percentage of all US companies' revenues, yearly - *NYSEFB*

US, aggregate, yearly - *NYSEFB*

Gross
individual companies, yearly - *MHCS*

Individual companies
quarterly and projection - *VL*
yearly - *SPSR, VL*
yearly, projection - *VL*

Individual industries
yearly and projection - *VL*

Operating
utilities, per share, yearly - *AH*

Per share
individual companies, yearly - *VL*
individual companies, yearly,
    projection - *VL*

Rial, Iranian—*see* Iranian rial

Ringgit, Malaysian—*see* Malaysian
    ringgit

Riyal, Saudia Arabian—*see* Saudi
    Arabian riyal

Rotary rigs running (Hughes)

weekly - *Barron's*

Round lots

New York Stock Exchange
price, average, yearly - *NYSEFB*

Rubber

Barron's Group Stock Averages
weekly - *Barron's*
companies and weights, irregularly -
    Barron's
range, yearly - *Barron's*

Rubber and tire industry

Financial statistics
yearly - *AH, VL*

Rupee, Indian—*see* Indian rupee

Rupee, Pakistani—*see* Pakistani
    rupee

Rupee, Sri Lankan—*see* Sri Lankan
    rupee

Rupiah, Indonesian—*see* Indonesian
    rupiah

Ryan Index

daily - *Barron's*

S

Safety rank

Individual stocks
weekly - *VL*

**Sale of property, plant and
equipment**

Individual companies and industries
yearly - *FD*

Sale price range

Bonds
Amex, individual bonds, monthly and
    year to date - *BQR*
NYSE, individual bonds, monthly and
    year to date - *BQR*

Stocks
individual stocks, by exchange,
    monthly and year to date - *BQR*

Sales—*see also* Short sales, Volume

All exchanges except NYSE and Amex
market value of shares, yearly -
    NYSEFB
market value of shares, percentage of
    all exchanges' sales, yearly -
    NYSEFB
number of shares, yearly - *NYSEFB*
number of shares, percentage of all
    exchanges' sales, yearly - *NYSEFB*

All registered exchanges
aggregate, monthly - *Barron's*

American Stock Exchange
daily - *Barron's*
yearly - *NYSEFB*
customers, odd lots, weekly - *Barron's*
floor traders, weekly - *Barron's*
individual stocks, daily - *NYT, WSJ*
individual stocks, weekly - *Barron's, CFC*
individual stocks, monthly and year to date - *BQR*
market value, yearly - *NYSEFB*
market value, percentage of all exchanges' sales, yearly - *NYSEFB*
members, weekly - *Barron's*
members, range and last, yearly - *AmexFB*
options principal members, range and last, yearly - *AmexFB*
percentage of all exchanges' sales, yearly - *NYSEFB*
specialists, weekly - *Barron's*

Amex companies
average and median, yearly - *AmexFB*
10 leading companies, yearly - *AmexFB*

Bonds
Amex, daily and weekly - *Barron's*
Amex, individual bonds, daily - *NYT*
Amex, individual bonds, weekly - *Barron's, CFC*
Amex, individual bonds, monthly and year to date - *BQR*
NYSE, daily and weekly - *Barron's*
NYSE, year to date - *WSJ*
NYSE, individual bonds, daily - *NYT*
NYSE, individual bonds, weekly - *Barron's, CFC*
NYSE, individual bonds, monthly and year to date - *BQR*
Pacific Stock Exchange, selected individual bonds, daily - *NYT*

Boston Stock Exchange
daily - *NYT, WSJ*
individual selected stocks, daily - *NYT, WSJ*
individual stocks, monthly and year to date - *BQR*

Business
monthly - *Barron's*

By segment
change, individual companies, yearly - *FD*
individual companies, yearly - *FD*
percentage of total sales, individual companies, yearly - *FD*

Change
effect on earnings per share, individual companies and industries, yearly - *FD*
year to year, individual companies and industries, quarterly, moving 12 months, and yearly - *FD*

Common stocks
for mutual funds, by stocks in the funds portfolio, monthly - *Barron's*

Companies, US
aggregate, yearly - *NYSEFB*

Corporate bonds
for mutual funds, monthly - *Barron's*

Department store
monthly and yearly - *SOSG*

Dow Jones Composite stocks
weekly - *Barron's*

Dow Jones Industrial stocks
weekly - *Barron's*

Dow Jones Transportation stocks
weekly - *Barron's*

Dow Jones Utilities stocks
weekly - *Barron's*

Foreign bonds
individual bonds, weekly - *Barron's*

Foreigners, to Americans
NYSE, foreign stocks, quarterly and yearly - *NYSEFB*
NYSE, US stocks, quarterly and yearly - *NYSEFB*

Government National Mortgage Association securities
for mutual funds, monthly - *Barron's*

Government securities
for mutual funds, monthly - *Barron's*

Incremental dollars per incremental dollar of working capital
individual companies and industries, yearly - *FD*

Individual companies
quarterly - *FD, SPSR, VL*
quarterly, projection - *VL*
moving 12 months - *FD*
yearly - *FD, VL*
yearly, projection - *VL*
change, annual rate, past 5 years, past 10 years, and projection - *VL*
per share, yearly and projection - *VL*

Individual industries
quarterly and moving 12 months - *FD*
yearly - *FD, VL*
yearly, projection - *VL*
per share, yearly - *AH*

Insurance
individual insurance companies, yearly
- *MHCS*

International
percentage of total sales, individual
companies, yearly - *FD*

Manufacturers
monthly and yearly - *SOSG*

Merchant wholesalers
monthly and yearly - *SOSG*

Midwest Stock Exchange
daily - *NYT, WSJ*
individual stocks, daily - *NYT, WSJ*
individual stocks, weekly - *CFC*
individual stocks, monthly and year to
date - *BQR*

Montreal Stock Exchange
daily - *NYT, WSJ*
individual stocks, daily - *NYT, WSJ*

Mutual funds
by type of mutual fund, monthly -
Barron's
shares for, monthly - *Barron's*

NASDAQ
individual stocks, daily - *NYT, WSJ*
individual stocks, weekly - *Barron's*

NASDAQ National List
individual stocks, weekly - *Barron's*

NASDAQ NMS
individual stocks, weekly - *Barron's*

NASDAQ OTC
daily and weekly - *Barron's*

NASDAQ Supplemental Stock Listing
individual stocks, weekly - *Barron's*

New York Stock Exchange
daily - *Barron's, SPIR*
weekly - *Barron's*
yearly - *NYSEFB*
customers, odd lots, weekly - *Barron's*
customers, odd lots, volume, number
of shares and value, monthly -
NYSEFB
floor traders, weekly - *Barron's*
individual stocks, daily - *NYT, WSJ*
individual stocks, weekly - *Barron's*

individual stocks, monthly and year to
date - *BQR*
market value, yearly - *NYSEFB*
market value, percentage of all
exchanges, yearly - *NYSEFB*
members, weekly - *Barron's*
members, round lots, monthly -
NYSEFB
members, round lots, trades originating
off the floor, monthly - *NYSEFB*
members, round lots, trades originating
on the floor, monthly - *NYSEFB*
members, stock, weekly - *Barron's*
odd lots, daily - *Barron's, DSPR*
percentage of all exchanges' sales,
yearly - *NYSEFB*
specialists, weekly - *Barron's*
specialists, round lots, monthly -
NYSEFB
stock, weekly - *Barron's*

NYSE companies
aggregate, yearly - *NYSEFB*
aggregate, percentage of all US
companies' sales, yearly - *NYSEFB*

Odd lots
weekly - *Barron's*

Options
by exchange, monthly - *BQR*

Pacific Stock Exchange
individual stocks, monthly and year to
date - *BQR*

Per dollar of average gross plant
individual companies and industries,
yearly - *FD*

Per dollar of average invested capital
individual companies and industries,
yearly - *FD*

Per dollar of average total assets
individual companies and industries,
yearly - *FD*

Per dollar of average working capital
individual companies and industries,
yearly - *FD*

Per employee
individual companies and industries,
yearly - *FD*

Per share
annual growth rate, individual
companies and industries, latest
year, 3 years, 5 years, and 10 years -
FD

change, individual companies and
industries, yearly - *FD*
individual companies and industries,
yearly - *FD*
least squares growth rate and
coefficient of determination,
individual companies and
industries, 5-year and 10-year - *FD*

**Percentage increase carried to pretax
income**
individual companies, quarterly - *FD*

Percentage of average assets
individual companies and industries,
yearly - *FD*

Percentage of average common equity
individual companies and industries,
yearly - *FD*

Percentage of gross assets
individual companies and industries,
yearly - *FD*

Percentage of industry sales
individual companies, yearly - *FD*

Philadelphia Stock Exchange
individual stocks, monthly and year to
date - *BQR*

Retail stores
monthly - *Barron's*

Retailers
monthly and yearly - *SOSG*

Securities
excluding common stock, held by
mutual funds, monthly - *Barron's*

State municipal securities
for mutual funds, monthly - *Barron's*

Toronto Stock Exchange
individual stocks, monthly and year to
date - *BQR*

Sales charge

Mutual funds
maximum percentage, monthly - *SOSG*

Sales offices

Member organizations, NYSE
number, by state, yearly - *NYSEFB*

Sales plus purchases

American Stock Exchange
members, yearly - *AmexFB*
members, percentage of total sales plus
purchases, yearly - *AmexFB*
odd lots, yearly - *AmexFB*
odd lots, percentage of total sales plus
purchases, yearly - *AmexFB*
specialists, yearly - *AmexFB*

Salomon Government/Corporate Yield Spread

weekly - *Barron's*

Saudi Arabian riyal

Exchange rate
daily - *BQR, NYT, WSJ*
weekly - *Barron's*

Savings and loan association holding companies

Financial statistics
yearly - *AH*

Savings and loan industry

Financial statistics
yearly - *VL*

Savings bonds—*see* United States savings bonds

Savings deposit yields

Top
weekly - *Barron's*

Savings due to common stock equivalents

Individual companies and industries
yearly - *FD*

Savings from common stock equivalents

Individual industries
per share, yearly - *AH*

Schilling, Austrian—*see* Austrian schilling

Scrap commodities prices

Moody's Index
monthly - *MIM*
monthly, graph - *MIM*
yearly - *MIM*
component commodities and weights,
  yearly - *MIM*

SDRs—see Special Drawing Rights

Seasonal borrowings

From Federal Reserve
weekly - *Barron's, WSJ*

Seats, exchange—see Exchange
  seats

Secondary distributions

weekly - *Barron's*

Number and total shares
yearly - *NYSEFB*

Securities

NASDAQ
number, yearly - *NASDAQFB*
number, by index classification, yearly
  - *NASDAQFB*
number, by type, yearly - *NASDAQFB*

NASDAQ National List
typical security profile, yearly -
  NASDAQFB

NASDAQ NMS
number, monthly and yearly -
  NASDAQFB
typical security profile, yearly -
  NASDAQFB

New
offered for cash sale, dollars, yearly -
  MIM

Securities brokerage companies

Financial statistics and ratios
individual companies, yearly - *MHCS*

Securities brokerage industry

Financial statistics
yearly - *VL*

Securities industry personnel

New York City
number, yearly - *NYSEFB*

New York State
number, yearly - *NYSEFB*

United States
number, yearly - *NYSEFB*

Securities Investor Protection Corporation

Assessment and advances
yearly - *NYSEFB*

Securities market credit

New York Stock Exchange
records, yearly - *NYSEFB*

Security credit

Quality
NYSE, monthly, graph - *NYSEFB*

Security issues

dollars, yearly - *MIM*

By industry
dollars, yearly - *MIM*

Security profits

Distributions per share from
mutual funds, yearly - *SOSG*

Segment data

Individual companies
yearly - *FD*

Sell (buy)

New York Stock Exchange
weekly - *Barron's*
net by members, weekly - *Barron's*

Sell volume

New York Stock Exchange
members, weekly - *Barron's*

Selling, general and administrative expenses

Individual companies
quarterly and yearly - *FD*

Individual industries
yearly - *FD*

Percentage of sales
individual companies and industries,
quarterly, moving 12 months, and
yearly - *FD*

Selling, general and administrative expenses margin

Change
effect on earnings per share, individual
companies and industries, yearly -
FD

Semiconductor industry

Financial statistics
yearly - *VL*

Senior capital

yearly - *MHCS*

Service industry

Financial statistics
yearly - *FD*

Services and goods bought—*see*
Goods and services bought

Settlement value

American Stock Exchange
options, yearly - *AmexFB*

Share Price Index—*see* Australia,
Share Price Index

Shareholders—*see also* Stockholders

Characteristics
NYSE, yearly - *NYSEFB*

Equity
Amex companies, average and median,
yearly - *AmexFB*

Amex companies, 10 leading
companies, yearly - *AmexFB*

Geographic distribution
NYSE, yearly - *NYSEFB*

Number
individual companies, quarterly -
SPSR

Shares

American Stock Exchange
market value, aggregate, yearly -
AmexFB

New York Stock Exchange
market value, aggregate, yearly -
NYSEFB
number listed, total and average, yearly
- *NYSEFB*
number listed, by industry, yearly -
NYSEFB
number listed, records, yearly -
NYSEFB
price, average, monthly and yearly -
NYSEFB

Offered by special methods
number of distributions and total
shares, yearly - *NYSEFB*

Volume
Amex, yearly - *AmexFB*
Amex, dollars, yearly - *AmexFB*
Amex, individual companies, 10
leading companies, yearly - *AmexFB*
blocks, Amex, yearly - *AmexFB*
Canadian issues, Amex, yearly -
AmexFB
Canadian issues, Amex, percentage of
total share volume, yearly - *AmexFB*
foreign issues, Amex, yearly - *AmexFB*
foreign issues, Amex, percentage of
total share volume, yearly - *AmexFB*

Shares outstanding

American Stock Exchange
individual companies, number, yearly -
AmexFB
individual companies, 10 leading
companies, yearly - *AmexFB*
number, yearly - *AmexFB*

Common stock
individual companies, quarterly - *VL*
individual companies, yearly - *VL*

Common stock and warrant issues
Amex, number, yearly - *AmexFB*

Individual companies
yearly - *FD, MHCS*

Individual industries
yearly - *FD*

Market value
individual companies and industries,
    quarterly, moving 12 months, and
    yearly - *FD*

NASDAQ
50 market value leaders, individual
    companies, yearly - *NASDAQFB*

Percentage traded
individual companies and industries,
    yearly - *FD*

Preferred stock
individual companies, monthly - *MBR*

Warrant issues and common stock
Amex, number, yearly - *AmexFB*

Shares per reported trade

New York Stock Exchange
average, records, yearly - *NYSEFB*

Shares per transaction

Specialists, Amex
average, yearly - *AmexFB*

Shares traded

Market value
individual companies and industries,
    quarterly, moving 12 months, and
    yearly - *FD*

Percentage of shares outstanding
individual companies, monthly - *VL*
individual companies and industries,
    quarterly, moving 12 months, and
    yearly - *FD*

Volume
individual companies, monthly, chart -
    SPSR

Shearson Lehman Brothers Auction Rate Preferred Index

weekly - *Barron's*

Shearson Lehman Treasury Bond Index

weekly - *Barron's*

Shekel, Israeli—*see* Israeli shekel

Shelf registrations

New
weekly - *Barron's*

Statistics
individual companies, weekly - *MBS*

Shipments, factory—*see* Factory shipments

Shipping industry

Financial statistics
yearly - *FD*

Shoes Index

Standard & Poor's
weekly, monthly, and yearly - *SPIR*
component companies, yearly - *SPIR*
range, yearly - *SPIR*

Shoes industry

Financial statistics
yearly - *AH, FD, VL*

Short interest

American Stock Exchange
monthly - *DSPR*

Individual stocks
monthly - *DSPR*

Largest percentage decrease
stocks listed, weekly - *Barron's*

Largest percentage increase
stocks listed, weekly - *Barron's*

NASDAQ
listings, weekly - *Barron's*

New York Stock Exchange
monthly - *Barron's, DSPR, NYSEFB*
yearly - *NYSEFB*
compared to average daily volume
    (5-week), weekly, last market
    bottom, and last market top - *VL*

compared to average daily volume
(5-week), range, 13-week and
50-week - *VL*
range, yearly - *NYSEFB*
records, yearly - *NYSEFB*

Short interest ratio

American Stock Exchange
weekly - *Barron's*
monthly - *DSPR*

Largest
stocks listed, weekly - *Barron's*

New York Stock Exchange
weekly - *Barron's*
monthly - *Barron's, DSPR*

Pacific Stock Exchange
weekly - *Barron's*

Short issues

American Stock Exchange
weekly - *Barron's*
volume, weekly - *Barron's*

New York Stock Exchange
weekly - *Barron's*
volume, weekly - *Barron's*

Pacific Stock Exchange
weekly - *Barron's*
volume, weekly - *Barron's*

Short position

Largest
stocks listed, weekly - *Barron's*

Largest changes
stocks listed, weekly - *Barron's*

Short ratio

American Stock Exchange
members/public, weekly - *Barron's*
specialists/public, weekly - *Barron's*

New York Stock Exchange
members/public, weekly - *Barron's*
specialists/public, weekly - *Barron's*

Short sales

American Stock Exchange
customers, odd lots, weekly - *Barron's*
floor traders, weekly - *Barron's*

members, weekly - *Barron's*
public, weekly - *Barron's*
specialists, weekly - *Barron's*
volume, weekly - *Barron's*

New York Stock Exchange
weekly - *Barron's*
customers, odd lots, weekly - *Barron's*
customers, odd lots, monthly and
yearly - *NYSEFB*
floor traders, weekly - *Barron's*
members, weekly - *Barron's*
members, records, yearly - *NYSEFB*
members, round lots, monthly and
yearly - *NYSEFB*
nonmembers, round lots, monthly and
yearly - *NYSEFB*
odd lots, daily - *Barron's, DSPR*
off-floor, records, yearly - *NYSEFB*
percentage of total volume, weekly, last
market bottom, and last market top
- *VL*
percentage of total volume, range,
13-week and 50-week - *VL*
public, weekly - *Barron's*
public, percentage of total short sales,
weekly, last market bottom, and last
market top - *VL*
public, percentage of total short sales,
range, 13-week and 50-week - *VL*
round lots, monthly and yearly -
NYSEFB
specialists, weekly - *Barron's*
specialists, percentage of total short
sales, weekly, last market bottom,
and last market top - *VL*
specialists, percentage of total short
sales, range, 13-week and 50-week -
VL
specialists, records, yearly - *NYSEFB*

Odd lots
weekly - *Barron's*

Short-term debt—*see* Debt

Short-term investments and
cash—*see* Cash and short-term
investments

Short-term loans

Ratings
Moody's, explanation, monthly - *MBR*
Moody's, individual loans, monthly -
MBR

Short-term price score—*see*
Moody's short-term price score

Short-term securities

Adjustable rate revenue
ratings, Moody's, weekly - *MBS*

Mutual funds
monthly - *Barron's*

Ratings
Moody's, changes, individual
  securities, monthly - *MBR*
Moody's, new, weekly - *MBS*
Moody's, reviewed and confirmed,
  weekly - *MBS*
Moody's, reviewed and revised, weekly
  - *MBS*
Moody's, withdrawn, weekly - *MBS*

Short-term trading index

American Stock Exchange
daily - *Barron's*

New York Stock Exchange
daily - *Barron's*

Short-term Treasury bills

Rate of return
weekly - *Barron's*

Silver

Continental
Sotheby's Art Index, weekly - *Barron's*

English
Sotheby's Art Index, weekly - *Barron's*

Prices
weekly - *Barron's*

Silver industry

Financial statistics
yearly - *VL*

Singapore, Straits Stock Index

weekly - *Barron's*

Singapore Stock Exchange

Listings, selected stocks
weekly - *Barron's*

Statistics
yearly - *NYSEFB*

Singaporean dollar

Exchange rate
daily - *BQR, NYT, WSJ*
weekly - *Barron's*

Sinking fund

Bonds
individual bonds, monthly - *MBR*

Preferred stocks
individual stocks, monthly - *MBR*

Size distribution of transactions

American Stock Exchange
yearly - *AmexFB*

Size of trade

Intermarket Trading System
average, monthly and yearly -
  NYSEFB

Soaps Index

Standard & Poor's
weekly, monthly, and yearly - *SPIR*
component companies, yearly - *SPIR*
range, yearly - *SPIR*

Soaps industry

Financial statistics
yearly - *AH, FD*

Sol, Peruvian—*see* Peruvian sol

Sotheby's Art Index

weekly - *Barron's*

South Africa, Johannesburg Stock Exchange

Listings, selected stocks
daily - *NYT*
weekly - *Barron's*

Statistics
yearly - *NYSEFB*

South African American Depository Receipts

Listings
daily - *WSJ*
weekly - *Barron's*

South African rand

Exchange rate
daily - *BQR, NYT, WSJ*
weekly - *Barron's*

South Korean won

Exchange rate
daily - *NYT, WSJ*
weekly - *Barron's*

Spain, Madrid Stock Index

weekly - *Barron's*

Spanish peseta

Exchange rate
daily - *BQR, NYT, WSJ*
weekly - *Barron's*

Special Drawing Rights

Exchange rates
daily - *WSJ*
weekly - *Barron's*

Special Drawing Rights Certificate Accounts

Federal Reserve banks
dollars, weekly - *Barron's, WSJ*

Special methods

Stock offerings
number of distributions and total
   shares, yearly - *NYSEFB*

Special offerings

Number and total shares
yearly - *NYSEFB*

Specialists

American Stock Exchange
number, yearly - *AmexFB*
number per unit, average, yearly -
   AmexFB
number of stocks per unit, average,
   yearly - *AmexFB*
options, number per unit, average,
   yearly - *AmexFB*
participation rate, yearly - *AmexFB*
participation rate, by type of option,
   yearly - *AmexFB*
purchases, weekly - *Barron's*
sales, weekly - *Barron's*
sales plus purchases, yearly - *AmexFB*
shares per transaction, number,
   average, yearly - *AmexFB*
short sales, weekly - *Barron's*
stabilization rate, yearly - *AmexFB*
options, contracts per transaction,
   number, average, by type of option,
   yearly - *AmexFB*
options, trade-to-trade price variations,
   by type of option, yearly - *AmexFB*
units, yearly - *AmexFB*

New York Stock Exchange
short sales, weekly - *Barron's*
participation rate, yearly - *NYSEFB*
purchases, weekly - *Barron's*
purchases, round lots, monthly -
   NYSEFB
purchases and sales, round lots,
   number of shares, yearly - *NYSEFB*
sales, weekly - *Barron's*
sales, round lots, monthly - *NYSEFB*
short sales, weekly - *Barron's*
short sales, percentage of total short
   sales, weekly, last market bottom,
   and last market top - *VL*
short sales, percentage of total short
   sales, range, 13-week and 50-week -
   VL
short sales, records, yearly - *NYSEFB*
stabilization rate, yearly - *NYSEFB*
trading, records, yearly - *NYSEFB*

Speculative Grade Industrials

**Moody's Preferred Stock Yield
Averages**
High Dividend Series, monthly and
   yearly - *MIM*

Splits, stock—*see* Stock splits

Spokane Stock Exchange

Seat prices
monthly - *BQR*

Seats outstanding
number, monthly - *BQR*

Spread—*see* type of spread (e.g., Yield spread)

Sri Lankan rupee

Exchange rate
daily - *BQR*

Stability

Stock price
individual companies, weekly - *VL*

Stabilization rate

American Stock Exchange
specialists, yearly - *AmexFB*

New York Stock Exchange
specialists, yearly - *NYSEFB*

Standard & Poor's Bond Yield Index

by rating groups, weekly, monthly, and yearly - *SPIR*

Range
by rating groups, yearly - *SPIR*

Standard & Poor's financial companies, composite

Financial statistics
yearly - *FD*

Standard & Poor's Financial Index

daily - *Barron's, DSPR, NYT, SPIR, WSJ*
weekly - *Barron's, SPIR*
monthly - *SPIR*
yearly - *SPIR, SPSR*

Component companies
yearly - *SPIR*

Dividends per share
monthly - *SPQDR*

Price-earnings ratio
weekly - *SPIR*

Range
weekly - *Barron's*
monthly, chart - *SOSG*
yearly - *SPIR, SPSR*

Yield
weekly, monthly, and yearly - *SPIR*

Standard & Poor's 500

daily - *Barron's, DSPR, NYT, SPIR, WSJ*
weekly - *Barron's, SOSG, SPIR*
monthly - *SPIR*
quarterly, graph - *AH*
yearly - *SPIR, SPSR*

Dividends
quarterly - *SPIR*

Dividends per share
monthly - *SPQDR*

Earnings
quarterly - *SPIR*

Financial statistics
yearly - *AH, FD*

Percentage change
yearly - *SOSG*

Price-earnings ratio
weekly - *Barron's, SPIR*
quarterly - *SPIR*

Range
weekly - *Barron's*
yearly - *SOSG, SPIR, SPSR*

Yield
weekly - *Barron's, SPIR*
monthly and yearly - *SPIR*
range, yearly - *SPIR*

Standard & Poor's 400

daily - *Barron's, DSPR, NYT, SPIR, WSJ*
weekly - *Barron's, SOSG, SPIR*
monthly - *SPIR*
quarterly, graph - *AH*
yearly - *SPIR, SPSR*

Book value
yearly - *SPIR*

Dividends
quarterly - *SPIR*

Dividends per share
monthly - *SPQDR*

Earnings
quarterly - *SPIR*

Financial statistics
yearly - *AH, FD*

Price-earnings ratio
weekly - *Barron's, SPIR*
quarterly - *SPIR*

Range
weekly - *Barron's*
yearly - *SOSG, SPIR, SPSR*

Yield
weekly - *Barron's, SPIR*
monthly and yearly - *SPIR*
range, yearly - *SPIR*

Standard & Poor's Industrial Bond Yield Index

by rating groups, weekly, monthly, and
   yearly - *SPIR*

Range
by rating groups, yearly - *SPIR*

Standard & Poor's 100

daily - *WSJ*

Put-call ratio
weekly - *Barron's*

Standard & Poor's Public Utilities Index

Yield
weekly, monthly, and yearly - *SPIR*
by rating groups, weekly, monthly, and
   yearly - *SPIR*
range, yearly - *SPIR*
range, by rating groups, yearly - *SPIR*

Standard & Poor's Railroad Index

daily - *SPIR*

Dividends
quarterly - *SPIR*

Earnings
quarterly - *SPIR*

Price-earnings ratio
quarterly - *SPIR*

Standard & Poor's ratings

Bonds
changes, weekly - *Barron's*

Commercial paper
individual companies, yearly - *FD*

Common stock
monthly - *SOSG*
changes, monthly - *SOSG*
definitions, monthly - *SOSG*

Corporate bonds
by class of debt, individual companies,
   yearly - *FD*

Individual companies
quarterly - *SPSR*

Preferred stock
monthly - *SOSG*
changes, monthly - *SOSG*
definitions, monthly - *SOSG*

Standard & Poor's transportation companies, composite

Financial statistics
yearly - *FD*

Standard & Poor's Transportation Index

daily - *DSPR, NYT, SPIR, WSJ*
weekly - *Barron's*
yearly - *SPSR*

Dividends per share
monthly - *SPQDR*

Range
weekly - *Barron's*
monthly, chart - *SOSG*
yearly - *SPIR*

Yield
weekly, monthly and yearly - *SPIR*
range, yearly - *SPIR*

Standard & Poor's utilities, composite

Financial statistics
yearly - *FD*

Standard & Poor's Utilities Index

daily - *Barron's, DSPR, NYT, SPIR, WSJ*
weekly - *Barron's*
yearly - *SPIR*

Dividends
quarterly - *SPIR*

Dividends per share
monthly - *SPQDR*

Earnings
quarterly - *SPIR*

Price-earnings ratio
weekly - *SPIR*

Range
weekly - *Barron's*
monthly, chart - *SOSG*
yearly - *SPSR*

State

Amex companies
headquarters per, yearly - *AmexFB*

NASDAQ companies
number of headquarters per, yearly - *NASDAQFB*

State bonds

Yield
by rating goups, monthly, graph - *MBR*

State municipals mutual funds

Sales
monthly - *Barron's*

Steel

Production
weekly - *Barron's*
rated capacity, weekly - *Barron's*

Raw, production
monthly and yearly - *SOSG*

Steel and iron

Barron's Group Stock Averages
weekly - *Barron's*
companies and weights, irregularly - *Barron's*
range, yearly - *Barron's*

Steel Index

Standard & Poor's
weekly, monthly, and yearly - *SPIR*
component companies, yearly - *SPIR*
range, yearly - *SPIR*

Steel Index (excluding USX)

Standard & Poor's
weekly, monthly, and yearly - *SPIR*
component companies, yearly - *SPIR*
range, yearly - *SPIR*

Steel industry

Financial statistics
yearly - *AH, VL*

Steel industry (excluding USX)

Financial statistics
yearly - *AH*

Steel industry (integrated)

Financial statistics
yearly - *VL*

Steel industry (specialty)

Financial statistics
yearly - *VL*

Stock, common—*see* Common stock

Stock, preferred—*see* Preferred stock

Stock/bond yield gap

weekly - *Barron's*

Stock distributions

New York Stock Exchange
yearly - *NYSEFB*

Stock dividends

Declared
listed, monthly - *VL*

New York Stock Exchange
number, by percentages, yearly - *NYSEFB*

resulting in increase in stock list, number, yearly - *NYSEFB*

Stock exchanges—*see* individual headings (e.g., Boston Stock Exchange, Cincinnati Stock Exchange, New York Stock Exchange, etc.)

Stock exchanges, foreign—*see also* individual headings (e.g., Brussels Stock Exchange, London Stock Exchange, etc.)

Listings
selected issues, daily - *NYT, WSJ*
selected issues, weekly - *Barron's*

Statistics
yearly - *NYSEFB*

Stock funds

Closed end
listings, weekly - *Barron's*

Stock index options

American Stock Exchange
calls, number, by index, yearly - *AmexFB*
close, individual indexes, monthly and yearly - *AmexFB*
contracts, number, total and daily average, by index, yearly - *AmexFB*
puts, number, by index, yearly - *AmexFB*
specialists, contracts per transaction, number, average, yearly - *AmexFB*
specialists, participation rate, yearly - *AmexFB*
specialists, trade-to-trade price variations, yearly - *AmexFB*

Calls
open interest, individual indexes, daily - *NYT, WSJ*
open interest, individual indexes, weekly - *Barron's*
volume, individual indexes, daily - *NYT, WSJ*
volume, individual indexes, weekly - *Barron's*

Listings
daily - *NYT, WSJ*
weekly - *Barron's*

Price range
individual indexes, daily - *NYT, WSJ*
individual indexes, weekly - *Barron's*

Puts
open interest, individual indexes, daily - *NYT, WSJ*
open interest, individual indexes, weekly - *Barron's*
volume, individual indexes, daily - *NYT, WSJ*
volume, individual indexes, weekly - *Barron's*

Convertible
industrial, yearly - *MIM*

Stock indexes—*see* individual headings (e.g., Airline Index, Beverages Index, Dow Jones Industrial Average, etc.)

Stock indexes, foreign—*see* individual headings (e.g., British Stock Index, Brussels Stock Index, Hong Kong Stock Index, etc.)

Stock list increases

New York Stock Exchange
sources, yearly - *NYSEFB*

Stock of record date

Dividends
individual stocks, quarterly - *SPQDR, SPSR*

Stock offerings

weekly - *Barron's*

Stock options

American Stock Exchange
specialists, contracts per transaction, number, average, yearly - *AmexFB*
specialists, participation rate, yearly - *AmexFB*
specialists, trade-to-trade price variations, yearly - *AmexFB*

Stock price

daily - *DSPR*

American Stock Exchange
average, yearly - *AmexFB*

Close
percentage of S&P 400, individual
  companies and industries, yearly -
  FD
percentage of S&P industry category,
  individual companies, year end - *FD*

Gains
individual companies, percentage,
  projection - *VL*

Individual stocks
30-week moving average - *DSPR*
projection - *VL*
relative strength, weekly - *DSPR*

Moody's utility stocks
monthly, graph - *MHCS*

New York Stock Exchange
most active stocks, average, weekly -
  Barron's

Publicly traded funds
weekly - *Barron's*

Range
individual companies, monthly, chart -
  MHCS, VL
individual companies, latest 52 weeks -
  MHCS
individual companies, yearly - *FD,
  MHCS, SOSG, VL*
individual companies, projection - *VL*
individual industries, yearly - *FD*
individual stocks, daily - *CFC, DSPR,
  NYT, WSJ*
individual stocks, weekly - *Barron's,
  DSPR*

Stability
individual companies, weekly - *VL*

**Stock Price Averages, Dow
  Jones**—*see* individual Dow Jones
  headings

Stock price indexes—*see*
  individual headings (e.g., Airline
  Index, Beverages Index, Dow Jones
  Industrial Average, etc.)

Stock purchase warrants

Industrial
yearly - *MIM*

Stock splits

American Stock Exchange
yearly - *AmexFB*
individual companies, year to date -
  BQR

Individual stocks
twice weekly - *MDR*
individual stocks, yearly - *MHCS,
  SPQDR*

Industrial
yearly - *MIM*

New York Stock Exchange
common stock, number, yearly -
  NYSEFB
individual companies, year to date -
  BQR
number, yearly - *NYSEFB*
resulting in increase in stock list,
  number, yearly - *NYSEFB*

Stock subscription rights

Individual stocks
monthly - *MDR*

Stockholders—*see also* Shareholders

Individual companies
number, quarterly - *MHCS*

Meetings
companies and dates, monthly - *MDR*

New York Stock Exchange
companies with largest number of
  common stockholders-of-record,
  number, yearly - *NYSEFB*

Rights
individual stocks, yearly - *SPQDR*

Stockholm Stock Exchange—*see*
  Sweden, Stockholm Stock Exchange

Stocks

At discount from liquidating value
listed, weekly - *VL*

Called
individual stocks, yearly - *MDR*

Leading
market value, NYSE, yearly - *NYSEFB*

Private placements
NYSE, yearly - *NYSEFB*

Straits Stock Index—*see* Singapore, Straits Stock Index

Strength

Financial
individual companies, quarterly - *VL*

Price
relative, individual companies, monthly, graph - *VL*

Relative—*see* Relative strength

Student Loan Marketing securities

Listings
daily - *NYT, WSJ*
weekly - *Barron's*

Yield
daily - *NYT, WSJ*
weekly - *Barron's*

Subsidiaries, unconsolidated—*see* Unconsolidated subsidiaries

Sucre, Ecuadorian—*see* Ecuadorian sucre

Sugar Refiners Index

Standard & Poor's
weekly, monthly, and yearly - *SPIR*
component companies, yearly - *SPIR*
range, yearly - *SPIR*

SuperNOW accounts

Average interest rate
weekly - *Barron's*

SuperNOW and NOW accounts

dollars, monthly - *Barron's*

Supplemental Stock Listing, NASDAQ—*see* NASDAQ
Supplemental Stock Listing

Surplus, capital—*see* Capital surplus

Surplus and common equity—*see* Common equity

Sweden, Japo Industrial Index

yearly - *NYSEFB*

Sweden, Stockholm Stock Exchange

Listings, selected stocks
weekly - *Barron's*

Statistics
yearly - *NYSEFB*
yearly - *NYSEFB*

Swedish krona

Exchange rate
daily - *BQR, NYT, WSJ*
weekly - *Barron's*

Swedish Stock Index

weekly - *Barron's*

Swiss franc

Exchange rate
daily - *BQR, NYT, WSJ*
weekly - *Barron's*

Forward exchange rates
daily - *NYT, WSJ*
weekly - *Barron's*

Swiss prime rate

daily - *WSJ*
weekly - *Barron's*

Switzerland, Basel Stock Exchange

Listings, selected stocks
daily - *WSJ*
weekly - *Barron's*

Switzerland, Credit Suisse Stock Index

daily - *NYT*
weekly - *Barron's*

Switzerland, Zurich Stock Exchange

Listings
selected stocks, weekly - *Barron's*

Statistics
yearly - *NYSEFB*

Volume
dollars, yearly, chart - *NASDAQFB*

Sydney Stock Exchange—*see* Australia, Sydney Stock Exchange

Sydney Stock Index—*see* Australia, All-Ordinary Stock Index; Australia, Share Price Index

T

Taiwanese dollar

Exchange rate
daily - *NYT, WSJ*
weekly - *Barron's*

Tax, income—*see* Income Tax

Tax-exempt bonds

Listings
daily - *WSJ*
weekly - *Barron's*

Yield
daily - *WSJ*
weekly - *Barron's*

Tax-free money market funds

Listings
weekly - *Barron's*

Tax rate

Change
effect on earnings per share, individual companies and industries, yearly - *FD*

Effective
individual companies, yearly - *SPSR*

Individual companies
quarterly - *FD*

Individual companies and industries
yearly - *FD, VL*
yearly, projection - *VL*

Tax status

Dividends
individual stocks, yearly - *SPQDR*

Technical new listings

New York Stock Exchange
companies and dates, yearly - *NYSEFB*

Technical rank

Individual stocks
weekly - *VL*

Technology Index

daily - *WSJ*

Telecommunications industry

Financial statistics
yearly - *VL*

Telephone industry

Financial statistics
yearly - *AH*

Telephone industry (excluding regional companies)

Financial statistics
yearly - *FD*

Television

Barron's Group Stock Averages
weekly - *Barron's*
companies and weights, irregularly - *Barron's*
range, yearly - *Barron's*

Term Eurodollars

dollars, monthly - *Barron's*

Term repurchase agreements

dollars, monthly - *Barron's*

Textile Index (apparel manufacturers)

Standard & Poor's
weekly, monthly, and yearly - *SPIR*
component companies, yearly - *SPIR*
range, yearly - *SPIR*

Textile Index (products)

Standard & Poor's
weekly, monthly, and yearly - *SPIR*
component companies, yearly - *SPIR*
range, yearly - *SPIR*

Textile industry

Financial statistics
yearly - *VL*

Textile industry (apparel manufacturers)

Financial statistics
yearly - *AH*

Textile industry (products)

Financial statistics
yearly - *AH*

Textiles

Barron's Group Stock Averages
weekly - *Barron's*
companies and weights, irregularly - *Barron's*
range, yearly - *Barron's*

Thai baht

Exchange rate
daily - *WSJ*
weekly - *Barron's*

Ticker symbols

quarterly - *MHCS, SPSR, VL*

American Stock Exchange
yearly - *AmexFB*

NASDAQ

yearly - *NASDAQFB*

Tickers and ticker displays

New York Stock Exchange
number, yearly - *NYSEFB*

Ticks, closing

American Stock Exchange
daily - *Barron's*

Dow Jones Industrial Average
daily - *Barron's*

New York Stock Exchange
daily - *Barron's*

Timeliness rating

Individual companies and industries
weekly - *VL*

Individual industries
changes, weekly - *VL*

Timely stocks—*see also* Untimely stocks

By rating groups
weekly - *VL*

In timely industries
listed, weekly - *VL*

Times interest earned

Individual industries
yearly - *AH*

Tires and Rubber Goods Index

Standard & Poor's
weekly, monthly, and yearly - *SPIR*
component companies, yearly - *SPIR*
range, yearly - *SPIR*

Tires and rubber goods industry

Financial statistics
yearly - *AH, VL*

Tobacco

Barron's Group Stock Averages
weekly - *Barron's*
companies and weights, irregularly -
  Barron's
range, yearly - *Barron's*

Tobacco Index

Standard & Poor's
weekly, monthly, and yearly - *SPIR*
component companies, yearly - *SPIR*
range, yearly - *SPIR*

Tobacco industry

Financial statistics
yearly - *AH, VL*

Toiletries/cosmetics industry

Financial statistics
yearly - *VL*

Tokyo Stock Exchange—*see* Japan, Tokyo Stock Exchange

Tokyo Stock Index—*see* Japan, TSE Stock Price Index and headings beginning Japan, Nikkei

Tools, machine—*see* Machine tools

Top savings deposit yields

weekly - *Barron's*

Toronto Stock Exchange—*see* Canada, Toronto Stock Exchange

Toronto Stock Index—*see* Canada, Toronto Stock Index

Total assets turnover

Individual industries
yearly - *AH*

Toy Manufacturers Index

Standard & Poor's
weekly, monthly, and yearly - *SPIR*
component companies, yearly - *SPIR*
range, yearly - *SPIR*

Toys and school supplies industry

Financial statistics
yearly - *VL*

Toys industry

Financial statistics
yearly - *AH*

Trade-to-trade price variations

Specialists, Amex
yearly - *AmexFB*
by type of option, yearly - *AmexFB*

Trades

Consolidated Tape
distribution, participating markets,
  yearly - *NYSEFB*

Executed
Intermarket Trading System, total and
  daily average, monthly and yearly -
  NYSEFB

NASDAQ NMS
number, monthly and yearly -
  NASDAQFB

New York Stock Exchange
total and daily average, monthly and
  yearly - *NYSEFB*
share volume, by size, monthly -
  NYSEFB
size, average, monthly and yearly -
  NYSEFB

NYSE-listed stock
number of shares and percentage of all
  NYSE-listed stock trades, by
  exchange, yearly - *NYSEFB*

Trading days

American Stock Exchange
monthly and yearly - *AmexFB*

NASDAQ
monthly and yearly - *NASDAQFB*
10 highest, dates and volume, yearly -
  NASDAQFB

Trading days and hours

New York Stock Exchange
yearly - *NYSEFB*

Transactions

New York Stock Exchange
monthly - *SPIR*
international, quarterly and yearly -
NYSEFB
value, monthly - *Barron's*

Transportation, Dow Jones Average—*see* Dow Jones Transportation Average

Transportation bonds

Listings
NASDAQ, monthly - *BQR*

Number of issues
weekly, six weeks, and projection -
MBS

Volume
dollars, weekly, six weeks, and
projection - *MBS*

Yield
individual bonds, monthly - *BQR*

Transportation companies

Security issues
dollars, yearly - *MIM*

Transportation Index (Airlines)

Standard & Poor's
weekly, monthly, and yearly - *SPIR*
component companies, yearly - *SPIR*
range, yearly - *SPIR*

Transportation Index (Amex)

Stock index options
close, monthly and yearly - *AmexFB*

Transportation Index (Railroads)

Standard & Poor's
weekly, monthly, and yearly - *SPIR*
component companies, yearly - *SPIR*
range, yearly - *SPIR*

Transportation Index (Standard & Poor's)

daily - *DSPR, SPIR, WSJ*
weekly, monthly, and yearly - *SPIR*

Price-earnings ratio
weekly - *SPIR*

Range
yearly - *SPIR*

Subgroups listed
yearly - *SPIR*

Transportation Index (Truckers)

Standard & Poor's
weekly, monthly, and yearly - *SPIR*
component companies, yearly - *SPIR*
range, yearly - *SPIR*

Transportation Indicator

New York Stock Exchange
daily - *BQR, DSPR, WSJ*
monthly - *BQR*
range, monthly - *BQR, NYSEFB*

Transportation industry

Financial statistics
yearly - *AH*

Treasury bill options

American Stock Exchange
specialists, contracts per transaction,
number, average, yearly - *AmexFB*
specialists, participation rate, yearly -
AmexFB
specialists, trade-to-trade price
variations, yearly - *AmexFB*

Treasury bills

Futures spread
vs. Eurodollar, weekly - *Barron's*

Rates
daily - *WSJ*
weekly - *Barron's, VL*
last market bottom and last market top
- *VL*
range, 13-week and 50-week - *VL*

Yield
by length of maturity, monthly, graph -
MBR, MBS
individual issues, daily - *NYT, WSJ*
individual issues, weekly - *Barron's,
CFC*
individual issues, monthly - *BQR*

Moody's Averages, weekly and
    monthly - *MBS*
Moody's Averages, range, yearly - *MBS*

Yield spread
vs. Treasury bonds, weekly, graph -
    MBS

Treasury Bond Index

Shearson Lehman
weekly - *Barron's*

Treasury bonds

Constant maturities
rates, weekly - *Barron's*

Listings
daily - *NYT, WSJ*
weekly - *Barron's, CFC*
monthly - *MBR*

Long-term
yield, monthly, graph - *MBR*

30-year
rate, weekly, graph - *VL*
yield, weekly, last market bottom, and
    last market top - *VL*
yield, range, 13-week and 50-week -
    VL

Yield
weekly, graph - *MBR, MBS*
individual issues, daily - *NYT, WSJ*
individual issues, weekly - *Barron's,
    CFC*
individual issues, monthly - *BQR,
    MBR*
Moody's Averages, daily and monthly -
    MBS
Moody's Averages, range, yearly - *MBS*

Yield spread
vs. Aaa corporate bonds, weekly, graph
    - *MBS*
vs. junk bonds, weekly, graph -
    Barron's
vs. municipal bonds, weekly, graph -
    MBS
vs. Treasury bills, weekly, graph - *MBS*

Treasury cash holdings

Federal Reserve banks
weekly - *WSJ*

Treasury deposits

With Federal Reserve banks
weekly - *Barron's, WSJ*

Treasury gold stock

Federal Reserve banks
daily - *WSJ*
weekly - *Barron's*

Treasury Issues

Yield
Moody's Averages, daily, weekly, and
    monthly - *MBS*
Moody's Averages, range, yearly - *MBS*

Treasury note options

American Stock Exchange
specialists, contracts per transaction,
    number, average, yearly - *AmexFB*
specialists, participation rate, yearly -
    AmexFB
specialists, trade-to-trade price
    variations, yearly - *AmexFB*

Treasury notes

Listings
daily - *NYT, WSJ*
weekly - *Barron's, CFC*
monthly - *BQR, MBR*

Yield
individual issues, daily - *NYT, WSJ*
individual issues, weekly - *Barron's,
    CFC*
individual issues, monthly - *BQR,
    MBR*
Moody's Averages, daily and monthly -
    MBS
Moody's Averages, range, yearly - *MBS*

Treasury statement

weekly - *Barron's*

Trucking industry

Financial statistics
yearly - *AH*

Trucking/transportation leasing industry

Financial statistics
yearly - *VL*

Trust companies

NASDAQ
listings, monthly - *BQR*
price-earnings ratios, monthly - *BQR*

Trusts, equipment—*see* Equipment
trusts

TSE Stock Price Index—*see* Japan,
TSE Stock Price Index

Turkish lira

Exchange rate
daily - *NYT, WSJ*

Turnover

Inventory
individual companies, quarterly and
yearly - *FD*
individual industries, yearly - *AH, FD*

Total assets
individual industries, yearly - *AH*

Turnover rate

New York Stock Exchange
yearly - *NYSEFB*
records, yearly - *NYSEFB*

Turnover ratio

American Stock Exchange
yearly - *AmexFB*

Twelve Federal Intermediate Credit Banks securities

Listings
monthly - *BQR*

Yield
monthly - *BQR*

Twelve Federal Land Banks securities

Listings
weekly - *CFC*
monthly - *BQR*

Yield
individual issues, weekly - *CFC*
individual issues, monthly - *BQR*

U

Uncapitalized leases—*see* Leases

Unchanged prices

Bonds
Amex, number, daily - *Barron's, WSJ*
NYSE, number, daily - *Barron's, WSJ*

Common stocks
NYSE, number, daily - *Barron's*

Stocks
Amex, number, daily - *Barron's,
DSPR, NYT, WSJ*
Amex, number, weekly - *Barron's*
Dow Jones companies, number, weekly
- *Barron's*
Dow Jones Industrial companies,
number, weekly - *Barron's*
Dow Jones Utilities companies,
number, weekly - *Barron's*
NASDAQ, number, daily - *Barron's,
DSPR, NYT, WSJ*
NASDAQ, number, weekly - *Barron's*
NYSE, number, daily - *Barron's,
DSPR, NYT, WSJ*
NYSE, number, weekly - *Barron's*

Unconsolidated subsidiaries

Equity in earnings of
individual companies and industries,
yearly - *FD*

Investments and advances
individual industries, per share, yearly
- *AH*

Unemployed

monthly - *Barron's*

Unemployment

monthly - *Barron's, SOSG*
average, yearly - *SOSG*

Unfilled orders

Statistics
monthly - *Barron's*

United Arab Emirates dirham

Exchange rate
daily - *NYT, WSJ*
weekly - *Barron's*

United Kingdom, Financial Times 500 Stock Index

daily - *NYT*

United Kingdom, Financial Times Industrial Index

daily - *WSJ*

United Kingdom, Financial Times Ordinary Share Index

yearly - *NYSEFB*

United Kingdom, Financial Times Stock Index

weekly - *Barron's*

United Kingdom, Financial Times 30 Stock Index

daily - *NYT*

United States Government Bond Price Index

Standard & Poor's
Taxable issues, by length of maturity,
    weekly, monthly, and yearly - *SPIR*
Taxable issues, range, by length of
    maturity, yearly - *SPIR*

United States Government Bond Yield Index

Standard & Poor's
Taxable issues, by length of maturity,
    weekly, monthly, and yearly - *SPIR*
Taxable issues, range, by length of
    maturity, yearly - *SPIR*

United States Postal Service bonds

Listings
monthly - *MBR*

Yield
individual bonds, monthly - *MBR*

United States savings bonds

Current semiannual yield
weekly - *Barron's*

United States Treasury—*see* Treasury

Units

Specialists, Amex
yearly - *AmexFB*

Untimely stocks—*see also* Timely stocks

Listed
weekly - *VL*

Uruguayan new peso

Exchange rate
daily - *NYT, WSJ*
weekly - *Barron's*

Uruguayan peso

Free exchange rate
daily - *BQR*

Utilities—*see also* Public utilities

Book value
individual companies, yearly - *MHCS*

Common equity percentage
individual companies, yearly - *MHCS*

Dow Jones Average—*see* Dow Jones
  Utilities Average

**Electric Power Companies Index,
  Standard & Poor's**
weekly, monthly, and yearly - *SPIR*
component companies, yearly - *SPIR*
range, yearly - *SPIR*

Financial statistics
yearly - *AH*

Gross for common percentage
individual companies, yearly - *MHCS*

**Natural Gas Distributors Index,
  Standard & Poor's**
weekly, monthly, and yearly - *SPIR*
component companies, yearly - *SPIR*
range, yearly - *SPIR*

**Natural Gas Pipe Lines Index,
  Standard & Poor's**
weekly, monthly, and yearly - *SPIR*
component companies, yearly - *SPIR*
range, yearly - *SPIR*

Operating income to net plant
percentage, individual companies,
  yearly - *MHCS*

Preferred stocks
ratings, Standard & Poor's, monthly -
  SOSG

Production
monthly - *Barron's*

Short-term debt
individual companies, yearly - *MHCS*

**Telephone Companies Index, Standard
  & Poor's**
weekly, monthly, and yearly - *SPIR*
component companies, yearly - *SPIR*
range, yearly - *SPIR*

**Telephone Companies (Excluding
  AT&T) Index, Standard & Poor's**
weekly, monthly, and yearly - *SPIR*
component companies, yearly - *SPIR*
range, yearly - *SPIR*

Utilities Companies Index

Standard & Poor's
weekly, monthly, and yearly - *SPIR*
range, yearly - *SPIR*
subgroups listed, yearly - *SPIR*

Utilities Indicator

New York Stock Exchange
daily - *BQR, DSPR, WSJ*
monthly - *BQR*
range, monthly - *BQR, NYSEFB*

Utility bonds

Number of issues
weekly, six weeks, and projection -
  MBS

Volume
dollars, weekly, six weeks, and
  projection - *MBS*

Utility company bonds

Domestic, Newly Issued
Moody's Weighted Averages of Yields,
  yearly - *MIM*

Utility stocks, Moody's

Dividends per share
monthly, graph - *MHCS*

Earnings per share
monthly, graph - *MHCS*

Prices
monthly, graph - *MHCS*

V

Value

Book—*see* Book value

Equity trading
selected foreign stock exchanges, yearly
  - *NYSEFB*

Large blocks traded
Amex, dollars, yearly - *AmexFB*
Amex, dollars, percentage of total
  dollar value of shares traded, yearly
  - *AmexFB*

Liquidating
stocks at discount from, listed, weekly
  - *VL*

Listed stocks
NYSE, monthly - *Barron's*

Market—*see* Market value

Net asset—*see* Net asset value

Par—*see* Par value

Preferred stock
individual stocks, monthly - *MBR*

Shares traded
Amex, dollars, yearly - *AmexFB*

Shares transacted
NYSE, monthly - *Barron's*

Value added

Incremental dollars per increased dollar labor costs
individual companies and industries, yearly - *FD*

Per employee
individual companies and industries, yearly - *FD*

Percentage of average invested capital
individual companies and industries, yearly - *FD*

Percentage of sales
individual companies and industries, yearly - *FD*

Value line

Individual companies
quarterly, graph - *VL*

Value Line cumulative advance-decline line

weekly, graph - *VL*

Value Line Industrial Index

daily - *VL*
weekly and monthly, chart - *VL*

Change
percentage, last four weeks - *VL*

Value Line Railroad Index

daily - *VL*
weekly, chart - *VL*
monthly, chart - *VL*

Change
percentage, last four weeks - *VL*

Value Line stocks

Advances
number, weekly - *VL*

Declines
number, weekly - *VL*

Dividend yield
median, weekly, last market bottom, and last market top - *VL*
median, range, 13-week and 50-week - *VL*

Highs, new
number, weekly - *VL*
number, weekly, graph - *VL*

Issues traded
number, weekly - *VL*

Price-earnings ratio
median, weekly, last market bottom, and last market top - *VL*
median, range, 13-week and 50-week - *VL*

Value Line Utilities Index

daily - *VL*
weekly and monthly, chart - *VL*

Change
percentage, last four weeks - *VL*

Variable annuities

Listings
weekly - *Barron's*

Variable life accounts

Listings
weekly - *Barron's*

Variations, price

Options
trade-to-trade, specialists, Amex, by type of option, yearly - *AmexFB*

Trade-to-trade
specialists, Amex, yearly - *AmexFB*

Variety and discount stores

Retail companies stock price index
quarterly, graph - *MHCS*

Venezuelan bolivar

Exchange rate
daily - *NYT, WSJ*
weekly - *Barron's*

Free exchange rate
daily - *BQR*

Volume

American Depository Receipts
NASDAQ, volume leaders, dollars,
  yearly - *NASDAQFB*
NASDAQ, volume leaders, number of
  shares, yearly - *NASDAQFB*

American Stock Exchange
daily - *Barron's, DSPR, NYT, WSJ*
10-day average, daily - *DSPR*
weekly - *Barron's, VL*
daily average, weekly - *Barron's*
monthly - *BQR*
10-week average - *VL*
monthly, chart - *MHCS, MIM*
year to date - *NYT, BQR*
yearly - *AmexFB, NASDAQFB*
daily average, yearly - *AmexFB*
advances, daily - *NYT, WSJ*
American Stock Exchange Index
  System, daily - *BQR*
bonds, monthly - *BQR*
bonds, dollars, daily - *WSJ*
bonds, dollars, monthly - *BQR*
bonds, dollars, year to date - *BQR,
  WSJ*
bonds, individual bonds, daily - *WSJ*
Canadian issues, number of shares,
  yearly - *AmexFB*
Canadian issues, percentage of total
  share volume, yearly - *AmexFB*
corporate bonds, principal amount,
  yearly - *AmexFB*
declines, daily - *NYT, WSJ*
dollars, yearly - *NASDAQFB*
dollars, percentage of all exchanges'
  dollar volume, yearly - *NASDAQFB*
foreign issues, number of shares, yearly
  - *AmexFB*
foreign issues, percentage of total share
  volume, yearly - *AmexFB*
government bonds, principal amount,
  yearly - *AmexFB*

individual companies, yearly -
  AmexFB
individual companies, 10 leading
  companies, yearly - *AmexFB*
large blocks, yearly - *AmexFB*
large blocks, number of shares, yearly -
  AmexFB
large blocks, percentage of total share
  volume, yearly - *AmexFB*
members, percentage of total volume,
  weekly - *Barron's*
options, monthly and yearly - *AmexFB*
options, contracts, monthly and yearly
  - *AmexFB*
options, percentage of underlying
  stock, monthly and yearly - *AmexFB*
percentage of all exchanges' volume,
  yearly - *NASDAQFB*
percentage of NYSE volume, weekly -
  VL
percentage of NYSE volume, 10-week
  average - *VL*
short sales, weekly - *Barron's*
stock sales, monthly - *BQR*

Bank-finance-insurance bonds
dollars, weekly, six weeks, and
  projection - *MBS*

Barron's Low-Priced Index
weekly - *Barron's, DSPR*
percentage of Dow Jones Industrial
  Average volume, weekly - *Barron's,
  DSPR*

Bonds
dollars, weekly, six weeks, and
  projection - *MBS*

Bonds and preferred stock
dollars, weekly, six weeks, and
  projection - *MBS*

Boston Stock Exchange
monthly and year to date - *BQR*

Composite, Amex
daily - *WSJ*

Consolidated Tape
yearly - *NYSEFB*

Corporate bonds and foreign bonds
dollars, weekly, six weeks, and
  projection - *MBS*

Dow Jones bonds
weekly - *DSPR*

Dow Jones companies
daily - *DSPR*

dollars, percentage of all exchanges'
    dollar volume, yearly - *NASDAQFB*
percentage of all exchanges' volume,
    yearly - *NASDAQFB*

New York Stock Exchange
daily - *Barron's, DSPR, SOSG, WSJ*
daily, chart - *WSJ*
daily, selected quarters and months -
    NYSEFB
10-day average, daily - *DSPR*
weekly - *Barron's, VL*
10-week average - *VL*
monthly - *NYSEFB*
monthly, chart - *MHCS, MIM, SOSG*
daily average, monthly - *NYSEFB*
year to date - *NYT*
yearly - *NASDAQFB, NYSEFB, SPIR*
hourly and daily averages, yearly -
    NYSEFB
advances, daily - *NYT, WSJ*
bonds, weekly - *Barron's*
bonds, monthly - *Barron's, BQR*
bonds, year to date - *BQR, NYT*
bonds, yearly - *NYT*
bonds, best grade, weekly - *Barron's*
bonds, dollars, daily - *NYT, WSJ*
bonds, individual bonds, daily and
    year to date - *WSJ*
bonds, intermediate grade, weekly -
    Barron's
bonds, par value, total and daily
    average, yearly - *NYSEFB*
bonds, par value, daily average,
    records, yearly - *NYSEFB*
bonds, par value, range, yearly -
    NYSEFB
by price groups, monthly - *NYSEFB*
by size of trade, monthly - *NYSEFB*
compounded growth rates, yearly -
    NYSEFB
customers, odd lots, purchases, number
    of shares and value, monthly -
    NYSEFB
customers, odd lots, sales, number of
    shares and value, monthly -
    NYSEFB
declines, daily - *NYT, WSJ*
distribution, by days, yearly - *NYSEFB*
distribution, most active stocks, yearly
    - *NYSEFB*
dollars, monthly - *BQR, NYSEFB*
dollars, year to date - *BQR*
dollars, yearly - *NASDAQFB, NYSEFB*
dollars, percentage of all exchanges'
    dollar volume, yearly - *NASDAQFB*
first-round shares, weekly - *Barron's*
futures contracts, daily average,
    monthly - *NYSEFB*

individual investors, daily average,
    selected quarters and months -
    NYSEFB
individual investors, percentage
    distribution, daily average, selected
    quarters and months - *NYSEFB*
institutional investors, daily average,
    selected quarters and months -
    NYSEFB
institutional investors, percentage
    distribution, daily average, selected
    quarters and months - *NYSEFB*
large block transactions, percentage of
    reported volume, yearly, chart -
    NASDAQFB
large block transactions, percentage of
    reported volume, records, yearly -
    NYSEFB
members, weekly - *Barron's*
members, percentage of total volume,
    weekly - *Barron's*
members, purchases, weekly - *Barron's*
members, sales, weekly - *Barron's*
most active stocks, yearly - *NYSEFB*
most active stocks, percentage of total
    volume, weekly - *Barron's, DSPR*
odd lots, number of shares, yearly -
    NYSEFB
odd lots, purchases, number of shares,
    yearly - *NYSEFB*
odd lots, purchases, value, yearly -
    NYSEFB
odd lots, records, yearly - *NYSEFB*
odd lots, sales, number of shares,
    yearly - *NYSEFB*
odd lots, sales, value, yearly - *NYSEFB*
odd lots, value, yearly - *NYSEFB*
odd lots, value, records, yearly -
    NYSEFB
percentage of all exchanges' volume,
    yearly - *NASDAQFB*
records, yearly - *NYSEFB*
short issues, weekly - *Barron's*
sources, quarterly - *NYSEFB*
stock sales, monthly - *BQR*
stocks, daily - *BQR*
stocks, monthly - *Barron's*
warrants, monthly - *Barron's, BQR*
warrants, total and daily average,
    yearly - *NYSEFB*
warrants, records, yearly - *NYSEFB*

**New York Stock Exchange Common
    Stock Index**
options, daily average, monthly -
    NYSEFB
options, daily average, monthly, graph
    - *NYSEFB*

W

Washington Metropolitan Area Transit Authority bonds

Listings
monthly - *MBR*

Yield
individual listings, monthly - *MBR*

West German mark

Exchange rate
daily - *BQR, NYT, WSJ*
rate, weekly - *Barron's*

Forward exchange rate
daily - *NYT, WSJ*
weekly - *Barron's*

West German prime rate

daily - *WSJ*
weekly - *Barron's*

West German Stock Exchange

Volume
dollars, yearly, chart - *NASDAQFB*

West German Stock Exchange Association

Statistics
yearly - *NYSEFB*

West German Stock Index—*see*
West Germany, Commerzbank Index; West Germany, Frankfurter Allgemeine Zeitung Stock Index

West Germany, Commerzbank Index

daily - *NYT*
weekly - *Barron's*

West Germany, Frankfurt Stock Exchange

Listings, selected stocks
daily - *NYT, WSJ*
weekly - *Barron's*

West Germany, Frankfurter Allgemeine Zeitung Stock Index

daily - *NYT*
yearly - *NYSEFB*

Wholesale Food Price Index

Dun & Bradstreet
weekly - *Barron's*

Wholesale industry

Financial statistics
yearly - *FD*

Wholesale prices

Index
monthly and annual average - *SOSG*

Wholesalers, merchant—*see*
Merchant wholesalers

Widest discounts from book value

Stocks listed
weekly - *VL*

Wilshire 500 Index

daily - *NYT, WSJ*

Wilshire 5000 Equity Index

daily and weekly - *Barron's*

Range
weekly - *Barron's*

Winnipeg Commodity Exchange—*see* Canada, Winnipeg Commodity Exchange

Won, South Korean—*see* South Korean won

Working capital

Change
individual companies and industries, yearly - *FD*

**Incremental dollars of sales per
    incremental dollar of working capital**
individual companies and industries,
    yearly - *FD*

Individual companies
yearly - *FD, MHCS, VL*
yearly, projection - *VL*

Individual industries
yearly - *FD, VL*
yearly, projection - *VL*
per share, yearly - *AH*

Percentage of sales
individual companies and industries,
    yearly - *FD*

Ratio to sales
individual companies, quarterly and
    five-year average - *VL*

Sales per dollar average
individual companies and industries,
    yearly - *FD*

World Bank—*see* International Bank
    for Reconstruction and
    Development

Worst performing stocks

last 13 weeks, weekly - *VL*

Worth, net—*see* Net worth

Y

Yen, Japanese—*see* Japanese yen

Yield

All stocks paying dividends
estimated, median, weekly, last market
    high, last market low, and 26 weeks
    ago - *VL*

American Stock Exchange
individual bonds, weekly - *Barron's*
individual bonds, monthly - *BQR*
individual stocks, daily - *NYT, WSJ*
individual stocks, weekly - *Barron's,
    CFC*

individual stocks, monthly - *BQR*

Bank for Cooperatives securities
monthly - *BQR*

Barron's 50-Stock Average
bonds, monthly - *Barron's*
bonds, best grade, weekly and monthly
    - *Barron's*
earnings, actual year end, weekly and
    monthly - *Barron's*
ratio, bonds/stocks, weekly - *Barron's*

Bonds
banks, monthly - *BQR*
individual bonds, monthly - *MBR,
    SOSG*
individual bonds, when issued - *MBR*
industrial bonds, monthly - *BQR*
minus average earnings yield, weekly,
    last market bottom, and last market
    top - *VL*
minus average earnings yield, range,
    13-week and 50-week - *VL*
Moody's Averages, by rating groups,
    monthly and yearly - *MIM*
Standard & Poor's Index, by rating
    groups, weekly, monthly, and yearly
    - *SPIR*
Standard & Poor's Index, range, by
    rating groups, yearly - *SPIR*

Common Stock
Public Utilities, Moody's Averages,
    weekly - *MBS*
Public Utilities, Moody's Averages,
    range, yearly - *MBS*

Convertible bonds
individual bonds, monthly - *BG*

Corporate Bonds
Distributed, Moody's Averages, by
    rating groups, monthly, graph -
    MBR
Distributed, Moody's Averages,
    composite and by rating groups,
    monthly - *MBS*
Moody's Averages, monthly, graph -
    MBR
Moody's Averages, Aaa, weekly - *VL*
Moody's Averages, Aaa, weekly, graph
    - *MBS*
Moody's Averages, Aaa, last market
    bottom and last market top - *VL*
Moody's Averages, Aaa, range,
    13-week and 50-week - *VL*
Moody's Averages, by rating groups,
    weekly, graph - *MBR, MBS*

Moody's Averages, by rating groups, monthly, graph - *MBR*

Moody's Averages, composite and by rating groups, daily - *MBS*

Moody's Averages, range, composite and by rating groups, yearly - *MBS*

Newly Issued, Moody's Averages, by rating groups, monthly, graph - *MBR*

Newly Issued, Moody's Averages, composite and by rating groups, monthly - *MBS, MIM*

Dividend

Barron's 50-Stock Average, year end, weekly - *Barron's*

Dow Jones Industrial Average, weekly, last market bottom, and last market top - *VL*

Dow Jones Industrial Average, quarterly and yearly - *Barron's*

Dow Jones Industrial Average, range, 13-week and 50-week - *VL*

Dow Jones Transportation Average, quarterly - *Barron's*

Dow Jones Utilities Average, quarterly - *Barron's*

individual companies, quarterly - *VL*

individual companies, moving 12 months and yearly - *FD*

individual companies, average annual, yearly and projection - *VL*

individual companies, range, yearly - *FD*

individual industries, moving 12 months and yearly - *FD*

individual industries, average annual, yearly and projection - *VL*

individual industries, range, yearly - *AH, FD*

NASDAQ National List, individual companies, weekly - *Barron's*

Value Line stocks, median, weekly, last market bottom, and last market top - *VL*

Value Line stocks, median, range, 13-week and 50-week - *VL*

Domestic Bonds

Newly Issued, Moody's Weighted Averages, yearly - *MIM*

Domestic Industrial Bonds

Newly Issued, Moody's Weighted Averages, yearly - *MIM*

Domestic Railroad Bonds

Newly Issued, Moody's Weighted Averages, yearly - *MIM*

Domestic Utility Bonds

Newly Issued, Moody's Weighted Averages, yearly - *MIM*

Dow Jones Bonds Average

weekly - *Barron's*

Dow Jones Industrial Average

weekly - *Barron's, DSPR*

monthly - *Barron's*

Dow Jones Industrial Bonds Average

weekly - *Barron's*

Dow Jones Transportation Average

weekly - *Barron's*

Dow Jones Utilities Average

weekly - *Barron's*

Dow Jones Utilities Bonds Average

weekly - *Barron's*

Equipment trusts

individual trusts, monthly - *BQR*

Farmers Home Insured Notes

individual issues, monthly - *BQR*

Federal Farm Credit Bank bonds

individual bonds, monthly - *MBR*

Federal Farm Credit Bank securities

individual issues, weekly - *Barron's*

individual issues, monthly - *BQR*

Federal Home Loan Bank bonds

individual bonds, monthly - *MBR*

Federal Home Loan Bank securities

individual issues, monthly - *BQR*

Federal Home Loan Mortgage Corporation bonds

individual bonds, monthly - *MBR*

Federal Home Loan Mortgage Corporation securities

individual securities, weekly - *Barron's*

Federal Home Mortgage Association securities

individual issues, monthly - *BQR*

Federal Intermediate Credit Debentures

individual issues, monthly - *MBR*

Federal Land Bank bonds

individual bonds, monthly - *MBR*

Federal National Debentures

individual issues, monthly - *BQR*

Federal National Mortgage Association bonds
individual bonds, monthly - *MBR*

Federal National Mortgage Association Participating Certificates
individual issues, weekly - *Barron's*
individual issues, monthly - *BQR*

Federal National Mortgage Association securities
individual issues, weekly - *Barron's*

Finance companies
bonds, individual bonds, monthly - *BQR*

Foreign bonds
individual bonds, weekly - *Barron's*
individual bonds, monthly - *BQR*

General Services Administration securities
individual issues, monthly - *BQR*

Government bonds
long-term, monthly, graph - *MBR*
3-5 year, monthly, graph - *MBR*

Government National Mortgage Association securities
individual issues, weekly - *Barron's*
individual issues, monthly - *BQR*

Government securities
monthly, graph - *MBR*

High
stocks listed, weekly - *VL*

Highest
non-utility stocks, listed, weekly - *VL*

Individual companies
percentage of S&P industry category yield, yearly - *FD*

Individual companies and industries
percentage of S&P 400 yield, yearly - *FD*

Industrial Bonds
Distributed, Moody's Averages, composite and by rating groups, monthly - *MBS*
Moody's Averages, by rating groups, weekly and monthly, graph - *MBR, MIM*
Moody's Averages, composite and by rating groups, daily - *MBS*
Moody's Averages, composite and by rating groups, monthly and yearly - *MIM*

Moody's Averages, range, composite and by rating groups, yearly - *MBS*
Newly Issued, Moody's Averages, composite and by rating groups, monthly - *MBS, MIM*
Standard & Poor's Index, by rating groups, weekly, monthly, and yearly - *SPIR*
Standard & Poor's Index, range, by rating groups, yearly - *SPIR*

Insurance companies
bonds, monthly - *BQR*

International Bank for Reconstruction and Development securities
individual issues, weekly - *Barron's*
individual issues, monthly - *BQR*

Midwest Stock Exchange
individual stocks, monthly - *BQR*

Money market funds
individual funds, weekly - *Barron's*

Mortgage-related securities
individual securities, weekly - *Barron's*

Municipal bonds
individual bonds, monthly - *BQR*
Moody's Averages, by rating groups, weekly, graph - *MBR, MBS*
Moody's Averages, by rating groups, monthly, graph - *MBR*
Moody's Averages, composite, weekly, graph - *MBS*
Moody's Averages, composite and by rating groups, monthly - *MBR, MBS*
Moody's Averages, range, composite and by rating groups, yearly - *MBS*

Mutual funds
from investment income, monthly - *SOSG*

NASDAQ National List
dividends, individual stocks, weekly - *Barron's*

NASDAQ NMS
individual stocks, weekly - *Barron's*

New York Stock Exchange
common stock, by percentage, number of issues, yearly - *NYSEFB*
common stock, median, yearly - *NYSEFB*
common stock, median, records, yearly - *NYSEFB*
individual bonds, weekly - *Barron's*
individual bonds, monthly - *BQR*
individual stocks, monthly - *BQR*

Tax-exempt bonds
individual bonds, daily - *WSJ*
individual bonds, weekly - *Barron's*

Tax-free money market funds
individual funds, weekly - *Barron's*

Top savings deposits
weekly - *Barron's*

Toronto Stock Exchange
individual stocks, monthly - *BQR*

Transportation bonds
individual bonds, monthly - *BQR*

Treasury bills
individual issues, daily - *NYT, WSJ*
individual issues, weekly - *Barron's*
individual issues, monthly - *BQR*
Moody's Averages, weekly and
    monthly - *MBS*
Moody's Averages, by length of
    maturity, monthly, graph - *MBR*
Moody's Averages, range, yearly - *MBS*
three-month, weekly, graph - *MBS*

Treasury bonds
weekly, graph - *MBS*
individual issues, daily - *NYT, WSJ*
individual issues, weekly - *Barron's*
individual issues, monthly - *BQR,*
    MBR
Moody's Averages, daily and monthly -
    MBS
Moody's Averages, range, yearly - *MBS*
30-year, weekly, last market bottom,
    and last market top - *VL*
30-year, range, 13-week and 50-week -
    VL

Treasury Issues
Moody's Averages, daily, weekly, and
    monthly - *MBS*
Moody's Averages, range, yearly - *MBS*

Treasury notes
individual issues, daily - *NYT, WSJ*
individual issues, weekly - *Barron's*
individual issues, monthly - *BQR,*
    MBR
Moody's Averages, daily and monthly -
    MBS
Moody's Averages, range, yearly - *MBS*

Twelve Federal Intermediate Credit
    Banks securities
individual issues, monthly - *BQR*

Twelve Federal Land Banks securities
individual issues, monthly - *BQR*

US Postal Service bonds
individual bonds, monthly - *MBR*

US Postal Service securities
individual issues, monthly - *BQR,*
    MBR

US savings bonds
semiannual, weekly - *Barron's*

Washington Metropolitan Area Transit
    Authority bonds
individual bonds, monthly - *MBR*

Yield gap

Barron's Confidence Index
vs. Dow Jones Industrial Average,
    weekly - *Barron's*

Yield spread

weekly, graph - *MBR*

Corporate bonds
among rating groups, weekly, graph -
    MBS
vs. Treasury bonds, weekly, graph -
    MBS

Junk bonds
vs. Treasury bonds, weekly, graph -
    Barron's

Municipal bonds
among rating groups, weekly, graph -
    MBR, MBS

Municipal composite bonds
vs. Treasury bonds, weekly, graph -
    MBS

Salomon Government/Corporate
weekly - *Barron's*

State bonds
vs. Treasury bonds, monthly, graph -
    MBR

Treasury bills
three-month, vs. Treasury bonds,
    weekly, graph - *MBS*
vs. Treasury bonds, monthly, graph -
    MBR

Treasury bonds
vs. Aaa corporate bonds, weekly, graph
    - *MBS*
vs. junk bonds, weekly, graph -
    Barron's
vs. municipal composite bonds,
    weekly, graph - *MBS*

vs. Treasury bills, weekly, graph - *MBS*
vs. Treasury bills, three-month,
   monthly, graph - *MBR*

Yuan, Chinese—*see* Chinese yuan

Yugoslav dinar

Exchange rate
daily - *NYT*

Z

Zurich Stock Exchange—*see*
   Switzerland, Zurich Stock Exchange

Zurich Stock Index—*see*
   Switzerland, Credit Suisse Stock
   Index

KAREN J. CHAPMAN is assistant commerce librarian at the University of Illinois Library, Urbana–Champaign. Her articles on business statistics and resources have appeared in *Reference Services Review* and *Behavioral & Social Sciences Librarian*.